*"Sometimes the answers to life's problems
are in the movies."*

—Gary Solomon, The Movie Doctor™

THE MOTION PICTURE PRESCRIPTION

Watch This Movie and Call Me in the Morning

by

Gary Solomon, MPH, MSW, Ph.D.

The Movie Doctor™

200 movies to help you heal life's problems

Aslan Publishing • Santa Rosa, California • 1995

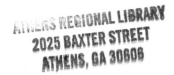

Published by
Aslan Publishing
3356 Coffey Lane
Santa Rosa, CA 95403
(707) 542-5400

For a free catalog of our other titles,
or to order more copies of this book,
please call (800) 275-2606.

Library of Congress Cataloging-in-Publication Data:

Solomon, Gary, 1947-
    The motion picture prescription : watch this movie and call me in
the morning / by Gary Solomon. -- 1st ed.
      p.   cm.
    Includes index.
    ISBN 0-944031-27-7 : $12.95
    1. Motion pictures in psychotherapy.   I. Title.
RC489.M654S65 1995
616.89' 165- -dc20   95-237
                                        CIP

Cover by Leslie Waltzer
Illustration by Matt Barna
Printed in the USA
First Edition

10 9 8 7 6 5 4 3 2 1

Table of Contents

Dedication

To Robin Huhn:

My friend, my confidante, and the love of my life. I could not have written this book without your everlasting support.

Robin, I love you dearly.

Acknowledgments

I want to acknowledge a few people who helped make this book what it is today. Without their suggestions and guidance, the journey may not have taken place.

To Joanne Flanagan, my editor at Aslan Publishing, who saw the light and made it that much brighter. It is because of Joanne's insight, fortitude, and editorial expertise that you are able to buy and read my book. I will always be grateful for her direction and interest in my work.

To Wayne Kritsberg, a fellow writer for whom I have an incredible amount of admiration and respect. Through his experience and wisdom I gained direction that I use in my everyday life. Today I am able to call him my personal friend. What a gift.

To all those at Aslan Publishing and Atrium Publishers Group who did the things that needed to be done to make this book everything it could be. Writing the book is part of the journey. Their work takes it the rest of the way.

To all my former patients and clients who expressed their sadness when I told them I was leaving but encouraged me to go forward with my personal aspirations of being a writer. I will never forget you.

AND...A very special thanks to all the actors, actresses, directors, writers, producers, and anyone else in the mystical, magical world of movie making. You have no idea how much your work has meant to so many people who need to see and hear your healing messages. It is my hope that this book is the beginning of the acknowledgment and appreciation for all the wonderful gifts you have given us in the area of emotional recovery. Please, never stop making your healing stories.

Preface

There have been special moments in my life. One of the most important took place a few years ago with the most important person in my world.

About three years ago my wife, Robin, and I were having a weekend to ourselves. A rare occasion, I might add. My psychotherapy practice had grown so large that we had very little time together, weekend outings were few and far between. Robin is a therapist and was very aware of my feelings about using movies as a form of therapeutic intervention.

"I have an idea for a book," she said. "Something that's never been done and is desperately needed in our field. I think you're just the person to make it happen." All said in the true spirit of someone who believes her mate can do anything.

Now let me tell you that was difficult for me to imagine—that there could be any new books under the sun in the areas of self-help and healing. For the most part, it seemed that the books that came out each year were well written by authors who had a great understanding of the problems and issues most therapists and their clients dealt with but that the books generally all repeated the same ideas in a slightly different structure.

"Darling, there are no new ideas," I said, absolutely sure I was correct.

"No," she said. "This is a brand new idea and it's right under your nose. You simply can't see it."

This is going to be good, I thought. I had been in private practice for a number of years, was teaching at Arizona State University, and was on the staff at a local psychiatric hospital. If it was under my nose then my sense of smell was shot to smithereens.

"Let's have it," I said. "You have my complete and undivided attention." And she began.

"Write a book on how to use movies as a way to help people deal with their problems. You know, share your healing movies with everyone. You've been using movies as a therapeutic tool for years," she exclaimed. "Now let everyone have a chance to see how they can use your list of movies and your therapeutic approach."

Other than the hum of the engine and traffic noise there was complete silence in the car. I was stunned. She was absolutely right. Therapists, counselors, and hospitals have been using movies and audio tapes for years in treating their patients and clients. I pulled the car to the side of the road, looked her straight in the eye, kissed her, and thanked her for the idea of a lifetime. It had been with me all the time. I simply could not see it—or smell it.

I immediately began making notes and structuring the book. Because I was so busy I could not concentrate completely on the writing. I closed my practice and began working on the project full time. I am grateful to Robin not only for her helping me to see my way to this idea but also for her support throughout this project.

I hope you will be as excited by my book of healing stories as I was when Robin suggested that I write it for you. No matter who you are—typist, plumber, lawyer, stock clerk, therapist, teacher, mechanic, motion picture producer, anyone on the road to self-improvement and recovery—you will experience growth and self-enrichment from *The Motion Picture Prescription*. Have fun with my book and enjoy your journey. Movies are our stories; they are a wonderful way to heal our past, help us enjoy today, and have a brighter future tomorrow.

Gary Solomon, MPH, MSW, Ph.D.
Portland, Oregon

Introduction

One of the questions people ask me is when did I begin writing my book. I actually started writing it a few years ago after my wife had this wonderful idea for a new book and suggested I take it to fruition. But thinking back I've come to realize that I really began writing this book many years ago when I was quite young. I'd like to share with you how it all began. Possibly after you read my story you may find yourself going into your past, getting in touch with the energy you had as a child, and uncovering a wonderful idea that's been tucked away all these years.

Why This Book

When I was a child there were some movies that touched me in a way that was different than all the westerns and war movies that were the popular cinematic features of the day. I liked movies that could make me feel things. Now, I didn't exactly know what my feelings were back then, but whatever was happening when I watched movies, I liked it. I found I was interested in biographies or real-life stories, which seemed more real to me. I liked hearing about people's lives, learning about their personal experiences, and sharing their emotions. *The Great Houdini, The Thomas Edison Story,* and *The Benny Goodman Story* all meant more to me than any action movie that everyone else was watching. I preferred movies that had a message, and when one of those movies came on the television, I got lost—lost in a world that protected me from the fear, pain, and abuse that were my constant reminders that life was not a happy place to be.

At school I struggled my way through, hated my way through—I didn't learn to read or write until I was twelve. In those days schools just passed kids like me along to the next grade; I simply became the next teacher's problem. It wasn't a very happy time, but I had my movies and eventually my music, so nothing else mattered. Even though I quit high school to go on the road with a rock band, by some miracle I learned to read and write, and eventually I graduated high school with my class. And somehow, some way, after two junior colleges and a state college, I made my way to the University of California at Los Angeles (UCLA) where I entered into the Department of Psychology. I wrote my papers, took my tests (went to the ever-popular war protests to meet girls), and struggled to pass my classes. Come hell or high water, I was going to get that piece of paper that everyone said would never be mine.

No matter what was going on in my life, my interest in movies was never far behind. It was the late sixties, times were changing, and so were the movies. I got entrenched in *Easy Rider,* especially the message it sent about drugs and the evil that drugs bring to anyone who sells or uses them. I got buried in *Clockwork Orange,* particularly the society in chaos portrayed in that movie. How could we evolve into such a negative, violent world? Surely Vietnam and the Beatles hadn't brought us to that point. My experience with movies kept calling me to watch more and more stories with special messages. I would go out on a date and take whomever I was seeing at the time to a movie. Afterwards we would sit and talk for hours about the movie's message. I learned that movies broke the ice on a date and also released the real me that was hiding inside. What was even better was that my dates and my new friends felt the same way.

As time passed I acquired a bachelor's degree in psychology and a master's in public health. Shortly after completing my academic work, I became disenchanted with the health care field and jobs were becoming scarce. For many years I took on more entrepreneurial endeavors and opened up a retail chain of coffee and cookie stores. I suddenly stopped going to movies and only did things that made me money. All of that made me a very successful businessman with lots of power, control, and prestige. Then, at thirty-seven, my world came tumbling down around me. It was a time when the interest rates skyrocketed. My needs had become obsessions and had taken me over. I lost a small fortune and was addicted to anything and everything—from alcohol, drugs, and food to sex and sick relationships. I was broke and broken. I didn't know why it happened. I surely didn't want to go on living that way. So I returned to an old friend of mine, the movies.

I had a mountain of movies to choose from, such as *The Boost, Less Than Zero, 9 1/2 Weeks,* and *The Big Chill.* Every one of them was a great comfort to me. They each had a special message for me about what I had done to myself and how I got to where I was in my life. They taught me that I wasn't alone, and knowing that was that much more healing. I was insatiable. I watched everything. *Clean and Sober* and *Jo Jo Dancer* told me I better stop doing what I was doing and start pulling back together what was left of my shattered life. I thought, if there were people out there who were writing stories that I could relate to, there must be other people who were suffering from the same things. So I started on a mission.

I applied to the University of Southern California (USC) and, lo and behold, got into a master's of social work program. Part of the requirements was that I do an internship. There I was, still on the road to my own recovery, and I'm seeing people who are having relationship problems, alcohol problems, drug problems, grieving over the loss of someone, or not knowing who their real parents were—you name it. I really could empathize with what they were going through. But if I was having problems, I wondered, how was I going to reach out and help them? Suddenly, I got an idea. If I gained comfort and help from the movies I was watching, wouldn't my clients experience the same healing?

"So it sounds like you're having problems with drugs. I'd like you to rent *The Drug Store Cowboy* and *The Man With the Golden Arm.* Tell me what you see and how the characters make you feel." "You're really struggling with your pain over saying good-bye to your father. There's a movie called *Dad* that I would like you watch. Let me know what happens emotionally as you're watching the movie." "What I hear from you is that you are struggling with some issues over lost relationships. I'd like you to watch *Same Time Next Year* and *Over Forty.* I think you will see some things you've never noticed before."

Between you and me, it felt like, "Take two movies and call me in the morning. If you don't feel better, try taking two a week until you're relieved of your symptoms." And while I only reflected humorously on that thought in the beginning, soon I was aware that the concept of prescribing movies really works.

What's going on here? I asked myself. I had neither read anything about this in my textbooks nor had any of my professors ever lectured about this concept. The results amazed me. My clients reported seeing themselves in the movies. The more I prescribed, the better they became, and the more quickly they healed. They came out of denial, and the recovery process moved much more quickly than I had anticipated, certainly faster than my peers reported they were experiencing with their clients.

I used movies as a therapeutic tool with my clients in both of my internships with positive results and rave reviews. I ended up completing my academic work at the University of Tennessee and immediately started my doctorate degree studies at Arizona State University. I wanted to find out what it was that made movies work in the treatment of my clients, and acquiring a more advanced degree seemed the best way to investigate the subject. Much to my disappointment, I received little support for doing research in this area. Although I continued my doctorate, I quickly realized I was going to have to research these phenomena on my own. I decided to go into private practice.

Again and again, my clients reported that the experience of using the movies I prescribed brought wonderful results. If someone was having problems over abortion I suggested they watch *Roe vs. Wade* and *The Baby Maker.* If they were dealing with problems over being adopted or adopting I recommended *Our Very Own, Immediate Family,* and *I Want to Keep My Baby.* When they would talk about being spied on or stalked I recommended *Fatal Attraction, A Cry for Help: The Tracey Thurman Story,* and *Sleeping with the Enemy.* For men and women dealing with issues related to abuse and rape I would prescribe *The Accused, Radio Flyer, Closet Land,* and so on. When my clients presented a problem, I had a movie to help them deal with whatever they were going through. It was time to bring all the pieces together.

With the support of my wife I closed my practice for a time and went full steam ahead on the book. About eighteen months later I had the first draft written. A year after that I produced the final draft as you see it today. So, now it's your turn to experience your own healing. I want you to have your own recovery through your local movie theater or at the press of the button on your television or VCR. We all have things that are bothering us, past or present, and everyone needs to experience recovery in some form or another. That's what makes my healing approach so universal; there are movies to help everyone with their healing. All one has to do is look up a movie and watch it.

Most people associate recovery with addictions like gambling or alcohol. But you don't have to have problems with drugs, alcohol, food, sex, work-aholism, or gambling to be in recovery. You may be recovering from the loss of a relationship, the loss of a parent who's recently passed away, or the pain of a lost friendship. You may be dealing with negative feelings or blocked emotions about abortion, adoption, or being related to a mentally or physically challenged person. Some of you are experiencing or have experienced an abusive relationship that's left emotional scars. Others are in a relationship or know someone who's in a relationship that is codependent. Or you may be in pain or denial over knowing that you or someone you know has AIDS or a serious illness. Can you see how we all have something to deal with and to recover from in our lives? We each have a burden we carry, but where do we go for help, at what price, and for how long?

One of the wonderful things about my book is that it is a helping guide to those movies that can empower you to make your own life choices, your own decisions. When you become caught up in the emotional life of the movies, you experience feelings that in turn lead to breakthroughs in negative thought patterns and the opening of new ideas. You can turn to yourself for your own healing and recovery whenever you want, as often as you choose, with whomever you would like to be with, and at a minimal expense.

By using *The Motion Picture Prescription* you can begin your own healing journey. If you are in therapy the movies make a great addition to your work. If you don't need traditional therapy or aren't in treatment because you can't afford to go or it's not your style, you can see any of these movies on television for free or for the cost of cable. You can go to your local video store and rent most of these movies for under two dollars—two dollars to open up the doors to some of those issues that have been burdening you and holding you back from growing.

So How Does It All Work?

Part One begins with an overview of how to view movies as healing stories. This is followed by the movies, some two hundred healing stories, each on its own page and in alphabetical order. For quick reference, you can find the title of any movie at the top of the page and the identifying themes or life problems of each movie (such as the loss of a loved one, money troubles, some kind of substance abuse, etc.) just below the title. Next, you will find the movie's cast, as well as the director and screenwriter, when possible. The summary (synopsis) and my comments detailing the healing themes in the stories make up the bulk of the text. These are some of the many points and issues I want you to see in each movie. Additionally, in the comments section, you may be asked a few questions about yourself and how the movie might relate to you or someone you know. And from those questions I have given you some directions to help you with your individual healing. Finally, I have added the year the movie was made, the running time, the movie rating, and, whether the movie is in color or black and white.

Part Two is designed to respond to the needs of those who will use movies in therapy and contains a special message for therapists, a Motion Picture Prescription List, alphabetically grouped by therapeutic issues, and a Motion Picture Prescription Pad. Here, I speak not only to my peers but also to those of you who are already working on emotional issues in traditional therapy, as well as those in recovery from addictions. I have made every attempt to make this section as informative as possible for the layperson, even addressing those who select movies for group situations.

At the end of the book you will find a glossary, an index to the movies (cross-reference guide), what I call my movie suggestion box, and a note on where to reach me for workshops/lectures. I certainly look forward to hearing from you.

Let me leave you with one last thought. The movies are not intended to take the place of therapy. If you or someone you know needs particular therapeutic attention or if watching a movie brings up a need for additional help, I urge you to seek an individual or an organization that can give you the help and support you need. GOOD LUCK. STAY IN TOUCH.

PART ONE

Movies as Healing Stories

Movies Are Our Stories

Movies have become the dominant art form in our culture; and like other art forms, movies reflect both the deep inner suffering and the unlimited capacity for joy that make up our humanness.

— Wayne Kritsberg

The purpose of *The Motion Picture Prescription* is to provide you, the reader, with a list of movies that are healing stories. As a result of watching these healing stories you will achieve self-enrichment and an increased awareness that will help direct you to your recovery. You're in store for a unique and wonderful treat. Your healing really took off when you bought my book. Now, let's take the next step.

What's Special About Movies?

We all have different ways of hearing healing messages, and each of us receives those messages in our own time. Some of us hear them when we're quite young, while others live nearly a lifetime before hearing a healing message. Sadly, some never get the message and live a life in pain, fear, and distrust of the world around them. Did you ever have a teacher, or store clerk, or neighbor who was very special to you? Maybe he or she was someone you could talk to about your feelings or share what was happening in your life. I had a couple of those people in my life. And on occasion they gave me some words of wisdom that I carry with me to this day. Listening to their words was soothing to me, getting me through some very difficult times. But imagine what it would be like if you could both hear and see those messages whenever you wanted and as many times as you liked?

You must have heard the phase, "A picture is worth a thousand words." Well, what do you think a moving picture is worth? Trillions of words? They're worth that and more. Here's an example we can all relate to: asking someone for directions.

"Well, let me see. Now you go down three miles until you get to the third stop sign. Or is it the fourth? Well, it's the third or the fourth, one or the other. You'll know you're there when you see the old burnt-out building. Or did they take that down? I was in that building when they just opened it. Anyway, go down two more miles and…." Frustrating and confusing, don't you think? You stopped listening halfway through and are already gearing up to ask someone else. But what if they gave you a map or drew one out for you so that you could see where you were and where you were going? Simple enough. That's what using movies as healing stories, to help with your recovery, is all about. The movie is your map and my stories supply you with some landmarks to make your journey easier and safer. You can see where you are and you know where you are going.

We each hear and see things differently. I say it's blue, you say it's dark blue. I say he's short, you say he's not very tall. We simply perceive things differently. What I have done in *The Motion Picture Prescription* is supply you with healing stories we can all see and still get the message, each in our own way, no matter who we are or what our beliefs.

Now, there are some images that are so strong that we can't help but agree on what these images mean. Do you remember this television commercial? It began with this guy holding an egg and saying something like: "Okay, let's try it one more time." (Holding up the egg and pointing to it.) "This is your brain." (He cracks open the egg and it drops onto a hot frying pan.) "This is your brain on drugs. Any questions?" I doubt if there is any question as to what the message meant: Drugs fry your brain. For most of us who saw it, it was a most unforgettable image, a powerful statement that hopefully brought a lot of people on drugs out of their denial about what they were doing to themselves. Well, that's what I want for you—the same powerful healing experience when you read my healing stories and watch the movie (or movies) I recommend.

Each movie offers a different message and brings that message to you in a way that will be eye opening and enlightening. And like the story about the egg, the healing messages will bring you out of denial, the denial that holds most people back from recovery. "I'm not an alcoholic. You just can't hold your liquor like me." "I'm not angry about what my parents did to me. I just like to eat, that's all." "Upset about my friends not calling me? No way. The heck with them. Who needs them anyway." Movies help break through the walls of denial in a very special way. They help us see and hear things that we were unwilling or unable to acknowledge on our own. Movies allow us to suspend our disbelief long enough to get the message. Suspend our disbelief? What's that you say? How about an example.

Do you remember when *Jurassic Park* came out? It was about this guy who owns a park where dinosaurs live. You think, *Yeah, right, dinosaurs. They've been extinct for millions of years. Now you want me to believe that these are real dinosaurs? You're nuts.* Well, the movie was so well done that it caused people to suspend their disbelief about the fact that dinosaurs are extinct. And for a time, if only while the movie was playing, they believed that there was a place called Jurassic Park and that dinosaurs lived in that park. Some people suspended their disbelief so long that they tried to find the park so they could take their family vacation in Jurassic Park. Suspension of disbelief is like coming out of denial.

By suspending our disbelief about ourselves or what's going on in our lives we have a chance to see things as they really are rather then the illusion we have created in our lives. It doesn't matter that an actor is an alcoholic in real life or not. In *When a Man Loves a Woman*, the actress Meg Ryan got us to suspend our disbelief and she became a raving, card-carrying alcoholic. Tom Hanks did the same thing for us in *Forrest Gump*. He, along with the rest of his movie-making-crew, got us to suspend our disbelief and accept that there really was a Forrest Gump who taught Elvis to dance, played Ping-Pong for the U. S. Olympic team, met two presidents, etc. You see, if I can get you to suspend your disbelief long enough, you will have the opportunity to see things as they are and to feel differently about life's problems, which means you will no longer be in denial. Now, given that you have the big picture—pun intended—who will benefit from this recovery approach?

Anyone and everyone will be able to grow from my healing stories. Hospitals and treatment center staff can enjoy turning the pages of my book and finding healing movies that apply to all of their patients and then airing them for everyone to see. Recovery groups and halfway house residents will be able to experience the healing messages. Prison and jail administrators can show movies to the inmates that will change the way they think, feel, and do things for the rest of their lives. Educators at all levels can show any of these movies to their students as they work to heighten the level of awareness in their students about specific problem areas in life. And people who counsel and give therapy will be able to use the movies as an adjunct in treating their clients.

If you are a therapist, counselor, treatment facilitator, minister, teacher, or anyone who is reaching out to help people through difficult times, you will now have a comprehensive list of movies with healing messages and a guideline by which to choose the movies for the people you are trying to help. To make things easy for you, I have included a motion picture prescription pad and a complete motion picture prescription list at the back of the book. Simply make copies of them from the book and give them to your clients as needed. I trust from my own experience as a therapist that you will find the list invaluable.

Hooray for Hollywood!

Hollywood's been making healing movies for years without knowing it. And the therapeutic community has been overlooking this body of therapeutic work. Well, those healing movies won't be passed over any more because we now have the beginnings of a master list of all their healing productions with more of my healing stories to come. I want you to experience the rich, emotional life in every movie from A to Z. And I would like you to enjoy the freedom that comes from finding the answers to your life problems and from finding recovery at your own pace. If it's true that there's no business like show business, then I think we have another reason to shout, "Hooray for Hollywood!"

Actors, actresses, writers, directors, the whole movie-making industry for that matter, gives us movies with healing stories that help us suspend our disbelief, come out of our denial, and direct us to look at ourselves and the world around us. That's what makes their work such an important part of our recovery process. I'm not even sure they know themselves how important their work is to our emotional lives. But I am hoping the movie industry will gain as much from my work as all of you will. Maybe there will be more of an incentive throughout the motion picture industry to create healing stories to show us how art can imitate life.

The Healing Stories in Movies

One of the reasons it's true that movies make powerful healing stories is because what happens to the characters in the movies can and often does happen to each of us in real life. Movies are a true example of how art imitates life. To begin the journey all you need to do is to identify those movies that apply to your individual life problem or those that will help you to self-nurture and grow. The movies will help you experience healing yourself and/or supporting family members and friends along their own healing path.

Now you may be thinking, why not just go out and buy some self-help and recovery books? Heaven knows there are more than enough of them out there! Many of them are well written. I must have two hundred or so on my bookshelf. The truth is I haven't had the time to read most of them. And I prefer watching a good movie with my wife and close friends to reading a book on my own. Let me explain more about why using movies as healing stories is more effective and easier than reading books.

Have you ever read a novel by an author like James Michener or Stephen King? How long did it take you to read those 750 plus pages? A week, a month, three months? I don't mind telling you that, as much as I love Michener's work, I have spent as long as six months reading one of his books. Yet, when Michener's *Space*, Stephen King's *It*, and the books by other authors are translated to the screen, I can see what they have written in about two hours. So, when you watch a movie one of the benefits over reading is that you experience the entire healing story in one sitting, whether you watch it on television or rent the video. In that sense a video library is no different than a book library. You simply pull it off your own shelf or rent it from a video store and pop it into a VCR. Two hours later you have experienced what might have taken weeks or months—with many interruptions—to understand if you read the book. Think, how many books are on your shelf today that you haven't read verses the number of movies you have rented that you didn't watch? The bottom line is that movies offer all of us the path of least resistance.

Here's another reason why I prefer the movies. I consider myself a fairly bright person. But when I read that 750-page book I tend to lose track of who the characters are and where the plot is taking me. "Now let's see, what did he do before? Where did he come from? Why did she decide to do that?" You get the idea. That rarely happens when you watch movies. I'll bet you can tell me in detail about the last five movies you watched—including the names of the actors and actresses. Can you do the same for the last five books you read? I wouldn't expect you to. When you choose to use movies in your recovery process you can focus your attention on the movie and embrace the story line with little or no effort. Accordingly you are able to direct your attention and energy to the healing messages in the movie and not the who did what to whom and where and when and so on in a book. Movies make it easy. All you have to do is take advantage of the process.

Seeing Is Believing

When a writer wants you to experience a character's anger he or she has to go into detail, describing every nuance and emotion, so that your mind's eye can capture the creative images. Yet you can see anger in a matter of seconds when it is portrayed in a movie. Just take a look at *Unspeakable Acts* and *Women on the Verge of a Nervous Breakdown*. In any one of these movies, you can't help but experience anger through the actor's character portrayal and the writer's words. There is no question about what these characters are going through. Someone can tell you he or she is enraged or hurt, but when the rage or hurt is accompanied by a visual image you know what is really happening with that person.

For years instructional videos and movies have been used to teach us everything from how to use computers or cook a meat loaf to showing us all how to be better drivers. (Don't you just hate getting a traffic ticket and having to watch those training films? Yuck.) Well, using movies as healing stories is the same idea. You're able to watch the movie as if it were a "how to" heal yourself story. *He Said, She Said* is the "how to" on relationships and love. *Mommie Dearest* is the "how to" on getting in touch with your feelings on abuse and abandonment. *My Name is Bill W.*

is the "how to" on alcohol and recovery. Each movie helps bring you out of denial and get in touch with your feelings, and confronts you with your own issues, often while you are being entertained at the same time. In many cases this takes place through a process that I call paradoxical healing. Don't worry, it's much simpler than it sounds.

All of us have experienced paradoxical learning in one form or another. As children we put our hands on a hot stove or walked on hot pavement. "Ouch! I won't do that again." You see, you have experienced paradoxical learning. You learned what not to do by doing it. The same thing is true for relationships. I know I've been in a few rough relationships in my life and would not get involved in a similar relationship because of the negative learning experience—or paradoxical healing. You may recall something similar to this idea as another learning tool known as negative reinforcement. By watching the movies you experience negative reinforcement, which leads to paradoxical healing.

In *The Boost*, James Woods plays the role of a man who gets hooked on cocaine. We watch him as he goes in and out of his addictive cycle. Eventually he succumbs to the cocaine and we are left with an image of a broken shell of a man who has become a full blown addict. How is that healing? you say. It's healing because we are left with a strong, indelible, visual image of what not to become; what not to let happen to us in our own lives. You see, this is paradoxical healing. We can come out of denial rapidly and, sometimes, learn best by seeing the exact opposite of a satisfying, rewarding, independent way of living.

How about another one? In *Lady Sings the Blues*, Diana Ross plays Billie Holiday, a real-life singer who fell prey to alcohol and heroin. We see her rise to stardom only to plummet, a victim of her own doing. Again, we experience paradoxical healing by seeing what not to do in our own lives. Simple, isn't it? I think you've got the idea. Let's move on.

Over the years I've met many people who've had a difficult time going through therapy. Some have difficulty because of their preconceived notion of what therapy is all about. Others are so entrenched in their own issues that the therapy just doesn't get through. Men can be resistant to therapy because they believe it's not a very manly thing to do. Women often receive resistance from their male counterparts because the men don't want their "dirty laundry" aired in front of a stranger. Still others don't believe in therapy. For some, seeing a therapist once or twice a week is simply not enough. They find they need more input and support. And for most people therapy is an unaffordable luxury. Whatever the reason, movies can often be the solution to many of these difficulties. You can watch the movies in the privacy of your own home, as often as you want, and for a fraction of the cost of therapy.

Movies are a help to almost everyone because they allow us to be with our emotions and our feelings in an environment that feels safe, such as our own home or that of a friends. If you have been in therapy you may be able to relate to the discomfort that comes from being in a foreign environment. A "safe" environment allows us to relax and more openly express and share our feelings.

Movies can help you deal with issues that you thought were resolved but are once again rearing their ugly heads. From time to time former patients or clients returned to my office years after they completed their personal work. They will complain of a backlash of depression, that they want to drink or use drugs, or that they feel as if they have lost control of their temper. The movies in my book offer immediate access to help and, oftentimes, a quick resolve to many old problems. If you have a friend to whom you want to reach out, watching a movie together can be the answer. Through a character or problem portrayed on the screen, you both have an opportunity to confront personal issues. The emotions portrayed in the movie open up feelings as you both watch, and you have a shared experience that can move towards resolution. The movies are a great way to turn a social event into a self-healing experience because the healing stories help you reach out to those who would not otherwise get involved in recovery.

Denial, Recovery, and Life Problems

You can see denial far more clearly when it is acted out in a movie than when you read about it in a book or if a therapist tries to explain it to you. Once you see what denial really looks like by observing an actor or actress playing a role, you can get in touch with your own denial. Watch James Cagney in *Come Fill the Cup*, Meg Ryan in *When a Man Loves a Woman*, or Jane Fonda in *The Morning After* to see people deal with their alcoholism. No more denial for them. What about *The Karen Carpenter Story* for problems relating to overeating and anorexia? How about *Sid and Nancy* and *Drugstore Cowboy* when dealing with drugs; or

Falling Down and *Postcards From the Edge* to look at depression and being pushed so far in life that it is possible to end up emotionally ragged? You have so many great movies to choose from; your options are limitless.

If you are questioning yourself about adoption and custody problems, why not watch *Kramer vs. Kramer, Baby Boom, Our Very Own,* and other movies with similar stories to help you break through some of the feelings that are keeping you stuck? A divorce may be stopping you from moving forward in your life, so you have *The Good Mother, Shirley Valentine,* and *The Way We Were* to help you confront some of your feelings. Maybe someone you know is trying to cope with a death in the family or their own mortality. *Adam, Doctor,* and *The Dollmaker* are all movies to help see you through this life problem.

You might decide to have a group of friends over to watch *The Big Chill* or *Grand Canyon* to deal with issues about friends and relationships. Have your family over to watch *The Gathering* to address issues of family conflict or *My Breast* to deal with abandonment or your fear of physical illness. The point is you have numerous options. All you have to do is exercise them. If you watch just one movie a week for the next two years, imagine the personal growth and recovery you could enjoy. That's not even half of the movies in my first book. And there are more books to come.

You will also find many movies that are great for children and adolescents. The movies are a wonderful way to open up a dialogue between parents and children. If either you or your children have difficulty talking about a particular problem, the movies can be used to create a foundation for future discussion. If a parent is suspicious that something is going on in their child's or adolescent's life, movies are great ice breakers. Try *Do You Know the Muffin Man?* or *Sarah T.: Portrait of a Teenage Alcoholic.* You will find that your child or adolescent will be less resistant to talking about what's going on in their life once they view the movie and realize that no one is ever alone.

Watching the Movie

Now that you've got the hang of selecting a movie, I'd like to give you an idea about how to watch the movie to get the most from the experience. First, I recommend that you make sure you will be undisturbed; take the phone off the hook or turn the volume to your answering machine off to avoid interruptions. Pin a DO NOT DISTURB sign on your door. Tell the kids it's adult time or tuck them in bed for the night. Even if you are watching the movies in a group, make the movie the primary focus of the evening. Avoid diversions that will take you away from your feelings and the messages the movie has to offer. Don't play a game, read a book, or have unrelated discussions while the movie is on. And please, if you are someone who has problems with substance abuse, keep your mind clear. No drinking, eating, smoking, drugging, etc. Focus. Focus. Focus.

Before viewing the movie, read what it's about in this book. Use the healing themes and comments sections as stepping stones to help you identify key ideas in the movie. Take some notes and highlight issues in the book that you want to look for in the movie. Keep a pencil and paper close by and journal what you're feeling as you watch the movie. Before you get started tell yourself you're going to focus on your feelings, especially those conjured up by memories of the past or current emotional issues.

So now you're ready to start watching your movie. If you're going to watch the movie from regular television programming, be sure to check your television guide for the exact starting time. Don't miss the beginning of the movie; the healing starts the moment the movie starts playing, including the opening credits. The same thing is true for videos. Watch the movie from beginning to end. This is no time to use that scan button. Hands off. Try to identify with a character or situation. What feelings do you experience? Look for the reasons that brought those feelings to the surface. What's happening on the screen that reminds you of something in your past or somebody you know or once knew? Have you been avoiding things or have you done something that has given you a sense of guilt, anger, sadness, etc.? Don't worry about how your notes look or what you're saying. Just get your thoughts down on paper. Use a tape recorder and record your thoughts if you prefer, but keep moving forward through the movie.

After the movie is over, turn off your television and/or your VCR and just be by yourself for a few moments—even if you're with friends or family. Don't rush off to do something else. Use the time to be introspective and self-exploring. Look at your notes and write more about what you are experiencing. Keep your notes in a place where you can reflect on them in the weeks and months to come; never destroy what you have written. Build a library of your thoughts in your own recovery movie book. Whether you watch the movies alone or in a group, in time you will experience tremendous growth and personal healing. Follow the steps that I have suggested, add your own style, and keep on watching.

Summing Everything Up

You have at your finger tips a list of movies to help you along the road to recovery. You can read my comments and remember my thoughts as you're watching each movie or you can come up with your own ideas. Your expense will be minimal, for you can rent two or three movies a week for about six dollars tops or watch movies as they're aired on television. In most cases if you check your television guide you will find that many movies air regularly, some even play back-to-back or at two different time slots for two days in a row. Have friends over and make a party of watching movies regularly. After you have worked through the issues spend some time discussing your feelings about the movie and the message. If you know someone who could use some suspending of their disbelief ask them to sit and watch the movie with you. Use these movies along with your private therapy or go it on your own. You can't go wrong, and I know you will grow by leaps and bounds. And here's one final message: Your healing begins with the first healing story you read and movie you watch. The controls are in your hands. Push the button and GET STARTED TODAY.

About Last Night

Healing Themes:

- Meeting, falling in love, and getting involved too quickly
- When friends interfere, learning not to let friends pressure you
- Trying to say you are sorry
- Refusing to accept an apology
- Leaving a relationship

Cast: Rob Lowe, Demi Moore, Elizabeth Perkins, James Belushi. Director, Edward Zwick. Writers, Tim Kazurinsky and Dennis Declue.

Synopsis: A group of young adults spend their days working and their nights on the prowl for relationships and sex. Danny Martin and Debbie Sullivan meet and fall in love on the fast-track. The relationship soon goes on the rocks and their friends offer little support.

Comments: More than anything this movie is about the course new relationships go through during those crucial beginning days. One of the biggest problems I see with relationships today is the lack of communication. Notice how Danny and Debbie never really set any boundaries or guidelines for the relationship. Neither of them really knows what the other person needs or wants; they simply move in together and set up house. And what about their friends? Maybe you have experienced the loss of a friend when he or she has found that "special someone." Watch how the friends undermine the relationship with little comments and control techniques. You can see and feel their frustrations. They're jealous of the new relationship and angry with the friend; having lost control, they simply transfer the anger to whomever is in the way. Make decisions for yourself. Don't be influenced by others who say they have your best interest at heart. Can you relate to feeling envious about someone else's relationship? There was a part of me that wanted to see what happened to each of the characters when the movie ended. This is a great movie to help you get in touch with how relationships work and what not to do. Give *He Said, She Said* a try. It's another good one. *About Last Night* was adapted from a David Mamet play entitled *Sexual Perversity in Chicago*.

Year: 1986
Length: 113 min
Rating: R
Color

The Accidental Tourist

Healing Themes:

- Letting someone into your life
- Learning to love again
- When you have trouble moving on
- Dealing with the death of a child
- Listening to your inner self
- Allowing yourself to become more spontaneous

Cast: William Hurt, Geena Davis, Kathleen Turner, Ed Begley, Jr., David Ogden Stier, Bill Pullman, Amy Wright. Director, Lawrence Kasdan. Writers, Frank Galati and Lawrence Kasdan.

Synopsis: Macon Leary, a perfectionist, writes books about how to travel efficiently. His own life is far from perfect: his son died, his wife leaves him, and his tired sister has taken on a caretaker role. By chance he meets Muriel Pritchett, who trains his dog. In time a relationship emerges and things change.

Comments: I hated this movie for the first half hour. What in the world are they talking about? Then it hit me. When Macon talks about being an efficient traveler, he's really talking about life and relationships, guiding us, step by step, through some of life's more difficult personal moments. There is a great deal going on in this movie. Notice how the sister is unable to let go of the role of caretaker. Maybe you know someone like her. Are you that person? Many people cannot move on. You will see that in Macon as he continues to grieve over the loss of his son and his wife. In contrast, Muriel is a reminder to all that you don't have to sit back and wait for someone else to take charge. Listen carefully to Macon's inner conflict as he goes from place to place. We see Macon beginning the healing that he needs to go through so that he can truly travel the emotional roads he writes about. Do you find yourself stuck in one place, unable to journey into the mainstream of life? Tell yourself you deserve all the happiness and emotional goodness that life has to offer. Watch this movie with a group of friends. You might want to pause the movie to discuss what you have seen and heard, or take a few notes and then go on. If you like the movie, I suggest you read the book by Ann Tyler.

Year: 1988
Length: 121 min
Rating: PG
Color

The Accused

Healing Themes:

- Dealing with rape and confronting the assailant
- Fighting against all odds
- When alcohol and drugs make life unmanageable
- Abuse of power
- Sending messages that backfire on you
- Being abandoned by someone who said they cared

Cast: Jodie Foster, Kelly McGillis, Bernie Coulson, Steve Antin, Leo Rossi. Director, Jonathan Kaplan. Writer, Tom Topor.

Synopsis: Sarah Tobias gets drunk while at the local hangout and is raped by four of the men who are at the bar. The assistant district attorney struggles with making a deal to close the case or taking it to trial to get the kind of justice Sarah feels she deserves. Justice is served when Sarah has her day in court.

Comments: If you're someone who is dealing with the terrible trauma of rape, *The Accused* is going to have quite an impact on you. On occasion I like to give a warning about some of the movies in my book. This is one now. I found a few of the scenes in this movie difficult to take. It's important that you prepare yourself to watch them. If you are in treatment for issues involving rape, check with your therapist or counselor before watching this movie. If you have been keeping your rape a secret, be assured you will have a strong reaction. Hold tight! In addition to the rape, *The Accused* confronts us with alcohol, lying, and the mistreatment of some victims in our judicial system. No matter how someone acts or what sexual messages they are sending, that does not mean they give up their rights to consent to having sexual contact or any physical contact for that matter. There is a lot of pain that comes with the memories of rape. Some people have problems living a normal life and being intimate again. But there is hope. You can experience healing from your painful ordeal through support groups, counselors, therapists, and ministers. It takes a lot of courage to move through your fears and get to the other side. Why not give this movie a try to gain a peace you thought lost because of the ordeal of rape.

Year: 1988
Length: 110 min
Rating: R
Color

Adam

Healing Themes:

- Coping with the senseless loss of a child
- Dealing with your rage
- When your world is turned upside down
- Rallying support and working to make changes
- Advocating for the rights of children

Cast: Daniel J. Travanti, JoBeth Williams, Martha Scott, Richard Masur, Paul Regina, Mason Adams. Director, Michael Tuchner. Writer, Allan Leicht.

Synopsis: Adam is a six-year-old with two loving parents, John and Reve Walsh. While on a family outing, Adam turns up missing. A search provides no leads. As the parents begin to accept the fate of their son, they lobby for more strict laws and better support for tracking down lost persons.

Comments: A child's kidnapping can bring the strongest of families to their knees over the pain that comes with grieving their loss. But there is healing and that's what I want you to experience through John and Reve Walsh. No doubt the name will sound familiar. John Walsh appeared on a number of TV shows and I had the honor of consulting on one involving children's safety. Let *Adam* help you get in touch with your own grieving from the loss of a loved one. Find yourself in John and Reve. Look for the healing that comes from going through the grieving process of shock, denial, anger, rage, and acceptance. The movie also gives us an opportunity to learn what we can do to help support those who are looking for someone who may have been abducted. John and Reve Walsh got so involved in the process they advocated for and founded the Missing Children's Bureau. Learn more about what you can do to protect yourself from those who are ill and would hurt your children or someone you care about. There's healing when you take action. You will feel better and your children will be safer. Take a lesson from *Adam*: One person can move mountains; John Walsh sure did.

Year: 1983
Length: 100 min
Rating: Unrated
Color

Alice in Wonderland

Healing themes:
- When fantasy leads to a greater reality
- Finding the child within you
- Realizing that life is full of many choices and experiences
- Making the journey

Cast: Carol Marsh, Stephen Murray, Pamela Brown, Felix Aylmer, Ernest Milton. Directors, Clyde Geronimi, Hamilton Luske, and Wilfred Jackson.

Synopsis: Alice, an average, everyday kind of girl, follows a rabbit down a hole and finds herself in Wonderland, where everyone and everything is not quite what it appears to be. By the end of her journey, Alice emerges from Wonderland having learned and grown from her adventure.

Comments: Now I don't know about you, but *Alice in Wonderland* takes me back to my college days. There was that inevitable discussion about what the book really meant. "It's a drug trip," or "It's a political satire," and one of my all-time favorites is, "Alice is really God and the hole is really the road to...." Oh please. Let's get real. The truth is that fables, like dreams, mean something different to every one of us. What I would like is for you to watch the movie in a way that parallels your own life. Alice goes on a journey. What kind of journey are you on in your life? Do you feel like Alice, falling into a deep, dark hole, not knowing where you are going? Maybe you're stuck in one place. Some people fix that problem through drugs, gambling, alcohol, sex, smoking, etc. Is that what you're doing? Alice runs into creatures who sit around and say or do crazy things. Are some of your friends into addictions and do nothing but vegetate? Do you ever have crazy conversations with crazy people who do crazy things? And does Alice learn from her experience that life is all about learning and growing? Just like Alice, do you feel small when things are closing in on you and tall when you take action? Give this one a try. Go back to how you felt as a child and experience this movie as a healing story. See if, like Alice, you can find the answer to some of life's crazy questions.

Year: 1950
Length: 83 min
Rating: PG
Color

Alien

Healing Themes:
- Confronting the evil in all of us
- Capturing your inner strength
- Saving yourself from those who would hold you back
- Preventing your own self-destruction
- Trusting your intuition

Cast: Sigourney Weaver, Tom Skeritt, Veronica Cartwright, Yaphet Kotto, Harry Dean Stanton, Ian Holm, John Hurt. Director, Ridley Scott. Writer, Dan O'Bannon.

Synopsis: Ripley is a member of a space freight crew which encounters a carnivorous creature that breeds in the bodies of other living animals. The crew wages war on the alien which kills everyone with the exception of Ripley and a cyborg, a human-like robot.

Comments: Sometimes science fiction movies have wonderful messages in them. As is the case with *Dr. Jekyll and Mr. Hyde* and *Star Wars*, *Alien* is about our other side, the evil in each of us. The symbolism in this movie forces us to look inside ourselves. It begs us to ask questions about how we live our lives. What aliens rear their ugly heads in your life? Are you lying in your relationship, having an affair? What does your alien do to you as a pay-off for your lying: Sleepless nights from worries over being caught? Maybe you're have some pains in your stomach? Maybe you're cheating on tests or not giving your employer what they're paying for? The alien is a reaction to your conscience. No matter what we do or how hard we try, our conscience is always aware of what we're doing. If your other side makes an evil choice, you can be assured your alien will get you one way or another. Sure there are ways to keep that alien quiet. Just keep it fed. You can use drugs, alcohol, gambling, smoking, food, etc., etc., etc. But as soon as you stop stuffing those feelings inside, that alien's going to want to be fed and you're back on the merry-go-round. Look for the alien in your life. Get in touch with what you're doing to keep your life in check. Force yourself to confront your alien and get rid of it for the rest of your life.

Year: 1979
Length: 116 min
Rating: R
Color

All That Jazz

Healing Themes:

- Living in illusion when drugs and alcohol take you to the end
- If relationships have no meaning
- Catering to someone's obsession
- Falling in love with someone who can't love
- Turning your back on the truth

Cast: Roy Scheider, Jessica Lange, Ann Reinking, Ben Vereen, John Lithgow, Wallace Shawn, Cliff Gorman, Leland Palmer, Sandahl Bergman. Director, Bob Fosse. Writers, Robert Alan Authur and Bob Fosse.

Synopsis: A talented and highly successful choreographer is a little too into himself, plus pills, alcohol, and cigarettes, for his own good. It all comes crashing down around him when his affairs and addictions finally do him in.

Comments: Here's a chance to see and hear all about the effects that drugs, alcohol, smoking, and sex have on one person's life. The choreographer has a special art for bringing out the best in his dancers. He also communicates his inner self through the interpretation of his dance routines. Sounds like a formula for success, but be prepared for a very different experience. There are those who might suggest that this is the nature of someone who is a genius at work. "Oh, I'm so creative I need things to help me," or "It's okay, I'm under a lot of stress." Maybe you know someone who uses those excuses to justify their behavior. Maybe it's you who's caught in the addictive cycle. Pay special attention to the fantasy scenes where he is looking in the mirror. We get inside the mind of this addict, living each day as if it were "show time," keeping up a front when he's falling apart. Watch his inability to make a commitment in his personal life. Are you with someone who can't commit to you or to their own recovery? This movie offers an almost surrealistic perspective on addictive behavior. If this one doesn't send you the healing message about life, keep trying. There are many more to choose from. Give yourself credit for taking that first step toward recovery.

Year: 1979
Length: 120 min
Rating: R
Color

An Affair to Remember

Healing Themes:
- Finding that special someone
- Feeling betrayed
- Giving yourself a chance to know that it is true love
- Seeing what true love is all about
- Telling another that you no longer love them
- Having it all come tumbling down just when you think you've made it

Cast: Cary Grant, Deborah Kerr, Richard Denning, Neva Patterson, Cathleen Nesbitt, Robert Q. Lewis, Charles Watts, Fortunio Bonanova. Director, Leo McCarey. Writers, Delmer Daves and Leo McCarey.

Synopsis: A playboy and a singer meet on an ocean liner. Both are engaged to others but fall in love. They make a pact to meet atop the Empire State Building three months after the boat docks, giving each other time to become independent. Unforeseen events forestall their meeting. When they do meet they must pass their own test of love.

Comments: In case this movie sounds familiar it's because, in part, it's what *Sleepless in Seattle* is based on. Most movies have separate healing messages. This movie is one beautiful message: When the right one comes along, nothing will keep you apart. But you'll have to work on it. A strong relationship is one where both partners are always working to make it all that it can be. At issue in this romance is trust. Both of them break their commitments to their prospective mates by having an affair. Simply because it was not a sexual relationship does not mean they were not having an affair. Affairs of the mind occupy the emotional space reserved for the person with whom you are involved. What about waiting the three months? Could you if you were in love? Do you think it was fair that she did not let him know what happened? If it were true love, would it have made a difference? Sometimes we get so caught up in just trying to get through the day we forget about romance. Romance heals in a very special way. Watch this movie as a couple and remind each other of your commitment to have an honest relationship with one another.

Year: 1957
Length: 115 min
Rating: Unrated
Color

Baby Boom

Healing Themes:

- Taking on responsibility
- Changing your life to suit your needs
- If your identity is wrapped up in how you earn your living
- Searching inside yourself for what you really want
- Realizing that money isn't everything
- Learning to love another

Cast: Diane Keaton, Harold Ramis, Sam Shepard, Sam Wanamaker, James Spader, Pat Hingle, Britt Leach, Mary Gross, Victoria Jackson, Paxton Whitehead, Annie Golden, Dori Brenner, Robin Bartlett, Christopher North. Director, Charles Shyer. Writers, Charles Meyers and Nancy Meyers.

Synopsis: J. C. Wiatt, a high-powered advertising executive, inherits a baby and tries to find someone to "take it off her hands." As she spends more time with her niece, her values change. J. C. learns that life is not all about business; it's more about love.

Comments: So you're just too darn busy with work. If there are any roses around, you would never notice. Well, *Baby Boom* is here to say make room for that hobby you put on the back shelf and take that trip you've been putting off for so many years. If you've had a chance to watch *The Closer* you have some idea of what this movie will teach you. This movie makes a statement to all those who have lost the reason why they're working so hard. Notice how this single event in J. C.'s life represents a catalyst for change. Instead of it being a baby, she could have experienced the death of someone close or a serious financial setback. It could have been an illness that forced her to slow down. Once J. C. allows the child's love in, she is able to have everything she wants, plus those things she never imagined. Those who get caught up in work are no different than those who lose their way to alcohol, gambling, etc. They're all just ways to avoid living life as it was intended. You can experience your own rebirth with *Baby Boom*. Oh, and on your way to rent this movie, why not stop off at a florist and smell some roses? Trust me, you've got the time.

Year: 1987
Length: 103 min
Rating: PG
Color

Baby M

Healing Themes:
- Making the difficult decision to give your child up for adoption
- Dealing with the pain of someone changing their mind
- Feeling betrayed by the legal system
- Standing up for your rights
- Deciding to adopt
- Doing what is in the best interest of the child

Cast: JoBeth Williams, John Shea, Dabney Coleman, Bruce Weitz, Robin Strasser, Anne Jackson, Bruce McGill, Jenny Lewis. Director, James Steven Sadwith.

Synopsis: A factual account of the first court challenge over surrogacy, especially the rights of a birth mother and her prerogative to change her mind. Elizabeth Whitehurst enters into a contract to be artificially inseminated but refuses to give William and Elizabeth Stern the baby. Each side deals with a great deal of pain and the courts hand down a decision in the best interest of the child.

Comments: Usually anything involving conception is sensitive for most people. Here's a fine movie that helps us focus on some of the issues dealing with adoption. Most adoptive parents are not psychologically prepared for any problems. Use *Baby M* as a tool to deal with the emotional investments you are taking into the adoption. Watch the Sterns as they become more involved in the anticipation of the arrival of the baby and then when the birth mother changes her mind. Ask yourself if this is an experience you are prepared to go through. Do you really know all of your rights? Be prepared for anything. Bringing a child into your home is a wonderful, enchanting experience. To lose that child could be overwhelming. If you are considering giving up your child, watch this movie and ask yourself these questions: Can I handle giving up my child for adoption? Can I let go of my baby? This is no time to go it alone. Seek counseling from someone with a background in adoptions. *Baby M* lends us a chance to heal our denial and inexperience before anything negative happens. Give this one a try. I think you will grow in the process. I also might suggest *The Baby Maker* and *Immediate Family*, two more movies with similar themes.

Year: 1988
Length: 200 min
Rating: Unrated
Color

Barfly

Healing Themes:

- When life is run by alcohol
- If you bury your feelings in a bottle
- If you are attracted to someone who drinks
- When refusing to see the problem endangers your life
- When you hang out with losers
- Abandoning your friends for your addiction

Cast: Mickey Rourke, Faye Dunaway, Alice Krige, Frank Stallone, J. C. Quinn. Director, Barbet Schroeder. Writer, Charles Bukowski.

Synopsis: Henry is a writer who can't seem to get his act together. When he's not at the bar, he bums around trying to get money for the next drink. Wanda is his girlfriend. They both live an existence of lost dreams and hopes which puts them going nowhere on a slow track back to their old friend, alcohol.

Comments: This movie is almost painful to watch because we see the way some people lose themselves in their addictions. Let me be honest here. When I see movies like *Barfly* or *Ironweed* I feel overwhelmed. If I were to ever fall prey to the course in life that Henry has taken I couldn't imagine being able to survive. That's why I feel so strongly about movies with paradoxical healing messages. Remember, we learn by seeing the opposite and then taking the proper road home. It's clear that Henry and Wanda took the wrong path in life. *Barfly* brings to light the misery that goes with the condition of alcoholism. It takes away all the glamour. We know that a lot of homeless people are caught up in the cycle of alcohol and drug addiction. Does this movie make you want to reach out to those who are less fortunate? Does it make you grateful for your own life? If you are having problems with drugs and alcohol, here's the total picture and an opportunity to avoid the inevitable downfall if you keep feeding your emotional problem. *Barfly* is a healing gift for those who can't seem to stop living on life's edge. Try to get involved with any number of support groups to help you with your alcohol or drug problem. There are Alcoholics Anonymous meetings all over the world. Start walking the road to recovery, TODAY!

Year: 1987
Length: 100 min
Rating: R
Color

Beaches

Healing Themes:

- Learning to trust your friends
- Being friends for life
- Being confronted with who you are
- Growing to your potential
- Learning that someone you love is about to die
- Taking over the responsibility of raising a child in the name of love

Cast: Bette Midler, Barbara Hershey, John Heard, Spalding Gray, Lainie Kazan, James Read. Director, Gary Marshall. Writer, Mary Agnes Donoghue.

Synopsis: C. C. Bloom is a loud, high-spirited girl who comes from a lower middle class family. Hillary Whitney is a sophisticated, soft-spoken girl from a wealthy family. They meet on the boardwalk in Atlantic City and become best friends. Over the years their friendship is put to the test, but never more than when Hillary becomes ill. Before she dies she turns to C. C. to take her child.

Comments: If this movie is difficult to watch it is because it speaks to one's heart and soul. It reaches inside of each of us, making us feel the pain that comes from losing a friend or lover or parent or child. Some may ask why I would pick this movie to be in the book? Through thick and thin, I want you to feel how deep a relationship between two people can be. More than anything we get the message of how important friendships really are. I encourage you to reopen the door and make contact with an old friend or relative. We can learn from watching and listening to the way these two friends interact with each other. We see how friendships are at risk for ending when confronted with problems. Notice how the process of dying is handled. Watch how she goes from denial to apathy then anger and final resolution. We will all have to deal with death at some time in our lives. Why is it that we are not taught how to handle death? After watching *Beaches* I suggest you call a friend that you've lost contact with over the years. I'm sure you'll feel better about yourself and your rekindled relationship. Make the call before it's too late.

Year: 1988
Length: 123 min
Rating: PG-13
Color

Benny and Joon

Healing Themes:
- Accepting people for their limitations
- Respecting the right for everyone to be happy
- Struggling with a mental illness
- Learning to let go of someone you've been over-protective of

Cast: Johnny Depp, Mary Stuart Masterson, Aidan Quinn, Julianne Moore, Oliver Platt, CCH Pounder, Dan Hedaya, Joe Frifasi, William H. Macy, Eileen Ryan. Director, Jeemia Chechik. Writer, Barry Berman.

Synopsis: Benny is quite a character. When Joon sees him she decides they are a lot alike. When Benny realizes he's in love with Joon, he runs into a great deal of resistance from Joon's brother, who tries to protect her from the evils of the outside world. But no power is strong enough to keep them apart.

Comments: There are times when people come into my office depressed because they feel there is no one in the world for them. "Doc, I'm never going to find anyone to love me. I'll be single for the rest of my life." Well, this movie is here to tell you that if Benny and Joon can find each other, your special someone is just around the corner. *Benny and Joon* is a love story; it teaches us that there is someone in this world for everyone. Notice the way Joon's brother takes care of her. While it is true she needs to be looked after, she doesn't get a chance to grow on her own. Were you over-protected? Were you held back? How are you handling that today? Are you still living at home with your parents? There's not a thing wrong with Benny except that he marches to the beat of a different drummer. People think he is "crazy." (We should all be so crazy.) What he does do is bring out the side of Joon that is capable of loving and living in the real world. Watch how he brings Joon and her brother out of their sadness. What a wonderful talent, making people laugh. You'll find yourself experiencing joy and hope from this movie. Let yourself enjoy all of Benny's and Joon's energy. Learn to kick hats down the sidewalk, and when you look up, someone special will be smiling their way into your life.

Year: 1993
Length: 98 min
Rating: PG
Color

Big

Healing Themes:

- Finding the child within us
- With freedom comes responsibility
- Trying to grow up too quickly
- Feeling left behind by your friends
- Learning that being an adult is not all it is cracked up to be
- Falling in love before you are ready

Cast: Tom Hanks, Elizabeth Perkins, John Heard, Robert Loggia, Jared Rushton, David Moscow, Jon Lovitz, Mercedes Ruehl. Director, Penny Marshall. Writers, Garry Ross and Anne Spielberg.

Synopsis: Thirteen-year-old Josh Baskin gets his wish and grows up overnight. He goes to work and becomes an executive. He finds life, sex, money, and the American dream, yet he realizes he has lost his childhood. He undoes the wish and returns to finish growing up.

Comments: Do you remember when you couldn't wait to be an adult? Adults got to stay up late, go to parties, and buy really good stuff. When I ask the classic question, "If you could go back and do it all again, would you?" some wouldn't for all the money in the world. Others would do it in a New York minute. Well, *Big* begs that question and more. It's a movie with very special messages. For the young the message is slow down, adulthood is just around the corner. For the adults it's remembering the years gone by. If you came from a home with few positive childhood memories, it's not surprising that you would want to grow up fast. Watch Josh's childhood friend as the stress of their new age gap pulls them apart. Is there someone you played with who helped make your childhood something special? Notice how Josh shows the adults some of the simpler things in life and how he learns honesty and the work ethic. We can get so much healing reaching into our past and embracing those years, whether they be good or bad. Memories are so important. They let us know where we've been and guide us to where we're going. All in all, they're a pretty BIG deal.

Year: 1988
Length: 98 min
Rating: PG
Color

The Big Chill

Healing Themes:

- Mourning the loss of a companion
- Comforting friends
- Learning to forgive
- Handling responsibility
- Getting a chance at a love that eluded you
- Going to a reunion
- Uncovering mysteries from the past

Cast: Tom Berenger, Glenn Close, Jeff Goldblum, William Hurt, Kevin Kline, Mary Kay Place, Meg Tilly, JoBeth Williams. Director, Lawrence Kasdan. Writers, Lawrence Kasdan and Barbara Benedek.

Synopsis: Seven former college classmates from the sixties get together at a friend's funeral. The gathering is a warm, playful, and sometimes tumultuous event as each of them re-examines the present, the past they shared, and their hopes for the future.

Comments: The process of reunion can be a wonderfully healing and cathartic experience, as you will see. Does anything that's going on in this movie remind you of what emotions you had or you thought you might have at a reunion of old friends? You can watch this movie ten times and see something different each time. Look for people you knew or know today in the characters portrayed in *The Big Chill*. What is it you could not see then that you can see now? What would you do differently? Are there some things you would like to say? Let yourself feel the experience of reminiscing the past. Would it be possible to have a reunion? Why not? Unpack that address book you've kept for so many years. Start making some phone calls and bring those old friends back together. You will be amazed at the healing you will experience through the memories you will share with one another. Here's another idea. How about having a party with some new friends? Play the movie, then spend some time talking about each other's past. You will find we are all the same. We all have memories that are both good and bad. Enjoy the journey. You will be glad you made it.

Year: 1983
Length: 108 min
Rating: R
Color

The Boost

Healing Themes:

- If you think you're not hurting yourself with your addiction
- When you get hooked on drugs
- Putting your life at risk
- Feeling insecure in a relationship
- Realizing it is too much, too soon
- Losing someone because of what you are doing to yourself

Cast: James Woods, Sean Young, John Kapelos, Steven Hill, Kelle Kerr, John Rothman, Amanda Blake, Grace Zabriskie. Director, Harold Becker. Writer, Darryl Ponicsan.

Synopsis: Lenny and his wife, Linda, are very much in love. Lenny gets his big break and begins the climb up the ladder. Along the way they find cocaine, they both become addicted, and lose everything. Lenny and Linda go through the process of kicking the habit but he becomes addicted again. She ultimately leaves him to his drugs.

Comments: *The Boost* is one of the best recovery movies I've ever seen. It has a very strong message. When I tested a few of the movies out on some of my willing clients, *The Boost* knocked more people off their feet and into recovery. Let's take a look at Lenny first. Can you see how slowly his drug use starts? How little by little it begins to consume his life? No one starts out wanting to be an addict. It happens over time. Lenny is constantly putting himself down. He has little or no self-esteem, so he can't accept that Linda really loves him. The drugs fill up the void of his missing self-esteem. Can you see that's what it's all about, using something or someone else to "make it all better." Maybe you're in a relationship with someone who uses drugs, alcohol, food, smoking, etc., to fill themselves up. You may see Linda as a victim. While it is difficult to understand, don't lose sight of the fact that she was attracted to his personality, who he was, which included his insecurity, low self-esteem, and his ultimate drug use. Linda needed to be with someone who had low self-worth. It was merely a reflection of her own needs. I can tell you this, that the ending is enough to stop anybody from doing drugs. What a wake-up call!

Year: 1988
Length: 95 min
Rating: R
Color

The Boy With Green Hair

Healing Themes:

- When your friends abandon you
- Learning you've lost your family
- Dealing with people's prejudices
- Special Messages: • Accept others for who they are
  - Not being a party to prejudice

Cast: Pat O' Brien, Robert Ryan, Barbara Hale, Dean Stockwell. Director, Joseph Losey. Writers, Ben Barzman and Alred Lewis Levitt.

Synopsis: A boy's hair turns green when he learns that his parents were killed. He tries to tell the people in the small town where he lives with his grandfather that even though he is different, he is still a human being. The town rejects him and makes him cut off his hair.

Comments: This movie brings back memories for me of sitting in front of the television watching this boy with the green hair and relating to being different. I had freckles. Lots of freckles. No one else in my class had freckles except me and I hated those freckles and myself for having them. And although my freckles eventually went away, I know now that being different can be a gift. That difference may have allowed me to take a path in life and see things in a way that ultimately allowed me to write this book. *The Boy With Green Hair* sends the wonderful message that it is okay to be different. We are confronted with our own prejudices when we watch the irrational behavior of the townspeople because of the green hair. But the green hair is only symbolic of people's differences. Have you ever been rejected for being or looking different? Learn to accept people for who they are and learn to accept yourself for who you are. That's one of the keys to being happy in life. The movie's message about peace and humanity is very strong and therapeutic. The movie is old, but it is as current as today's news. Take special note of the way his grandfather supports his struggle to keep his green hair. Make a pact with yourself to never be a party to an act of prejudice. Accept your uniqueness in life and use it to your advantage. What better healing than the healing of self-acceptance?

Year: 1948
Length: 82 min
Rating: Unrated
B/W

The Boys in the Band

Healing Themes:

- When friends gather
- Dealing with our individual problems
- Getting inside relationships between people of the same sex
- Accepting that we all have different lifestyles
- Coming out of the closet
- Seeing yourself for who you really are

Cast: Frederick Combs, Cliff Gorman, Lawrence Luckinbill, Kenneth Nelson, Leonard Frey. Director, William Friedkin.

Synopsis: A group of gay men get together one evening to celebrate the birthday of a friend. As the party goes on the men start to share some of their intimate and personal feelings. When the party is over two men are left to work through their personal relationship problems.

Comments: If you are someone who struggles with your sexual identity, this movie can offer a sense of unity and healing by letting you know you're not alone. *The Boys in the Band* is really the first major motion picture to deal with the issues of homosexuality. I've had several opportunities to help people make safe emotional transitions in their life with respect to their sexual identity. It's never an easy journey. Having movies available like this one makes the healing process that much easier. The movie is honest and for the most part the issues presented come right to the point. Maybe you find yourself isolated because you are afraid of what people will think. Possibly you are the friend or parent of someone who is gay and you are trying to gain a grasp on understanding their lifestyle. Do you find if difficult to accept who they are? Were you brought up to believe that alternative sexual lifestyles were wrong? Ask yourself if they're really different than anyone else. As you will see, this group of gay men have found support by being with each other. Notice they experience the same issues as heterosexuals. Give the movie a try. Enjoy the power that comes from knowing you're not alone. Embrace the idea that you can learn to accept the people in your life just as they are. There is great healing in acceptance.

Year: 1970
Length: 120 min
Rating: R
Color

The Breakfast Club

Healing Themes:
- You still have feelings no matter how popular you are
- Finding yourself
- Making new friends
- Learning that the judgment you placed on people was all wrong
- Realizing that people's personal lives affect their social lives

Cast: Ally Sheedy, Molly Ringwald, Judd Nelson, Emilio Estevez, Anthony Michael Hall. Director, John Hughes. Writer, John Hughes.

Synopsis: Five students from different cliques in a Chicago suburban high school serve out one day of detention together. They delve into each other's thoughts. By the time the day is over they gain a new level of maturity and come to understand more about themselves than they ever thought possible.

Comments: *The Breakfast Club* focuses on an incredibly diverse group of kids. Do you see yourself in any of the characters? Were you the snob, the nerd, the jock, the outcast, or the tough kid? Were you really that person or were you playing a role? How do you feel as this group of young people gets to know each other? Are you envious? Maybe there was a time when you finally got to know someone who you thought was so different from you but, who like you, was just trying to find themselves. Watch how the individual personalities emerge over time. What kinds of feelings and memories come back when you listen to them talk? Do you have any regrets about the way you might have treated people when you were younger? Maybe you have some anger about the way you were treated? Possibly people never really spent the time to find out who you were as a person. Here's the lesson we gain from this movie. We can miss out on many valuable relationships by letting our first impressions and preconceived notions about people get in the way of future relationships. When you watch movies like this you really get a chance to see who you were, which in turn helps you look at yourself today. It helps you feel things that you thought were long gone and buried. And when those feelings come to the surface you experience your own healing from knowing you made it through a difficult time of your personal growth.

Year: 1985
Length: 97 min
Rating: R
Color

Bright Lights, Big City

Healing Themes:
- If drugs rule your life, take a look in the mirror
- Focusing your energy on unhealthy habits
- Bending over backwards to help a friend
- Turning your back on your family
- Taking care of yourself first

Cast: Michael J. Fox, Kiefer Sutherland, Phoebe Cates, Frances Sternhagen, Swoosie Kurtz, Tracy Pollan, Jason Robards, Jr., John Houseman, Dianne Wiest, Charlie Schlatter, William Hickey. Director, James Bridges. Writer, Jay McInerney.

Synopsis: Jamie Conway works during the day on a conservative magazine and parties at night, all night. To loosen up he drinks more than he should and uses cocaine, partly to deal with the reality that his wife has left him. Unable to keep up a front at work, Jamie is forced to look at himself.

Comments: This movie is an excellent example of what happens to cocaine and alcohol abusers. The drugs and alcohol work for a while, but eventually they consume any one who is addicted to them. Jamie's in his early twenties, hooked on cocaine, and ready to tell you: Don't do drugs. This is another of those paradoxical healing stories. Take note of the way he becomes more and more desperate as he continues to use drugs. Drug users lie. They simply are not capable of telling the truth. Watch how Jamie constantly lies about his life to get what he wants. Do you know anyone like Jamie? Don't you find that you can never trust them no matter what they say? When a family member comes to town to see Jamie, he runs away because he can't stand the thought of being confronted. Also, watch as codependency plays a role in his relationship with a friend at work. She covers up for him in the hopes that their relationship will grow. His wife sure had enough. Were you angry that she left or did you respect her courage for getting out of the relationship because it was in her best interest? Get in touch with what you're doing to yourself. Learn the healing messages and make them work in your own life. You can make the bright lights shine on you, but you've got to do the work.

Year: 1988
Length: 108 min
Rating: R
Color

Broadcast News

Healing Themes:

- Following your convictions, being moral and ethical against all odds
- When someone you love creates a false image
- Building a career and having time for nothing else
- Realizing you cannot control every aspect of your life
- Letting go

Cast: William Hurt, Albert Brooks, Holly Hunter, Robert Prosky, Lois Chiles, Joan Cusack, Peter Hackes, Jack Nicholson. Director, James Brooks. Writer, James Brooks.

Synopsis: Jane Craig, a top news producer with high standards, falls for Tom Grunick, a newsman on his way up who is not who he appears to be. Jane runs into conflict when she is forced to choose between Tom and her ethics.

Comments: *Broadcast News* is a great movie, but I want us to focus our attention on just two ideas offered in a few scenes. Watch for two scenes where Jane is alone and she decides it's time to have an emotional release, so she cries. WOW! Is she put together well or what? Just seeing her cry may seem like a simple, strange concept to you, but crying is so healing. It can allow you to self-nurture and rejuvenate yourself. Women are much more willing to let themselves go and just cry. Men get lots of messages while they're growing up that tell them it's not okay to cry. Jane reveals the fine art of letting go, and she lets go when she needs to just as she eats when she's hungry. Now, connected to this idea is Jane's very strong moral conviction that tears are from the heart. To her they have spiritual meaning and are not to be abused. When she's confronted with the reality that Tom lied about his tears, she realizes she has no choice but to let him go. Jane has a philosophy which she has strong convictions about. Do you have an idea of what you believe, then change that idea as soon as you meet someone you want in your life? You must know who you are and what you want in order to be a healthy, complete person in life. Don't hesitate to use that rewind button on your VCR. That's why it was invented, so that you could watch the good parts again and again.

Year: 1987
Length: 131 min
Rating: R
Color

The Burning Bed

Healing Themes:

- Living in an abusive relationship
- Fighting back
- Dealing with life or death situations
- When your life has become unmanageable
- Coming to the end of your rope
- Choosing between two evils

Cast: Farrah Fawcett, Paul LeMat, Penelope Millford, Richard Masur. Director, Robert Greenwald. Writer, Rose Leiman Goldenberg.

Synopsis: A battered wife who, after years of abuse, sets fire to the bed with her husband in it. She is arrested and tried for murder. Her attorney portrays her as a woman who is truly battered and fearful for her life, asking the judge and jury to find her not guilty.

Comments: Abuse of any kind is unconscionable. *The Burning Bed* is an important movie to watch for those involved in spousal abuse, for both the abuser and the abused. It is important to begin the healing process by coming out of denial before it's too late. We can soon realize the wife is being abused. Can you relate to what she is going through? Stay in touch with your feelings as you're watching this movie, your anger at him for abusing her, your anger at her for staying. And what of the children who are also experiencing the abuse? They're the real victims. Maybe you grew up in a home where there was abuse. It could be that you find yourself being drawn to relationships of abuse and mistreatment so you can relive your early childhood. You might be a parent whose children are following in your footsteps. Can you see they're returning to the thing in life they're most accustomed to—being abused or being the abuser. I was so angry at the legal system for not understanding why she was left with only one means to protect herself. Do you think you could ever get to the point she did? You don't have to, for there are organizations that can help you get the protection you need. There are safe houses where you can live until you get back on your feet. Call the police, get some support, and start on a healing path of freedom from an abusive relationship.

Year: 1984
Length: 100 min
Rating: Unrated
Color

Call Me Anna

Healing Themes:

- Being addicted to drugs and alcohol
- Dealing with depression
- When you are pushed over the edge
- Going from one chaotic relationship to the next
- If you where abused by a parent
- Living with the memory of your past
- Realizing your problems and getting a grip

Cast: Patty Duke, Howard Hesseman, Millie Perkins, Deborah May, Ari Meyers, Jenny Robertson, Arthur Taxier, Karl Malden. Director, Gilbert Cates.

Synopsis: Patty Duke portrays herself from a rocky start as a teenage television star, through her adult life where bouts of depression mixed with extreme highs throw her and her family into chaos. Patty finally finds help for her problems and begins living free from self-destruction.

Comments: Patty Duke in real life suffers from manic depression. As a personal choice and campaign, she shares her problem with the world so that others do not have to experience what she has gone through. There have been other stars who have talked about their problems in an effort to help those who are still suffering: Rod Steiger, Richard Dreyfuss, Mac Davis, and Mary Tyler Moore, to name but a few. What I want you to see in *Call Me Anna* is what manic depression looks like and how it can drive one's life. Notice how it seems to come from nowhere. One moment she is fine, the next she is down, and the next she's all over the place. The mood swings can be so painful they can drive you to suicide. How about Patty's addiction? You can't help but notice the drugs and alcohol. Do you abuse substances? Are you self-medicating, hiding in your addiction? That's exactly what Patty is doing. You will see that she uses alcohol and drugs as a way to manage her depression, but it is making things worse. There are several medications today that can help those with depression. There are doctors, clinics, and counselors who will help get you on the right path. Remember, one way to heal yourself is to reach out for help and support. Don't be embarrassed to say that you need help.

Year: 1990
Length: 100 min
Rating: Unrated
Color

Carnal Knowledge

Healing Themes:

- When your best friend cheats on you
- Taking a look at your past and seeing yourself for who you really are
- Manipulating other people and hurting them in the process
- When sex is all that you live for

Cast: Jack Nicholson, Candice Bergen, Arthur Garfunkel, Ann-Margret, Rita Moreno, Cynthia O'Neal, Carol Kane. Director, Mike Nichols. Writer, Jules Feiffer.

Synopsis: Jonathan and Sandy are best friends in college. Their main goal in life is to meet women and get laid. As time passes Sandy turns to a younger woman to find happiness while Jonathan ends up with a prostitute in his attempt to find his manhood.

Comments: *Carnal Knowledge* has become a cult classic. I first saw it in college, and when I saw the movie in my mature years, it touched me again. I was able to look back at myself and see some things I had forgotten. Don't be concerned about whether or not you went to college or if you're male or female. You'll get the message and get in touch with some old stuff that keeps holding you down. Can you find yourself in one of the four main characters? There is one character, Jonathan, who has the greatest loss. He has one goal in life: to have sex, lots and lots of sex, at any cost—even at the expense of his friendship. How did you feel when Jonathan lied and had an affair with his best friend's girlfriend? Watch and feel the chaos in Jonathan's life. He couldn't get it together when he was young and he can't get it together as an adult. Look at his relationships. He takes them hostage and doesn't know what to do with them. Do his involvements remind you of some of your relationships? There's a lot to this movie. I've pointed out just a few things to get you started. This one's great for a group. Gather a few friends together and share some memories. Doing something like this is great for the healing process. When you get in touch with your past you become more free to live your future. Enjoy.

Year: 1971
Length: 96 min
Rating: R
Color

Chantilly Lace

Healing Themes:

- Enjoying the gathering of friends
- Learning that a friend is gay
- Accepting that everybody has a different way of living life
- Finding out that one of your friends is dying

Cast: Lindsay Crouse, Jill Eikenberry, Martha Plimpton, Ally Sheedy, Talia Shire, Helen Slater, JoBeth Williams. Director, Linda Yellen. Writer, Gisela Bernice.

Synopsis: A group of women gather at a cabin for the weekend to talk and reminisce about old times and current happenings. Tragedy hits when one of them discloses that she is dying. They bond together and experience the death of their friend, which ultimately brings them even closer.

Comments: One of the things which makes this movie unique is that the actresses were allowed to improvise. Because of their spontaneity, we capture the free floating, true-to-life intimacy between all of them. You're in for a real treat. Stay close to your feelings as each character emerges on the scene. Go inside yourself and look for the character or combination of the characters you identify with and experience your feelings through them. When they present a problem or are confronted by one another, ask yourself what you would have done. How would you have handled it? Use their response as a tool for yourself in the future. A bombshell is dropped when one of them comes out of the closet about her homosexuality. Would you feel threatened? Could you continue the friendship? Maybe you're someone who is gay but has not told your friends? Why? If they're truly your friends they will accept you for who you are. How did you cope with the video from one of the women telling the group she was dying and would be dead by the time they saw the video. What a devastating experience. Did you feel the closeness among them? It was a very special moment. Notice the way they used each other to deal with this overwhelming emotional experience. Use their bond of friendship as a guiding light on your own friendships. We were not put on this earth to be alone. Our friends, our lovers, and our families are here to see us through life's journey.

Year: 1993
Length: 102 min
Rating: R
Color

A Child's Cry for Help

Healing Themes:

- If you are giving your problems to your children
- When children become ill because of their parents
- Confronting the memories from the past
- Struggling to save an innocent child

Cast: Veronica Hamel, Pam Dawber, Daniel Hugh Kelly, Lia Jakub, Cynthia Matells, Daniel Benzali, James Pickens, Jr., Jeff Williams, Zachary Charles, Tobery Maguire, Lois Hicks, James Gale.

Synopsis: When a doctor decides to investigate the real cause of a child's illnesses, she uncovers a dark secret: The boy's mother suffers from a psychological illness that drives her to make her child ill. The boy is ultimately spared the pain of being the victim of his mother's condition.

Comments: How is it possible that a parent or guardian would intentionally make a child ill? When we understand why it happens and what the child goes through, we can emerge from some of our deep, dark secrets into a brighter, healing light. To get on our own road to recovery sometimes we travel down very crooked paths. Each of us has dealt with a trauma from our past. Some of you are working on issues of abuse and some of you are feeling the results of abandonment by parents who where simply never around. And in each case at least one result might be that you needed attention. *A Child's Cry for Help* is a look at one way an adult who came from a home where her parents were emotionally unavailable might get that attention. This movie shows us what happens when her emotional upheaval is transferred to her child. And what of the doctor? How quick were you to judge her actions? She was trying to do her best to protect the child but she got little support. The point is some wounds are so deep they require a very special person to admit that they exist or a rare person who is willing to spend the time to unearth the problem. Give this movie a try. There is no other movie like it. (By the way, in case you're interested, the condition this mom has is known as Munchausen syndrome, also known as factitious disorder by proxy.)

Year: 1994
Length: 100 min
Rating: PG
Color

A Christmas Carol

Healing Themes:

- Taking a look at your past/knowing there's more to life than money
- Getting a second chance at life
- Accepting that life is full of love
- When it's all work and no play

Cast: Alastair Sim, Jack Warner, Kathleen Harrison, Mervyn Johns, Hermione Baddeley, Clifford Mollison, Michael Hordern, George Cole, Carol Marsh, Miles Malleson, Ernest Thesiger, Hattie Jacques, Peter Bull, Hugh Dempster. Director, Brian Desmond Hurst. Writer, Noel Langley.

Synopsis: On Christmas Eve Ebaneezer Scrooge—mean, cruel, uncaring, and greedy—is visited by three ghosts who show him his past, present, and future. Amazed and terrified, he takes his one chance to mend his thoughtless ways.

Comments: Now I know most of you have seen *Scrooge,* which is based on *A Christmas Carol.* There are at least five movie versions of this classic Charles Dickens' story, and we are inundated with them over the holidays. My question is have you ever really spent the time to learn what this movie is telling you? Is the world passing you by? Are you really enjoying your life? Will you leave this earth having done little good for anyone but yourself? And what of those around you? Are you overlooking people who are trying to reach out to you? Why? In following Scrooge's journeys with the three ghosts through his past, his present, and his bleak future he is given a second chance. And here's my second chance to you. Don't wait for the holidays to see this movie; watch it now. Listen to the message: Live life to the fullest with all the joy and happiness it has to offer. Pull back the curtains and let the bright, vibrant light of the rest of your life shine in and never, ever lose its glow. This is my healing gift to you: Don't be a Scrooge with yourself, your money, or your future. Enjoy the time you have. There isn't a moment to spare. No more humbug!

Year: 1951
Length: 86 min
Rating: Unrated
B&W

Clean and Sober

Healing Themes:
- Taking it one day at a time
- Recognizing your limitations
- Realizing that drugs and alcohol ruin your life
- Destroying friends and relationships because of your disease
- Standing in the way of someone recovering from their problems

Cast: Michael Keaton, Morgan Freeman, M. Emmet Walsh, Kathy Baker. Director, Glenn Gordon Carson. Writer, Tod Carroll.

Synopsis: Daryl Poynter's life is in shambles over the use of cocaine. He wakes up one day to find the woman he went out with the night before is dead. He has been stealing money from the company he works for to pay for his habit. In an attempt to hide he decides to check into a rehabilitation center and begins the long and painful process of recovery.

Comments: What a great healing movie this is! When it came out all I heard was, "Did you see *Clean and Sober*? I want to get sober like that." What an incredible impact this movie had on so many people who were trying to become well from their addictions. I think it's one of the best movies ever made dealing with addiction and recovery. We get to see how denial works on the mind of the addict and how the slips that Daryl experiences—returning to using drugs—eventually move him towards recovery. While the language is a little strong, I really recommend that this movie be shown to everyone, including the whole family, dealing with addiction and the denial that goes with it. Notice how hard Daryl works to avoid what he has known all along: He has a problem with life. Cocaine addiction is simply one of the symptoms. What's he really avoiding? Watch his friends lose patience with his perpetual lying and manipulation. Can you see how he is destroying his life in so many ways? And what of the death of the woman? Have you lost someone to his or her own addiction? Maybe you've brought yourself to the edge one too many times. Please, listen to the healing message from this movie. Take advantage of the lesson Daryl learns. And while you're at it, give *When a Man Loves a Woman* and *The Boost* a try. You won't go wrong.

Year: 1988
Length: 124 min
Rating: R
Color

The Closer

Healing Themes:

- When your whole life is nothing but work, power, and money
- Losing touch with your family and friends
- When your parents haven't got time for you
- Feelings that come from remembering the parent who was never around

Cast: Danny Aiello, Michael Pare, Joe Cortese, Justine Bateman, Diane Baker, James Karen, Rick Aiello, Michael Lemen. Director, Dimitri Logothetis. Writers, Robert Kents and Louis LaRusso II.

Synopsis: Chester Grant is a big shot businessman whose very existence is the next deal. On his way to the top he has lost touch with his family by being a domineering father and husband. The family falls apart and Chester is left alone with his empty domain.

Comments: *The Closer* lets us see what effects someone like Chester can have on those who are around him. While the idea of being rich and powerful or the process of working towards greater wealth looks attractive, you can see that it all comes at a very high price. As a therapist I would often recommend this movie to those who had lost track of why they were working so hard. Can you relate to this man? Why did you want to acquire wealth and power? He never takes the time to enjoy it, much like the subject of *Regarding Henry*. What effect has money had on your family and friends? Are you really enjoying life or are you hiding from life? Maybe you are someone who is fed up with a friend or family member who's lost all sight of the true meaning of life. Listen to the pleas of the children as they try to be heard by a man who has long since lost his ability to listen to anyone but himself. Notice how they abandon him and give up on the struggle to have a family experience with him. Did you grow up in a home where a family member ruled the roost with money and power? How do you feel about yourself today? As you watch *The Closer* are you angry at the way you were treated like a possession or an asset? This movie helps put life in perspective. You will grow in the process and become more aware of the destruction that comes with this kind of family crisis.

Year: 1990
Length: 95 min
Rating: R
Color

Closet Land

Healing Themes:

- Memories of physical and psychological abuse
- If you've ever felt as if you were a prisoner to your feelings
- Escaping from someone who is abusing you
- When you feel like there's no way out

Cast: Madeleine Stowe, Alan Rickman. Director, Radha Bharadwaj. Writer, Radha Bharadwaj.

Synopsis: A woman is tortured by a political faction to get her to admit that she is a political activist. To avoid feeling the pain she escapes to the same place she created in her mind to deal with her abusive childhood. When her oppressors can't get her to confess, they keep her locked up and away from the people they believe she is trying to reach.

Comments: Before I start, I have a warning. Please, if you are someone who is in treatment for abuse of any kind, check with whomever you're working with before watching this movie. Without a question of a doubt, *Closet Land* is the most emotionally difficult movie I have ever watched, bar none. If you are not in treatment, watch this movie with a friend. You do not want to go this one alone. There are two themes of abuse that are important to see in this movie. One is clear: People are being tortured because of their political beliefs. This movie was, in part, funded by Amnesty International for this reason. The second reason is why this movie has such a powerful healing value. As a child whenever she was molested she was forced into a closet where she would escape into fantasy to avoid the reality of what was happening to her. As an adult she wrote books based on those fantasies to deal with the emotional pain. She uses the tool of escapism to endure her present torture just as she did as a child. This is how children who are molested learn to survive the experience(s). As adults they may escape by drinking, eating, smoking, shopping, sexual promiscuity, etc. And some have problems with intimacy. The healing comes with confronting your feelings and moving forward with your life, not escaping. There are groups and organizations to help you through the pain.

Year: 1990
Length: 95 min
Rating: R
Color

The Color Purple

Healing Themes:
- Looking at the extremes of prejudice
- Experiencing sex against your will and being abused
- Learning to be your own person
- Never forgetting a lost sibling
- Triumph over tragedy

Cast: Whoopi Goldberg, Oprah Winfrey, Danny Glover, Margaret Avery, Willard Pugh, Akosua Busia, Adolph Caesar, Rae Dawn Chong, Dana Ivey. Director, Steven Spielberg. Writer, Menno Meyjes.

Synopsis: Celie is still a child when she is married to Mister, who is more of a master than a husband in the rural South of the early '20s. In time, she learns the ways of the world and finds the courage to gain her independence. With her freedom comes the return of a lost sister.

Comments: I don't mind telling you I was so taken by all that is packed into this movie that just thinking about it brings tears to my eyes. That's what makes this movie so healing; it's the tears that remind us how to feel, how to recover from our guarded self. How did you feel when Mister chased Celie's sister away? Those of you who have lost family members to adoption, custody decisions, serious illness, or accident will really get in touch with their emotions when the sister is chased out of the house. Mister treated Celie as if she were property. Have you ever felt like you were in a relationship where you had no control or equality? Did you feel her strength as she gains her own sense of self? What of her intimate relationship with the family friend? Were you bothered by it or did you feel it wasn't important? Sofia is introduced as a strong-willed character. What did you experience emotionally when her rights were taken away from her just because she was "colored"? My wish for each of you is that *The Color Purple* leaves you with a richer sense of self. Trust that it is right to have your own identity and commit to never being a party to repressing anyone's rights or life choices. And most importantly, keep all the colors in your life glowing and full. When the colors remain the healing is complete.

Year: 1985
Length: 155 min
Rating: PG-13
Color

Come Fill the Cup

Healing Themes:

- When alcohol has taken over your life
- How to reach out to someone who needs some help
- Taking a long look in the mirror at real sobriety
- Picking yourself up out of the gutter and getting on with life

Cast: James Cagney, Phyllis Thaxter, Raymond Massey, James Gleason, Gig Young. Director, Gordon Douglass. Writers, Ivan Goff and Ben Roberts.

Synopsis: A has-been news reporter spends most of his time in bars until he meets a man who is a recovering alcoholic. When he gets the support he always needed, he sobers up and gets back on his feet. The test comes when he has to spend time around a playboy alcoholic just to get a story. Real sobriety is experienced as he gets his life in order.

Comments: I found this one in the process of doing my research for the book. As you can see it's a relatively older movie. To the best of my knowledge it's one of the first movies made that deals with the problem of addiction and recovery. *The Lost Weekend* was also made around the same time and both are excellent for those of you who are struggling with these issues. *Come Fill the Cup* is so entertaining you can't help but get the message. Watch this alcoholic as he pushes people away. Only one man is able to reach him. Recovery and healing can be about that one person or that one moment in time. You have to be ready to hear the message. One of my favorite scenes is when our alcoholic goes to live with his "new friend" to sober up. He finds a bottle in the kitchen cabinet. His friend explains that he keeps it there to remind himself he's just one drink away from being a practicing alcoholic again. There's a lesson and a lot of support from just this one scene. This is an area that most recovering addicts do not understand. Recovery is for a lifetime, one day at a time. That's what meetings like Alcoholics Anonymous, Overeaters Anonymous, etc., are all about. It's being able to see in others what is going on with ourselves. It's knowing that there's someone out there to help you down a healing path and into recovery for a lifetime.

Year: 1951
Length: 113 min
Rating: Unrated
Color

Cries From the Heart

Healing Themes:

- If you're feeling overwhelmed from taking care of your child
- When your child has more than the average childhood needs
- Autism and some of its problems
- Confronting those who molest children
- Finding someone who really wants to help
- Knowing when it's time to reach out for some help

Cast: Patty Duke, Melissa Gilbert, Bradley Pierce, Markus Flanagan, Lisa Banes, Roger Aaron Brown, Peter Spears, Joe Chrest, Troy Evans, Shelly Morrison, Raye Birk. Director, Michael Switzer. Writer, Robert Inman.

Synopsis: A young mother trying to raise an autistic child seeks the help of a special school for autistic children. She meets a woman who takes a special interest in the child. Although they struggle over the control of the child, they work together and finally learn to communicate with him.

Comments: Raising a child is a full-time job, but when a child has special needs the job can be overwhelming. Let's look at the focal problems offered through this movie. We have a chance to deal with an autistic child, an enabling mother, a caregiver, and sexual abuse. For some years it was believed that autism was caused by inappropriate parenting. Today we know that this is not the case. We are able to treat autistic children to some positive levels of success. Are you the parent of a challenged child? Give yourself credit for the strength it takes to work with this additional challenge in life. It is difficult to imagine that someone would sexually abuse anyone, especially a challenged child. However, pedophiles make their way into all areas of life. Children like Michael are easy targets. What did you want to see done to this guy? One final note, the treatment approach, facilitated communication, is relatively new and unproved. In the last three years there have been several court cases charging, in part, that therapists are bilking money out of unwitting parents by leading them to believe that the children are communicating with them.

Year: 1994
Length: 100 min
Rating: G
Color

Crimes of the Heart

Healing Themes:

- Reunions with your family
- If you haven't seen your siblings in a long time
- If you have an abusive spouse
- When you want to feel connected to those who were an important part of your past
- Never saying it's okay to be ignored

Cast: Sissy Spacek, Jessica Lange, Diane Keaton, Sam Shepard, Tess Harper, Hurd Hatfield. Director, Bruce Beresford. Writer, Beth Henley.

Synopsis: Three sisters, Lenny, Meg, and Babe, meet at the home where they grew up; the place where Lenny lives because Babe is up for murder. All three tell a different story about what they remember from their childhood. Together they experience a re-bonding.

Comments: *Crimes of the Heart* is very special for those who grew up in homes with brothers and sisters. If you were one of three sisters this movie will be a real gift. Can you see yourself in Lenny, Meg, or Babe? Were you the shy one like Lenny, always taking care of everyone else, making sure things were in order? How about Meg? Were you the wild one, never conforming and forever acting innocent? I loved the scene where she ate the chocolates. How telling about her self-centered personality. And what about Babe? She's straight-laced and proper on the outside, with a whole lot going on behind everyone's back. How is it that three children can live in the same house, with the same parents, and grow up to be so different? I've seen many people who don't or won't talk to their brothers and sisters. They have lots of anger about one thing or another. But deep down inside they don't want to break that unique bond. Is that what it's like for you? Give this a try. Call your brothers and sisters and have a "let's revisit our growing up" party and play *Crimes of the Heart*. If you can't do that invite some friends over and do the same thing. You may be able to find your brothers and sisters in your friends. What a wonderful way to get in touch with not only your friends but your childhood. In the last scene you will see them bond again as sisters. Get yourself a big cake and rejoice with them.

Year: 1986
Length: 105 min
Rating: PG-13
Color

Cry for Help: The Tracey Thurman Story

Healing Themes:

- Realizing the person you love is abusive
- When you've had enough of an abusive relationship
- Learning that it's okay to reach out for help
- If someone is stalking you
- Dealing with an ex-spouse who won't leave you alone

Cast: Nancy McKeon, Dale Midkiff, Graham Jarvis, Yvette Heyden, Philip Baker Hall, Bruce Weitz. Director, Robert Markowitz. Writer, Beth Miller.

Synopsis: A young woman is a battered and abused wife whose experience of being stalked and almost killed by her husband led to the creation of the Connecticut Thurman Law.

Comments: Many who have experienced this kind of horrible abuse have a difficult time trusting they can ever have a normal, healthy relationship again. People who have not experienced this kind of problem can't relate to Tracey's ordeal. Well, ask yourself this question: Does anyone ever intend to be stalked, molested, raped, or abused in any way by anyone, let alone by someone who claims to love them? If you're honest with yourself, the answer is no, and therefore it can happen to anyone. So use Tracey's story as a way to see what it might be like to go through this kind of nightmare. If you have ever been pursued by an ex-lover or someone who feels they can't live without you, this movie will reach some feelings you've tucked away. Notice how subtle her husband's abuse is at first. It's a push, a shove, or a slap in the face. And from there it gets worse and worse. Secondly, did you find yourself getting mad at the police when they did little to protect her? It almost appears as if she is the one to blame. Finally, it seems in some cases that a person literally has to give up their life before people will stand up and take notice. Possibly you are someone who is terrified of leaving the person you are with, for fear of repercussion. Get help and support so you can get out of the relationship safely. There are halfway houses and shelters to protect you. If it's not too late, see a counselor or a therapist as a couple. Watching this movie will take courage, but healing will follow.

Year: 1989
Length: 100 min
Rating: Unrated
Color

Dad

Healing Themes:

- Knowing when it's time to say good-bye
- Letting go of old resentments
- If a parent is getting old and is ill
- How to grieve over a parent who has died

Cast: Jack Lemmon, Ted Danson, Ethan Hawke, Olympia Dukakis, Kathy Baker, Zakes Mokae, J. T. Walsh, Kevin Spacey, Chris Lemmon. Director, Gary David Goldberg. Writer, Gary David Goldberg.

Synopsis: John Tremont learns that Jake, his father, with whom he has not been close in years, has had a heart attack. John and Jake spend their last days together getting close to each other and saying good-bye. Family wounds are healed as John grieves over the loss of his dad.

Comments: Having used movies as a healing method for some time, I have only on rare occasion found movies that help us look at issues involving men. With *Dad* we're lucky to experience the healing between a father and son. In some ways this movie is the male perspective of *Steel Magnolias*, *Chantilly Lace*, and *Terms of Endearment*. Are you at a time in your life where your parents may not be around much longer? Do you have things you want to get off your chest but have been keeping them inside? Isn't this a good time to reach out and make contact with your parents and put some of that old stuff behind you? *Dad* shows us the way to reach a parent we've shut out of our lives. So many people live with the regret of not talking with their parents before they died. Dying is different for everyone, but there are some common threads, mainly emotional ones, we all must go through. Finally, notice how John's mother handles her husband's aging and dying. It is very difficult for one spouse to lose the other. So this movie can be wonderful for couples. It can touch the memories of your relationship and help you feel what it's like to say good-bye to someone you love. After you've watched this one alone try watching it with your father or your family. You may find that the doors open to a bond and relationship you never thought could exist.

Year: 1989
Length: 117 min
Rating: PG
Color

Damage

Healing Themes:

- When your obsession takes over
- Forgetting your responsibilities
- Betraying those who trust you
- Hurting yourself and those you love

Cast: Jeremy Irons, Juliette Binoche, Miranda Richardson, Rupert Graves, Ian Bannen, Leslie Caron, Peter Stormare, Gemma Clark. Director, Louise Malle. Writer, David Hare.

Synopsis: Dr. Steven Fleming, obsessed with his son's fiancée, has an affair with her. Martyn finds out and dies in a tragic accident while confronting them. Steven is left to live out his life obsessed over a woman he can never have.

Comments: Occasionally someone will come to my office who has lost their ability to function. Like *Fatal Attraction*, *Damage* looks at what happens when someone's life is consumed by another person. Your first reaction might be that Steven's obsession came from nowhere; it just happened when he met Ingrid. But look closer. Wasn't he obsessed with his work and the control he had over his family? Do you see that they're all the same? Steven merely focused his obsession on something else. Can you see that his obsession with Ingrid becomes that much more unconscionable when he cheats on his wife and his son. What did you feel when Martyn died? Part of me was shocked and sad over Martyn's death. Dying must have been the only way out at the time. Did it ever occur to you that it wasn't an accident but rather suicide? The other part of me thought Steven got what he deserved. Did you experience that reaction? Throughout the whole movie Ingrid got to be the innocent bystander, someone along for the ride. What was incredible to me is the way she just went on with her life. Now how corrupt is Ingrid's character? But no matter who you are, the person with the obsession or someone who was cheated on, why not seek the support of a therapist or friends to see you through the difficulties and enjoy living life as it was intended, undamaged?

Year: 1992
Length: 111 min
Rating: R
Color

Dante's Inferno

Healing Themes:

- What life after death might be like
- If you have fears of dying
- Being moral and ethical in your life
- Having a chance to change your life course

Cast: Harry Lachman, Spencer Tracy, Claire Trevor, Henry B. Walthall, Alan Dinehart, Scotty Beckett. Director, Harry Lachman.

Synopsis: A man is the owner of a successful carnival show. Things are going well for him as he rakes in the profits. He doesn't seem to care much about anyone or anything but himself. He is forced to take a look at himself and his life. The images that occur change him forever.

Comments: Some people are obsessed with visions of what this place called Hell is like. The force is so strong that they live every day in fear of what their life after death will be like. It is not my intent to offer a deep healing message by suggesting *Dante's Inferno*. Rather I want to give those of you who have curiosity about life after death an opportunity to see an image created in one person's mind. And when you're done, put the movie aside and simply accept the image for what it is, a reflection of one man's realization of the life he is leading. What is your image of life and does it control your existence? Do your fears of tomorrow get in the way of enjoying your life today? I would not presume to tell you what life is like after death or if there is life after death. I can tell you that you have your life today. You can't do any more than live your life with high moral and ethical standards. And when you do you have no fear about what tomorrow will bring or what life after death holds for you. Knowing that I can live in the here and now and don't have to be afraid about what tomorrow will bring is enough healing for me. *Ghost, Defending Your Life,* and *Flat Liners* will give you some additional ideas about the life after death experience. Note: There is another version of this movie. However, this version has images that are much more strong and clear.

Year: 1935
Length: 88 min
Rating: Unrated
B&W

Darkness Before Dawn

Healing Themes:

- When you are consumed by drugs
- Neglecting your children and putting them in danger
- Trying to keep up a front and not being able to make it work
- Remembering growing up in a chaotic house

Cast: Meredith Baxter, Stephen Lang, Gwynyth Walsh, L. Scott Caldwell, Chelsea Hertford, Bill Applebaum, Michael Bryan French, Lee Tergesen, Natalie West, Robert Desiderio. Director, John Patterson, Writer, Karen Hall.

Synopsis: A nurse, who is addicted to pills, marries a heroin addict she is helping to treat. He finally turns his life around and kicks the habit. But she can't quit. He is left with no choice but to save himself and their children from her dangerous and chaotic drug life.

Comments: *Darkness Before Dawn* is one of the best movies I've seen to show that anyone can become an addict. Many people assume that because someone is a nurse or a lawyer or a doctor or…they're above being addicted to drugs. This movie is going to help you get beyond that myth. The truth is some individuals are drawn to these professions so they can feed their addiction; the food addict to the restaurant business; the gambler working in a gambling institution; the pedophile working in a day-care center. Here is a case where a nurse is the abuser. Watch how she uses the drugs to keep her childhood memories in check. Can you relate? Are you someone who hides your feelings in alcohol, drugs, food, gambling, sex, etc.? It's time to do good things in your life and confront your addictive behaviors. Listen to the denial as they fight the urges that drive their addiction. Watch as she ignores their children at the expense of getting drugs. Watch as she jeopardizes her patients' well-being to get drugs for herself. You'll find this movie painful to watch, but it will help you get out of denial. There are support groups and meetings to help you, your significant others, and friends to help you find your way out of the black hole of addiction. If you're in a support group try using this movie as the focal point for one of your meetings. What a wonderful enlightening gift on the road to recovery.

Year: 1993
Length: 100 min
Rating: PG
Color

David's Mother

Healing Themes:

- Overwhelmed with responsibilities if your children have special needs
- When things are coming at you from every angle
- Refusing to do what's in the best interest of your children
- Working towards letting go

Cast: Kristie Alley, Sam Waterson, Stockard Channing, Michael Goorjian, Chris Sarandon, Phylicia Rashad.

Synopsis: A single mother's new relationship with a loving man is put to the test when the state wants to put her son, David, in a home for the mentally challenged (learning impaired) and she must decide what is in the best interest of her son.

Comments: David is a challenged child. For those of you who have a child with special needs like David, this movie will let you know you're not alone and there sure is healing when we know we're not alone. Do you have a place to go to for support when you're feeling that raising your child is too much? Notice the role the mother takes. She is his full-time caretaker. She has no outlet and no place to go for support. We experience the emotional roller coaster she goes through in trying to handle David's special needs while warding off a government agency that wants to take him away. How did you feel about the father? It seems to me he just abandoned David and left him to grow up the best way he could. Look at how exhausting the job of raising this child is and how it affects her new relationship; she no longer has a life of her own. Can you see how she has lost her identity in her child? She's so tired that she can't see what's right for David. *David's Mother* will really help you get in touch with what you're going through in raising a challenged child. If you know someone who could use some guidance, why not recommend this movie to them. You will find that your relationship with them will grow to a new level of closeness. Remember, you can experience your own healing when you reach out to someone who could use some love and support.

Year: 1994
Length: 100 min
Rating: PG
Color

The Days of Wine and Roses

Healing Themes:

- Falling in love for the wrong reasons
- If you drink too much
- When your partner can't stop his/her alcoholic behavior
- Losing track of your responsibilities
- Getting a brand new start in life

Cast: Jack Lemmon, Lee Remick, Charles Bickford, Jack Klugman. Director, Blake Edwards. Writer, J. P. Miller.

Synopsis: An advertising man becomes entrenched in the use of alcohol to get through the day. His soon-to-be-wife also starts drinking. They start losing days, then weeks to their alcoholism. In time the husband decides that he can no longer handle alcohol in his life. Things appear to be getting better. But then she returns to the bottle and he realizes he needs to get on with his life.

Comments: Once in a while a couple will come to me seeking help for their addiction. Some are addicted to drugs, others to food or gambling. *The Days of Wine and Roses* may be the most telling story for those who are caught in their addiction to alcohol. The climb to recovery can be a difficult one, but the healing that comes from knowing you are beyond your addiction is a spiritual experience. In this movie you will see the effects that alcohol addiction has on work, relationships, and health. Notice how pleasant and loving personalities turn into abusive and violent ones. You can see the denial in their addictive/codependent behavior; they support each other in their disease. Some of you may find this movie difficult to watch. Ask yourself why you're having trouble dealing with this movie. What's going on that disturbs you so much? Here are a few suggestions. Ask yourself what role you play in your relationship. Look for some of the effects the alcohol or drugs are having on your life. Maybe your children are being affected and you hadn't realized what was happening to them. Consider joining a 12-step group to deal with your issues of drug abuse or alcoholism. You can begin by watching *The Days of Wine and Roses*, then keep on going by watching *The Boost, Clean and Sober,* and *My Name is Bill W.* to name a few.

Year: 1962
Length: 117 min
Rating: Unrated
B&W

Dead Poets Society

Healing Themes:
- Meeting someone whom you'll never forget
- Pushing your children too hard
- Feeling like it's okay to express your thoughts and feelings
- If someone is thinking of committing suicide
- When people are close-minded

Cast: Robin Williams, Ethan Hawke, Robert Sean Leonard, Josh Charles, Gale Hansen, Kurtwood Smith, James Waterson, Dylan Kussman. Director, Peter Weir. Writer, Tom Schulman.

Synopsis: A former student, John Keating, returns to his old school as an English teacher inspiring his students with his unconventional methods. A group of his students reform the Dead Poets Society, a club started when John was a student. John is falsely blamed for the suicide of one of the students and released of his teaching duties.

Comments: You may recall one teacher, when you were a student, who stood out from all the rest. My guess is that as soon as you read that sentence a teacher came to mind. John Keating is a metaphor for all those teachers who reached us in a way no one else could. They were the ones who told us we had the brains, creativity, and strength to make a difference and stand out in a crowd. Listen to Mr. Keating as he challenges his students to grow, think for themselves, and seize the day. How many times in your life have you missed your chance to do what you wanted in spite of everyone's opinion? How about your children? Look at the many ways you can teach them to be original and unique. Don't follow in the footsteps of the father who pushed his son too far. He took the fire from his son and his son decided not to live without that fire. Teach your children to take chances and to grow from every experience. The school needed to find a scapegoat so they would not have to take responsibility for repressing the student's creativity and personal growth. But John could not and would not compromise himself. Be courageous and take chances in your life. That's what living is all about. *Carpe Diem*. "Seize the day." What better healing than to live your destiny.

Year: 1989
Length: 128 min
Rating: PG
Color

Defending Your Life

Healing Themes:

- Taking a look at your past
- Feeling good about what you have done in your life
- If someone passes judgement on you
- Having to explain your actions
- Wanting a second shot at making your life better

Cast: Albert Brooks, Meryl Streep, Rip Torn, Lee Grant, Buck Henry, George D. Wallace, Lillian Lehman, Peter Schuck. Director, Albert Brooks. Writer, Albert Brooks.

Synopsis: Daniel Miller dies in a car crash and is sent to heaven where he has to sit before a life committee that will decide his next life. Problems arise when his new-found love, Julie, is allowed to go on to the next level. Daniel fights the committee's decision to hold him back.

Comments: As is the case with *Made in Heaven, Defending Your Life* offers us a look at what may happen when we die. So what do you think happens? Do you think we get recycled and returned to earth to do it again and again until we get it right? Maybe you believe when it's over it's over. Some of you may think it's more like *Dante's Inferno*, where we end up in heaven or hell. In truth you may be terrified about what happens after death. I invite you to hear that we all need to live life in the moment. If we get lost in worrying about another life we can't live in the one we have. But if you imagine for a moment you have to go through what Daniel is coping with, how would you defend yourself? Is there a lot of "stuff" you think would hold you back from the next level? *Defending Your Life* is symbolic of a rather basic concept: What have we learned from our mistakes and are we prepared not to make those same mistakes again? Have you noticed there are those around you who get into the same type of relationships or can't seem to keep a job or…? You get the point. They're stuck in a pattern because they never learned from their past experience (or is that past life?). Life offers us many opportunities to learn. How we take advantage of those opportunities is up to each individual. Accountability is the name of the game. While we're on this earth it is important to keep the slate as clean as possible.

Year: 1991
Length: 100 min
Rating: PG
Color

Dialogues with Madwomen

Healing Themes:

- Being pushed too far
- Appreciating your own sanity
- Hearing stories and seeing where they fit in your life
- Learning about the plight of other people
- Getting in touch with a dysfunctional past

Cast: Documentary. Interviews with various women. Director, Allie Light.

Synopsis: Five women who have spent some portion of their lives in a mental institution are interviewed. As each woman is interviewed they paint images of what their lives have been like. Each one has taken a different direction to make their own peace in life.

Comments: *Dialogues with Madwomen* is an extraordinary movie/documentary. Here were five woman who were not actors sharing their most intimate secrets on the road to their insanity. Now I don't think there is one of us, myself included, who hasn't felt at some time that we were going insane. For starters, if you can think you're going insane, you're not. Insanity is a slow decent into madness with a painful climb back to sanity. The wonderful thing about this movie is you don't need to be a psychologist or a therapist to understand what's going on or to see where some of your own emotionally based issues come from. What do these women talk about that reminds you of yourself? Really work to stay in touch with yourself as these women speak. It took a great deal of courage for these five women to share their lives with us. And in the process they experienced the healing power that comes from self-disclosure. You don't have to be strong and hang tough in a life that's no longer working for you. You can have the same self-healing experience and emerge free from the emotional chains that are dragging you down. Call someone to share your very personal feelings and fears. There are therapists, treatment centers, and support groups to help you deal with the parts of your life that are no longer working. Start your own dialogue today and you will experience a wellness tomorrow. Also, give *Postcards From the Edge* and *Falling Down* a try. You may appreciate the dialogue in those movies, too.

Year: 1993
Length: 75 min
Rating: PG
Color

Do You Know the Muffin Man?

Healing Themes:

- When your children have to keep a secret
- Remembering being molested as a child
- Standing up for the rights of your children
- Dealing with the guilt over a child who has been sexually abused
- Getting help for a child who has been exploited

Cast: Pam Dawber, John Shea, Stephen Dorff, Anthony Gear, Matthew Laurance, Georgann Johnson, William Prince, Brian Bonsall. Director, Gilbert Cates. Writer, Richard Freudenberger.

Synopsis: Children in a preschool are starting to have problems and some of the parents believe their children are being sexually abused. The community gets involved, an investigation takes place, and the children are spared any more abuse.

Comments: As a therapist I find some of the most painful issues are those relating to childhood molestation. The stories are always different and yet they're all the same: One human being taking advantage of another weaker human being to meet their own sick needs. If you're in denial, *Do You Know the Muffin Man?* will help. Like *Unspeakable Acts*, we have an opportunity to get in touch with our own feelings as the children, their families, and the community attempt to work through this horrible experience. Are you someone who was molested by a parent, teacher, relative, friend, religious leader, or stranger? How are you coping with the memories of what happened to you? Have you sought help? Many people who were molested complain of problems with relationships and intimacy. Others turn to different kinds of behavior to avoid thinking about their past such as becoming an work-aholic, gambler, sex addict, food-aholic, or obsessions with cleanliness. Watch as people become aware of the problem by observing some unusual behavior in the children. How about the parents? Can you get in touch with their pain? Use this movie as a way to educate yourself. Before you place a child in someone's care, learn how to identify any behavior your child might exhibit that would let you know something is wrong.

Year: 1989
Length: 100 min
Rating: Unrated
Color

The Doctor

Healing Themes:

- Falling off a pedestal
- Getting real
- Realizing you're not immortal
- Learning to treat other human beings with respect
- Getting a second chance to live a better life

Cast: William Hurt, Elizabeth Perkins, Christine Lahti, Mandy Patinkin. Director, Radha Haines. Writer, Robert Casewell.

Synopsis: Jack, a pompous doctor, develops throat cancer and experiences being treated the same way that he treats his patients. He meets June who is a cancer patient dealing with the same problems. This sobering experience changes his outlook and makes Jack a new man.

Comments: This movie should be mandatory viewing for any doctor, therapist, counselor, teacher, or health care provider. The movie is based on a book written by a doctor who experienced the events. Professionals often forget they are working on human beings. In doing so they lose their sensitivity and compassion. I have observed my own behavior and constantly remind myself that everyone is different, which means that everyone heals in different ways and in their own time. There is no excuse for being uncaring. And, as *The Doctor* points out, sometimes we need a little reality check in order to become compassionate. Can you relate to his experience? Have you gone to someone in the medical profession, been told to wait, shown little or no concern for your feelings? Part of the healing process comes when you take charge and stand up for what you believe in. Tell your therapist, counselor, doctor, etc., that you need and want their support and compassion. Let them known how you feel about the way you're being treated. Tell them exactly what you expect from them, and if you don't get it move on. Before I begin working with anyone I let them know the following: You don't have to like your mechanic or the person who reads your meter, but you've got to like your therapist. And if you're not comfortable you need to let me know so I can help you find someone you can work with. Scary, but it's so important to your well-being.

Year: 1991
Length: 125 min
Rating: PG-13
Color

The Dollmaker

Healing Themes:

- One woman's courage
- If you've lost a child
- Nurturing that special talent
- Living with the loss of a child
- Appreciating what you have in your life
- Wanting the best for your children

Cast: Jane Fonda, Levon Helm, Amanda Plummer, Susan Kingsley, Ann Hearn, Geraldine Page. Director, Daniel Petrie. Writers, Susan Cooper and Hume Cronyn.

Synopsis: It's the mid-1940s and times are very difficult for a Kentucky family. Gertie, a wife and mother of five, finds joy in carving dolls out of wood. The husband finds a job in Detroit, where Gertie sells her dolls. When one of their children is killed in a train accident, Gertie leaves her husband and moves back to the hills of Kentucky with her four children.

Comments: *The Dollmaker* is a beautiful, moving story about courage and the importance of family. Have there been times when you've felt like giving up? Life can be very trying and sometimes it helps to see someone else's courage to get reconnected with our own. Gertie shows us how we can live through the most difficult of times. She makes us keep going against all odds and reminds us about the importance of family and a place called home. Gertie also lets us know that life is not without its overwhelming disappointments. How much of you is in Gertie? Are you able to keep the family together against all the odds? Do you feel unsupported by a spouse who believes he or she has only one role in the family—to make money? How would you cope with the loss of a child? Could you have gone on the way Gertie did? Maybe you have lost a child and you're struggling with carrying on with your life. Stay with her courage. Gather her strength and make it your own. I know some of you will have difficulty relating to being this impoverished woman, but work to get beyond her circumstances. Look for your own message and experience the healing that comes from gathering your courage and going forward with your life.

Year: 1984
Length: 140 min
Rating: Unrated
Color

Dr. Jekyll and Mr. Hyde

Healing Themes:

- When your dark side emerges
- Being confronted with the effects of drugs
- Hiding who you really are
- Getting life's bigger message in a different way

Cast: Spencer Tracy, Ingrid Bergman, Lana Turner, Donald Crisp. Director, Victor Fleming. Writer, John Lee Makin.

Synopsis: Jekyll, a gentle doctor who does laboratory research, decides to do drug experiments on himself. He becomes Mr. Hyde. His evil self takes over as he spends more time as Mr. Hyde. Dr. Jekyll's life ends when Mr. Hyde is caught and killed.

Comments: *Dr. Jekyll and Mr. Hyde* is not just a horror film. Like *The Portrait of Dorian Gray, Alien,* and *The Nutty Professor,* it begs us to look inside ourselves to find out what we may be hiding. Have you ever known someone who seemed to switch personalities at the snap of a finger? Are you in a relationship with someone who turns hot and cold for no reason at all? Did you grow up in a home where you ended up hiding under the bed every time your dad stepped into the house not knowing who he would be that night? Maybe your mother was kind to you one moment and abusive the next. Some people change for no reason at all; others, when they start drinking or taking drugs. Some have personality changes when they don't get that cup of coffee, have that cigarette, make that bet, or get that piece of cake. You get the idea. Dr. Jekyll was under the influence of drugs which brought out his evil side. What about you? Have people told you that you become mean when you don't get your fix on whatever it is that fixes you? It's important to capture the symbolism of this movie. The reality is that drugs can turn people into monsters; drugs turn people inside out. What comes along with the drugs is the inability to have control over yourself, the need to satisfy every desire no matter what the cost. Dr. Jekyll's life ended up in disaster. Stop what you're doing before it's too late. Note: There are a number of versions of this story. I suggest seeing it in black and white for the strong reality of good and evil.

Year: 1941
Length: 113 min
Rating: Unrated
B&W

Drop Dead Fred

Healing Themes:

- Revisiting your childhood
- Remembering a special friend from your past
- If you're a parent who can't let your child grow up
- When it's time to let go and move on

Cast: Phoebe Cates, Rik Mayall, Tim Matheson, Marsha Mason, Carrie Fisher, Daniel Gerroll, Ron Eldard. Director, Ate DeJong. Writers, Carlos Davis and Anthony Fingleton.

Synopsis: Elizabeth's husband leaves her and she is told to come home by her domineering mother. She rediscovers her protector, Drop Dead Fred, who was sealed up in a Jack-in-the-Box many years ago when her mother locked him away. Once he is set free Elizabeth finally grows up.

Comments: CONGRATULATIONS! You have finally made it to one of my all-time favorite movies. You never ever heard of it, you say? Not many people have. This movie is a real gift for anyone who wants to let go of the past. Do you remember when you were a kid? Did you have an imaginary friend who kept you company? What happened to him or her? When did you leave them behind? Maybe your imaginary friend got locked away in the deepest recesses of your mind. That's what happened to Elizabeth and for that reason she always stayed a little girl and everyone treated her that way, too. Did you notice her husband and her mother telling her what to do and how to do it? When you're around your parents, do you revert to being a little kid again? Do you turn your power over to them and follow their rules as if they had control over you one more time? I loved the one in the doctor's waiting room. The best scene of all is when she finally takes charge of her life and lets Drop Dead Fred know he's no longer needed. Watch how the person she hugs good-bye is herself, the little girl inside. Sure, you can act like an adult and have a job and get married. You can even have children yourself, but you will never feel like an adult until you come to terms with your past. You may want to give *Harvey* a try, too. Oh, Harvey is Drop Dead Fred's best friend. You'll get the hang of it.

Year: 1991
Length: 103 min
Rating: PG-13
Color

Drugstore Cowboy

Healing Themes:

- Understanding the violence that can come with addiction
- Being confronted with a death from an overdose
- Trying to clean up your act
- What it's like for your past to catch up with you

Cast: Matt Dillion, Kelly Lynch, James Remar, William S. Burroughs. Director, Gus Van Sant. Writers, Gus Van Sant and Daniel Yost.

Synopsis: Bob Hughes is the Drugstore Cowboy, the leader of a gang of drug addicts who rob drugstores to maintain their habit. Along the way one of the gang members dies of a drug overdose. Bob attempts to go clean but he is shot by some of his former drug customers.

Comments: When I work with teenagers and young adults I like to use movies that reach out to them and touch them. Like *Sid and Nancy* and *Less Than Zero*, this movie cuts to the chase on issues of drugs and self-destruction for young and old addicts alike. You will see Bob Hughes and his gang as they live and die for their drugs. First, notice how their entire existence is based on drugs, including their personal relationships. Do you know anyone whose life revolves around the use of drugs? Have you noticed they can't seem to talk about anything but drugs and getting the next score? Also, notice the risk they put themselves in as they rob the drugstores. It's hard to imagine that someone would want to live this lifestyle, but some people do. Can you see all their chaos? The death of the girl is a real eye opener, isn't it? A positive note is when Bob attempts to break away and get off the drugs. It is important for all of us to see their reality and not deny the message: You're killing yourself. What about showing this one to a friend or a family member who can't see what they're doing to themselves. Hopefully you or your friend will make the move towards experiencing the healing that Bob tried to have. If you or someone you know is caught-up in this lifestyle, there is a way out. There are support groups and recovery houses to show you the way out. There is no need to destroy yourself. Why not start being a clean and sober member of the human race today!

Year: 1989
Length: 100 min
Rating: R
Color

A Duet for One

Healing Themes:

- Having your dreams fall apart
- Realizing you're not really living life
- Being confronted by an illness
- Accepting your fate and enjoying being alive
- Dealing with your rage over your destiny

Cast: Julie Andrews, Max Von Sydow, Alan Bates, Liam Neeson. Director, Andrei Konchalovsky. Writers, Tom Kempinski, Jeremy Lipp, and Andrei Konchalovsky.

Synopsis: A famous concert violinist, Stephanie Anderson, learns that she has multiple sclerosis and will no longer be able to play her violin. She becomes depressed and obsessed with what the future will bring until the love from an old friend helps her embrace her destiny.

Comments: We all have hopes and aspirations for our future. But when they are interrupted for reasons we have no control over, life can become overwhelming, leaving us with so many unanswered questions. Listen to Stephanie as she talks about life, its meaning and worth. Her being was tied up in her violin. Nothing else seemed to matter. You don't have to be a concert violinist to relate to Stephanie. Are you so wrapped up in your work that life is just passing you by? Are you so busy you don't have time for family, friends, or lovers? Would it take finding out that you were going to die for you to slow down and enjoy all the wonderful things life has to offer? Watch as Stephanie faces her impending death. We all experience denial, anger, resistance, remorse, avoidance, and eventually acceptance. It doesn't matter whether it's happening to someone we love or if you are the one who is dealing with your own reality of death. Experience your feelings through Stephanie. Let her teach you that it's not too late to start living life one day at a time. Don't turn your life into a duet for one. Rather, enjoy the beauty and vibrancy that come from living in the moment. I would also suggest *Dying Young, Dad,* and *Rocket Gibraltar* to help you get in touch with some of these issues.

Year: 1986
Length: 108 min
Rating: R
Color

Dying Young

Healing Themes:

- Learning you have a terminal illness
- Dying with dignity
- Living for the moment
- When all you have is today with the one you love

Cast: Julia Roberts, Campbell Scott, Vincent D'Onofrio, Colleen Dewhurst, Ellen Burstyn, David Selby. Director, Joel Schumacher. Writer, Richard Friedenberg.

Synopsis: Hilary O'Neil answers an ad to care for Victor, who is dying of leukemia. They fall in love. When Hilary and Victor accept that his death is imminent they learn to enjoy the time they have left together.

Comments: It's inevitable. At one time or another each and every one of us is going to be confronted with the death of a loved one. And when that happens a piece of us is taken away that can never be replaced. Most people are not prepared for death—our own or the death of someone else. They live in a state of denial. Did you ever wonder why people keep smoking, drinking, drugging, overeating, etc., even though they know their behavior can be harmful to their health. Denial! Victor can't afford to take any risks. He knows that "death happens," yet you will hear his denial. He starts acting as if nothing's wrong. Hilary gets caught up in his denial, too. Maybe she can't handle dealing with the reality now that she's fallen in love with him. Many people can't get close to anyone because of their fear of losing that person. Maybe that's one of the reasons you're having a difficult time with intimacy. Are you afraid that once you let them into your heart they'll leave you, even if the leaving is in death? Stay with your feelings as you take this path with Victor and Hilary. Experience the roller coaster of their highs and lows and the inevitability of Victor's death. Your tears will help you get connected to the healing that comes with your own feelings about death. Enjoy the time you have on this earth. You cannot control what tomorrow will bring.

Year: 1991
Length: 111 min
Rating: R
Color

Eating

Healing Themes:
- Listening to women's thoughts
- If food is all there is to life
- Being betrayed
- Having a common bond with people

Cast: Frances Bergen, Lisa Richards, Nelly Alard, Gwen Welles, Mary Crosby, Marlene Giovi, Marina Gregory, Daphan Kastnre, Elizabeth Kemp, Toni Basil. Director, Henry Jaglom. Writer, Henry Jaglom.

Synopsis: A documentary filmmaker interviews her friends on the subject of food at a birthday party. Each woman reveals much more about herself than she would ever have expected.

Comments: I am constantly on the prowl for movies that send healing messages in different ways. If we get the same message the same way over and over again, there is a tendency to ignore what we're hearing. So when I came across *Eating* I was thrilled. Here's a movie for women about women. The good news is men will gain a lot from this movie, too. And for those who have ever had problems with food, this movie is going to touch you that much more. Because the women experience the safety of a women's-only party, they seem to feel free to let go and say what's on their minds. What makes this movie unusual is the main theme. But from that main theme comes all the other issues you might expect to hear: relationships, affairs, money, loneliness, men, FOOD, FOOD, FOOD, and more about men. Say, do you think food and men are the same thing? I wonder. They can both be filling for all the wrong reasons. What makes this movie excellent for both men and women is that women can learn they're not alone in their thoughts and feelings, and men can learn something about what women are dealing with in their lives. What I also like about this movie is that the characters are very real; they're like you and me. Gather a group of your friends together and give *Eating* a try. The healing comes when you let yourself be honest and take action toward getting healthy and enjoying life.

Year: 1990
Length: 110 min
Rating: Unrated
Color

Enchantment

Healing Themes:

- Letting someone slip through your fingers
- Grieving the loss of a parent
- Coping with a sadistic person
- Living in the fantasy that life will get better

Cast: David Niven, Teresa Wright, Evelyn Keyes, Farley Granger, Jayne Meadows, Leo G. Carroll. Director, Irving Reis. Writer, John Patrick.

Synopsis: As his niece's romance grows, an elderly man reflects on his past and realizes how he left behind the one love he knew. He is stuck with the pain of not being able to recapture his lost love.

Comments: Do you have any regrets because you aren't with the person of your dreams? Maybe a parent didn't approve of the person you wanted to be with and stood in the way of the two of you getting together. *Enchantment* will help you get in touch with some of those memories and more. You won't be able to help getting caught up in the lives of these characters. Are you the angry, jealous sister, the adoring son, or the down-to-earth parent? Maybe you're the lost child who always felt as if you were at the mercy of someone else's decisions. Get in touch with the pain and sadness for the little girl who lost her family. Have you had a devastating loss only to have others ignore your pain? Maybe you lost a parent and never felt like you could grieve over that loss. Where did you bury the pain and what do you do to keep it stuffed inside of you? Are you affected by the anger of the other young woman? Notice how manipulative and controlling she is. Has there ever been anyone like this in your past? What about the brothers and the way they kowtow to their sister? Do you find yourself getting mad at them for putting up with her? And how about the little girl? Notice how she never seems to take charge. Finally, what of the lost love this older man lives with? Why did he allow that to happen? You don't have to live with loss. You can get lost in *Enchantment* and enjoy the healing that comes from taking charge of your life.

Year: 1948
Length: 102 min
Rating: Unrated
B&W

Extremities

Healing Themes:
- Being stalked
- When confronted with rape
- If you've ever been attacked
- Feeling like you have no control
- Taking revenge

Cast: Farrah Fawcett, Diana Scarwid, James Russo, Alfre Woodard. Director, Robert Young. Writer, William Mastrosimone.

Synopsis: A middle-class, single woman becomes the focus of a rapist. He breaks into her home and in the process the tables are turned and she decides to kill him. She is confronted by her friend and realizes she must turn him over to the authorities.

Comments: You don't have to be a woman to get the message from this movie. It will kick up feelings of rage and indignation in everyone. Those who have been victimized by rape or have had an attempted rape will especially be touched. *Extremities* is extremely graphic in its portrayal of a woman under attack. If you are in therapy, ask your therapist or counselor if you are ready to see this movie. If you have decided to deal with your feelings on your own, be gentle with yourself and take it very slow. This movie may be too much too soon. Movies such as this one can bring up feelings to such an intensity that your emotions can get the best of you. We're all tired of the violence that's taking place around us. But that violence is really brought home when we watch this woman's struggle with her attacker. How did you feel when she got the upper hand? What would you have done? Even as I'm typing some feelings about this story are being brought up in me and I can feel my own rage. Notice how her friend confronts her with what she is doing. Does she have the right to be judge and jury? It is much easier for people who are not dealing with these feelings to be logical. This is also an important movie for those who are dealing with wanting to molest or abuse people. Movies such as this one may bring you out of denial and send you into your own recovery. By the way, this movie was adapted from a play in which Fawcett gained critical acclaim.

Year: 1986
Length: 83 min
Rating: R
Color

Face to Face

Healing Themes:

- Therapists are human
- Having to confront your issues
- Feeling like you can't hold on one more day
- Professionals seeking professionals
- Trouble dealing with your emotions

Cast: Liv Ullmann, Erland Josephson, Gunnar Bjornstrand, Aino Taube-Henrikson, Kari Sylwan, Sif Ruud. Director, Ingmar Bergman.

Synopsis: A woman who is a consummate psychiatrist has a nervous breakdown and is directed into therapy herself. She grows in the process and discovers that she, too, has her own issues to work on. When she is done with her work she is a better, more forgiving person.

Comments: When people enter into therapy they tend to see the therapist as someone who has "his or her act together." In time, if the therapeutic relationship moves forward, the patient/client sees the therapist as an all-knowing Guru. The truth is that therapists are only human. In spite of the role of counselor and caregiver, he or she has personal problems, and some, like you, have unresolved issues. Over the years I have seen more than one therapist who I felt should have sought help before continuing practice. *Face to Face* offers a nice portrayal of a therapist whose own issues have caught up with her. View the whole movie as an opportunity to take therapists off the pedestal and put them on a more human level. Are you concerned your therapist is having too many problems to help you with yours? It happens. Maybe you're afraid to say anything. Isn't that the way you've felt with your parents or teachers, that they had too much power or authority for you to question? A good, healthy therapeutic relationship consists of mutual trust and knowing it's okay to say how you feel and what you need. Isn't that why you're in therapy? I believe in this field true knowledge comes from firsthand experience. Seek a therapist who has investigated his/her own issues and knows what it's like to sit where you are sitting. Healing comes from empowering yourself in all areas of your life.

Year: 1976
Length: 136 min
Rating: R
Color

Falling Down

Healing Themes:

- Turning to rage because you can't take it anymore
- Being pushed to the edge
- Trying to cope with all of life's pressures
- Knowing that you're not alone

Cast: Michael Douglas, Robert Duvall, Barbara Hershey, Frederic Forrest, Tuesday Weld, Rachel Ticotin, Lois Smith, Michael Paul Chan, Raymond J. Barry, D. W. Moffett, Brent Hinkley, Dedee Pfeiffer, Vondie Curtis-Hall, Jack Kehoe, John Diehl. Director, Joel Schumacher. Writer, Ebbie Roe Smith.

Synopsis: Bill Foster, a man pushed to the limit, abandons his car in a traffic jam and goes on a violent rampage. He decides he wants to be a part of his daughter's birthday even though he has been told to stay away. Pursued by a cop and backed up against the sea, he decides to check out completely.

Comments: Have you ever felt like you've just had it, had it with the people, traffic, taxes…had it with the world? Look at Bill's face the moment he makes his decision to call it quits. You will see how the events in his life drive him farther and farther over the edge; the store clerk, the fast food employee, the robbers, etc. Notice that Bill reaches the point of no return. He runs amuck and just starts going after anyone who's in his way. Have there been times when you have wanted to reach through the phone and strangle the person on the other end because of the way they were treating you? Absolutely! But you never want to let your life get to that point. It can take a movie like *Falling Down* to bring us back to reality. Do things to balance out the stress and strain of everyday living. Go to the museum, take a walk in the park, listen to music that is soothing to the ear, keep fresh flowers in your home, keep healing colors in your environments, and learn to stay free from those people who try to bring you down. If you're feeling as if you need help or a place to just vent, see a counselor, therapist, or minister. Bill waited too long to see the healing message. His journey was the wrong way to go.

Year: 1993
Length: 115 min
Rating: R
Color

Family of Strangers

Healing Themes:

- Finding out you may have a serious illness
- Learning that you were adopted
- If you feel abandoned
- Searching for your real parents
- Realizing you can't hide from your past

Cast: Patty Duke, Melissa Sue Gilbert, William Shatner.

Synopsis: A young woman needs an operation and is hit with two bombshells. First, she learns that she was adopted. Second, she learns that she is the product of a rape. The woman she believes to be her birth mother denies it. In time they confront each other's fears and work to discover who the father is.

Comments: Over the last few years we have seen numerous cases come before the courts relating to adoption. I have been called in to consult on a few. I can assure you they're never easy and are always laced with emotional issues. *Family of Strangers* really gets deep inside the feelings of all the people involved: the adoptive parents, the adopted child, and those who give up their children for adoption. I've talked before about how important it is to heal from the experience of adoption. Those who were adopted can be made to feel different from other people and often attest to feeling abandoned. When adoptive parents decide not to tell their child that he or she is adopted, there is always a potential for problems. It is clear this young woman is angry. But what of the birth parents? How did you feel about the way her birth mother initially handled learning that her daughter was looking for her? How would you handle being confronted by your child after so many years? That she was a product of a rape is devastating, making the child's journey even more difficult. Let yourself feel every moment of what you see. If you are someone who was adopted or you have been raped, the movie will be an important experience. Possibly you are looking for your parents. Try reading *Birthbond: Reunions Between Birth Parents*. Also try *Adoptees and Search*. Both of these books may lend you the support you need.

Year: 1993
Length: 100 min
Rating: Unrated
Color

Fatal Attraction

Healing Themes:

- Repercussions of an affair
- Hurting those who are innocent
- Being stalked
- Knowing you're obsessed
- Putting all the pieces back together again

Cast: Michael Douglas, Glenn Close, Anne Archer, Stuart Pankin, Ellen Hamiton-Latzen, Ellen Foley, Fred Gwynne, Meg Mundy, J. J. Johnston. Director, Adrain Lyne. Writer, James Dearden.

Synopsis: Dan Gallagher, a married attorney, has an affair with a very seductive woman, Alex Forest. He sees the affair as an innocent weekend fling. Alex has other designs. She becomes obsessed with him and will stop at nothing, including murder, to get him. Alex goes after Dan and his family, and ultimately drowns in her own obsession.

Comments: If you were ever thinking of having an affair, this movie will change your mind. If you have ever been stalked, check with your therapist. If you're not seeing a therapist, watch the movie with a trusted friend who can keep you centered as you attempt to deal with your emotions. It's real easy to get caught up in the story and forget that this all happened because Dan had an affair while Beth was out of town. Can you see that his behavior has put not only him and Beth at risk but also his child? Now, let's look at some of the issues in this movie. We see Dan's codependency when he runs to Alex's aid during her melodramatic attempted suicide. We also get a clear picture of what something like this can do to interrupt a person's life; Dan is unable to work or function as a husband and father. Note how Dan does not take responsibility for what he's done. Also, watch Alex as she loses perspective. Individuals end up stalked and murdered each year for the reasons portrayed in this movie. If you are being stalked, get the support you need from the police and other legal systems. If you are someone who is obsessed with another, get help. The healing comes when you do something about the things that are creating chaos in your life.

Year: 1987
Length: 120 min
Rating: R
Color

The Father of the Bride

Healing Themes:

- When your daughter marries
- If you're having trouble letting go of your children
- Keeping up with the Joneses
- Accepting your son or daughter-in-law

Cast: Steve Martin, Diane Keaton, Martin Short, Kimberly Williams, Kieran Culkin, George Newbern, B. D. Wong, Peter Michael Goetz, Kate McGregor Stewart, Martha Gehman. Director, Charles Shyer.

Synopsis: Annie, the daughter of an upwardly mobile couple, is going to get married. George and Nina have a difficult time letting go of her. It all comes together at the wedding when Nina and George see what a wonderful job they've done in raising their children.

Comments: Okay, you've taken the family to ball games, ballet practice, band rehearsals, etc., applauding every time your child did something. So now what? *The Father of the Bride* is for those parents who are having a difficult time letting go of their children. Even though this issue is handled in a humorous manner, the problems portrayed are very real. George and Nina deal with everything from the cost of the wedding and who will be invited, down to their feelings, mainly George's, that Annie's too young. If you are a parent you will find yourself relating to all of his hysteria. Notice the calm, logical position Nina takes. This is where life has led her daughter and she is going to support Annie's process of moving on with her life. And that is the key, to allow your children to make their own choices after you have given them the proper foundations by which to live their lives. I'm a little uncomfortable with the stereotyping of the caterer. Would it have been okay if he looked and acted like a football player? This is what stereotyping is all about; blonds are one way, weight lifters another, and religious groups another. You get the point. Gather the family and watch this one early in your children's lives. Prepare them for the future and then let go. Movies are wonderful healing tools. Learn to use them to enjoy bonding between the family. There is an earlier version of this movie. They're both good.

Year: 1991
Length: 105 min
Rating: PG
Color

Fear Inside

Healing Themes:

- When you can't go outside
- Confronting your fears
- If your life is consumed by an illness
- When others try to hurt you
- If problems stop you from having a relationship with your children

Cast: Christine Lahti, Dylan McDermot, Jennifer Rubin, David Ackroyd, Thomas Ian Nicholas, Paul Linke. Director, Leon Ichaso. Writer, David Birke.

Synopsis: Meredith Cole, a graphic book artist, can't leave her home. She is agoraphobic. Two psychopathic killers hold her hostage as they destroy her home and terrorize her. When she realizes her son is at risk she takes a monumental step: she leaves the house.

Comments: Sometimes people have problems that are difficult to comprehend. Most people cannot imagine someone being afraid to ride an elevator or cross a bridge. Meredith is terrified to leave her home; she's agoraphobic. To someone who does not have this problem, the solution seems simple: open the door and walk outside. But let's not be so quick to judge. Aren't most of you afraid of something—spiders, snakes, heights, relationships, etc.? Everybody's got a fear they need to confront. Meredith gives us her fear and makes us look at ourselves in the process. Her fear has affected her marriage and the relationship with her son. What fears have altered the experiences you might have had with your family? Was there a time when your family could have taken a trip down a steep, coastal mountain road but you wouldn't go? The bottom line is, these fears stop you from having a normal life. What happens to her in her own home is a metaphor for our own self-confrontation. She is attacked by two corrupt souls who feed off of her sickness. How did you feel when they taunted her? Meredith confronts the fear that holds her back. And that's what each one of you must do in your own lives. Ask yourself, what is the worst thing that can happen? Finally, if you are stuck in your home, get the help of a professional. Confronting your fears is the beginning of living you own life free from terror. You have the right to live a rich, healed life.

Year: 1992
Length: 115 min
Rating: R
Color

Ferris Bueller's Day Off

Healing Themes:

- A movie to make you feel good
- Learning to just have fun
- Being with friends

Cast: Matthew Broderick, Alan Ruck, Mia Sara, Jeffery Jones, Jennifer Grey, Cindy Pickett, Lyman Ward, Edie McClurg, Charlie Sheen, Del Close, Max Perlich, T. Scott Coffery, Louis Anderson. Director, John Hughes. Writer, John Hughes.

Synopsis: Ferris Bueller is an extraordinary teenager. He defines the phrase, "the life of the party." He decides to take a day off from school with a couple of his friends and the party begins. This boy can do no wrong. After a day of adventure, Ferris returns home to the arms of his loving parents who have no idea what their darling boy is all about.

Comments: In one way or another all the movies will make you feel good by helping to heal you of issues that stand in the way of your living life as it is intended, with spiritual peace and happiness. But *Ferris Bueller's Day Off* is an opportunity to just relax and experience a different kind of healing. Like *Rocky*, this movie brings out a special energy that's a little hard to define. Now be honest, isn't there just a little part of you that would like to be like Ferris? He's inventive, creative, popular, lovable, funny, mischievous, devilish…I could go on. He's filled with a positive energy and I want you to share that energy with him. Maybe you've known someone like Ferris, someone who did whatever they wanted when they wanted to do it. So how about you? Why not put a little Ferris in your life? Don't be afraid to join that singing group at church. Just do it. Don't just think about taking a day off from work to go shopping or biking or feed the ducks. Just do it. Ask that person you've being eyeing in the next office out on a date. Don't think about it. Just do it! Tell yourself, if Ferris Bueller can take the day off so can I. What better healing power than the power of fun and laughter. So here's today's prescription: Every time you've got a chance to have some fun and laugh, JUST DO IT.

Year: 1986
Length: 103 min
Rating: PG-13
Color

Field of Dreams

Healing Themes:

- Never letting go of your dreams
- Learning to listen to your inner self
- Getting your life in order to face the challenges
- Loving someone enough to make their dream come true

Cast: Kevin Costner, Amy Madigan, James Earl Jones, Burt Lancaster, Ray Liotta, Timothy Bushfield. Director, Richard Brooks. Writer, Richard Brooks.

Synopsis: Ray Kinsella is barely making his Iowa farm work. One day he gets a message to build a baseball field, and famous ball players who have died start playing on his field. Ray realizes that building the field is really about a personal mystery he needs to solve when he meets the father he never knew and reaches his own inner peace.

Comments: *Field of Dreams* is a beautiful story. A true gift to each and every one of us. We're all born into a field of dreams, surrounded by hopes, aspirations, and excitement for the future. But life can play some mean tricks on us and in time we can get diverted from our dreams. We put them on hold in the process of trying to survive in this world. That's what happened to Ray. He struggled to make his farm work, but it just wasn't going to happen until he put to rest the one thing in his life that was holding him back from fulfilling his dreams. And there are times when each of us is reminded that we too had those dreams. When you get centered in your life you hear the message more clearly. "If you build it, they will come," is a message that exists inside all of us. What things are you avoiding in your life that would allow you to solve your personal conflicts: If you write that letter it will open up the door to solving a painful issue; if you fill out the resume and send it, it will force you to confront your fears of rejection or acceptance; if you stop drinking, you will see the way out of your pain and into the light. In Ray's case he needed to put to rest a relationship with a man he never really knew. Allow yourself to search out those areas of your life you are avoiding. Never give up hope on the way to your dream. If you listen you will hear.

Year: 1989
Length: 106 min
Rating: PG
Color

The Fisher King

Healing Themes:

- Losing something that's important to you
- If you push someone too far
- Getting humble
- Making friends with someone you would normally turn your back on
- Understanding what life is all about
- Everyone deserves to be in love
- Listening to a special life story

Cast: Robin Williams, Jeff Bridges, Amanda Plummer, Mercedes Ruehl. Director, Terry Gillian. Writers, Richard Lagravenese and Terry Gillian.

Synopsis: Jack, an egotistical, drug- and alcohol-using talk-show host, finds himself on the streets when one of his listeners goes haywire and kills patrons in an uptown restaurant. His life is turned around when he meets Parry, a man who became psychotic from the shooting, who asks Jack to get what he thinks is the Holy Grail.

Comments: We all need to get our healing messages in different ways. In *The Fisher King* we experience healing through the lives of Jack and Parry, two lost souls in need of each other. They confront us with so many important issues: alcoholism, codependency, love, relationships, obsession, mental illness, friendship, hopelessness, and desperation. Rarely do I suspend my disbelief, but I sure did with these two. You will see that Parry fights demons and Jack struggles with his alcohol; he's got his demons too. We've all known people like Jack who don't seem to care who they hurt to get what they want. Were you happy to see him hit rock bottom? And how did you feel that Parry, like Humpty Dumpty, had a great fall and there weren't any doctors who could put him back together again? I'd take Parry any day of the week over some other people I know who refer to themselves as sane. Get absorbed in the characters as they come to recognize their love for each other. Please listen closely to the story Parry tells of the Fisher King, an example of a healing story within a healing story.

Year: 1991
Length: 138 min
Rating: R
Color

Flat Liners

Healing Themes:

- Looking at life after death
- Knowing there is a past that was never resolved
- Understanding that we don't have control over our destiny
- Confronting your fears
- Learning that we're not alone in life and in death

Cast: Kiefer Sutherland, Julia Roberts, William Baldwin, Oliver Platt, Kevin Bacon, Kimberly Scott, Joshua Rudoy. Director, Joel Schumacher. Writer, Peter Filardi.

Synopsis: A group of medical students decide to experiment in secret with the out-of-body experiences reported to accompany death. One by one they experience death while the others make sure that they bring them back before it is too late. They are confronted with their own issues and learn that the afterlife is a place they do not belong, yet.

Comments: In recent years people have become intrigued with the idea of life after death. Like *Ghost, Dante's Inferno,* and *Defending Your Life, Flat Liners* invites us to look at life after death through someone's imagination and the minds of these four young medical students. It is not for me to say whether these images have any real meaning. What is important in *Flat Liners* is the idea that when it's all over, we must still pay the piper. If something's been left undone you will have to resolve it before you move on. Rachel has unresolved issues with her father. Nelson has a violent past to contend with. What about you? Were you teased as a child by some kids who would never let you alone? What would you do to them in the afterlife? Possibly you never knew your real parents. Would you like to find out what happened and why they didn't keep you as their child? The big message in *Flat Liners* is that we must finalize our business in this life before we can move on to the next. And while there's no way to prove that any of this is true, why not work to keep your life in balance. If you have some unresolved issues work to resolve them. I wonder if this is just another way to keep us going on our healing journey? What do think?

Year: 1990
Length: 111 min
Rating: R
Color

For the Love of Nancy

Healing Themes:
- If food is ruling your life
- Being afraid to grow up
- Parents who try too hard to run their children's lives
- Paying the price for not expressing your feelings

Cast: Tracey Gold, William Devane, Jill Clayburgh, Cameron Bancroft, Michael MacCray.

Synopsis: A very anxious high school graduate decides to take charge of the only part of her life she has control over—food. Nancy is anorexic and exists near death. Her family struggles with her and the disease. Eventually she is able to work through the issues that drove her to anorexia.

Comments: I am so touched by those with Nancy's pain. It is very easy to be impatient with people like her. But I can tell you that patience is what it takes to get on the other side of the emotional crisis that comes with anorexia. I have firsthand experience. A member of my own family died from complications due to an eating disorder. Listen to the parents try to talk Nancy into eating. They can't hear that Nancy no longer has control of her food; rather, food has control over her. It doesn't matter whether you're someone who can't eat or can't stop eating, it's an addiction like gambling and alcohol. Notice Nancy's isolating, constant exercising, and sudden outbreaks of temper. These are all signs of an addictive behavioral cycle. Notice the way her mother takes control of Nancy's life. Maybe you're someone who can't step back from a friend or family member who is struggling with this problem to see your own role in their disease. Can you see that every time you try to stop them from hurting themselves they simply take more control? This is a family disease, and that means if the child is young, the whole family must experience the healing before the disease can take another course. There are support groups such as Overeaters Anonymous to help you and your family. Also, give *Kate's Secret* and *Eating* a try to help you get your life back.

Year: 1994
Length: 100 min
Rating: PG
Color

Forrest Gump

Healing Themes:

- Realizing your special qualities in life
- Learning about life's wonderful message
- Falling in love with someone who can't fall in love with you
- Being successful at whatever you go for

Cast: Tom Hanks, Sally Fields, Gary Sinese, Robin Wright, Mykelti Williamson. Director, Robert Zemeckis. Writer, Eric Roth.

Synopsis: Forrest Gump is a mildly retarded boy who grows to be a man in a world that doesn't know quite how to take him. Yet he learns more from each experience than most people do in a lifetime. Forrest finally gets his dream girl but learns life's lesson one more time when she dies, leaving him a son.

Comments: Like most people, I fell in love with this movie. When I can get lost in a story I know I'm home. Forrest challenges us with his own challenges. We can all be a little embarrassed for the prejudice and attitude of the people around Forrest. Why must people be so cruel to those who are different? Forrest teaches us not to stuff our feelings inside us and not to give credit to those who would do anything to hurt us. Notice how he sees the good in people and that he always wants to be the best that he can be. That's the lesson Forrest learned and those are lessons he can teach us. More than anything this movie teaches us it's the little things in life that are important. Forrest also teaches us about giving, kindness, and love; love of family and love of others. It seems to me Forrest doesn't have an unkind bone in his body. What a tremendous thing to aspire to, not being judgmental of others. How is it someone so challenged in life could be such an inspiration? This is a special movie, one that I would like all of you to watch more than once. You cannot help but grow from the experience. One final note: *Forrest Gump* is a fictional story. However, the film production is so well done there is a tendency to believe that Forrest is a real person who encountered everyone you see in the movie. Enjoy the fantasy, learn the lessons, and use them as a map for the rest of your life.

Year: 1994
Length: 142 min
Rating: PG-13
Color/B&W

The Four Seasons

Healing Themes:

- Accepting changes in your friend's life
- Realizing that not everyone stays married forever
- Trying to recapture your youth
- Learning about friends and relationships

Cast: Alan Alda, Carol Burnett, Sandy Dennis, Len Cariou, Jack Weston, Rita Moreno, Bess Armstrong. Director, Alan Alda. Writer, Alan Alda.

Synopsis: Three couples take all of their vacations together. Their individual quirks make their way to the surface when one of the men decides to leave his wife for a younger woman. The couples grow as people when they learn that the four seasons are really about their own lives.

Comments: Friends and their friendship can be put to the test, which is the focus of this movie. Especially for those who are a little older, you will see a bit of yourself in at least one of the characters. Notice how each member has a role to play within the group. Who are you: the leader, the follower, the aggressor, the joker? When you're with your friends do you act differently? I was fascinated with the way the movie dealt with each marriage, how different the couples were with one another. Do you keep up a front like these couples? That's normal. People struggle in their relationships to gain their own identity and autonomy. Do you ever feel lost in your partner? What's it like when you try to gain equal power? Are you shot down? And what of the couple who broke up? How do you think the group handled it? And why is she out and not him? I thought the new member did a great job of taking care of herself when she confronted the group about the way they all treated her. But all and all the members of this group care for each other. We experience healing when we have good, reliable, and nurturing friends we can turn to for support. I would also suggest watching *Over Forty, The Big Chill,* and *Grand Canyon.* These movies all have similar themes and are presented in a way that will allow you to hear their message. Invite some friends over. Pop this one in the VCR. You're in for a whole new experience.

Year: 1981
Length: 108 min
Rating: R
Color

Frances

Healing Themes:

- If a parent abuses you or your family betrays you
- When you lose control over your choices in life
- Being pushed to the limit
- When all you have to live for are drugs and alcohol
- Using sex in place of love

Cast: Jessica Lange, Kim Stanley, Sam Shepard. Director, Graeme Clifford. Writers, Eric Bergen, Christopher Devore, and Nicholas Kazan.

Synopsis: A domineering, neurotic mother, little by little, drives Frances over the edge. Frances uses drugs, alcohol, and sex to get through each day of her chaotic existence. In and out of mental institutions, she is given a lobotomy in an attempt to keep her under control.

Comments: Some of you may remember Frances Farmer, a popular movie actress during the mid-forties and fifties. She was so wild that some people decided she needed to be calmed down. I don't think that destroying part of her brain was the answer. I was working on a master's degree at UCLA when some controversial research was being done on prisoners who were given lobotomies. I will spare you my opinion on the subject. However, if Frances were alive today she would not be treated this way. Knowing that you do not have to submit yourself to any kind of abuse, even if it is in the name of science, is healing. Frances was led down the false path of believing there weren't any other options. Today we have Alcoholics Anonymous, therapists, counselors, and support groups to see you through your healing. Wellness comes in many ways, and one way is to see yourself in someone else. I call this paradoxical healing—seeing what we do not want to be like so that we can be who and what we want to be. Each of us has a special energy, a vibrancy to share with the universe. When people around you try and force you to live without your individuality, like Frances Farmer, you are conforming to someone else's rules. I'm not saying we should live without rules, but that we must not give up who we are in order to be what others want us to be.

Year: 1982
Length: 134 min
Rating: R
Color

The Gambler

Healing Themes:

- When nothing else matters but the role of the dice
- Refusing to see that your life is pure chaos
- You can't see you're fostering someone else's addictive behavior
- Allowing your addiction to cancel out all other aspects of your life

Cast: James Caan, Lauren Hutton, Paul Sorvino, Burt Young, James Woods. Director, Karel Reisz. Writer, James Toback.

Synopsis: James Caan plays the role of Axel, a professor with a gambling problem, who is pursued by the mob as he gets deeper into debt. Rescued by his mother, he goes on another disastrous gambling spree, hitting rock bottom when he tries to destroy himself in a New York ghetto.

Comments: Many of you can't imagine someone being so addicted to gambling they could and would lose their house, job, and family. But it happens every day and it can happen to anyone. It happened to Axel, who's a college professor. Some may think that because he's intelligent he's beyond being addicted. Let's clear up that myth right now: Addictions have no bounds and addicts like Axel cannot help themselves. They are sick with the addiction of gambling and they are in denial about their disease. Have you ever known anyone like Axel? This is the type of personality who pushes everything to the edge—himself, his family, and the people whom he calls his friends. How did you feel about the mother giving him the money? Were you angry at her or him or both of them? People who are addicted will lie, do and say anything to get their fix; they'll make that bet at any cost. But it doesn't have to be that way. Not anymore. There are support groups to help you heal the wounds, fill up the emptiness with a better life beyond the addiction of gambling. Reach inside and grasp your own positive energy, then use that force to get you to the other side of your disease. Another excellent movie that deals with this issue is *The Great Sinner*. While it is an older movie, the messages are the same: Don't gamble. Watch both *The Gambler* and *The Great Sinner*. Get started on the healing today!

Year: 1974
Length: 111 min
Rating: R
Color

The Gathering

Healing Themes:

- Bringing your family back together again
- Getting over the wounds from the past
- Coping with your anger at a parent
- Facing your past and moving on
- Realizing you're not the parent you thought you were

Cast: Edward Asner, Maureen Stapleton, Lawrence Pressman, Stephanie Zimbalist, Bruce Davison, John Randolph, Gregory Harrison, Veronica Hamel, Gail Strickland. Director, Randal Kleiser. Writer, James Poe.

Synopsis: It's Christmas time and Adam, a father and husband, knows he hasn't got much time left to reunite his family before he dies. Adam seeks the support of his wife, Kate, who tries to help him accomplish his dream. Though the job of accomplishing the gathering is painful, the family experiences the joy of coming together.

Comments: Each year when the holiday season draws closer, the therapy sessions I have with my clients begin to change their focus. People become worried, angry, and upset over the idea of spending the holidays with their relatives. It seems most people have very high expectations about the family gatherings that take place over the holidays. I would like you to watch *The Gathering* as it relates to your own experiences. Feel the resentment and anger of the children. Listen to the way they speak to each other. You can't help but notice the resistance to going home on the part of the children. For them, the holidays and home mean discomfort and unhappiness, not safety and joy. That's going to really hit home for some of you, and it cannot all go away in a few holiday gatherings. Here's a suggestion. Bring everyone together a little early this year and watch *The Gathering* as a family. Work to get in touch with your feelings and open up a discussion that, in time, leads to the resolution of the family issues. Set some guidelines and boundaries and commit to working through all of the past problems and do the healing as a family for all the futures you have together. We have so little time together. Make it quality time.

Year: 1977
Length: 92 min
Rating: Unrated
Color

Ghost

Healing Themes:

- Losing the love of your life
- Still feeling connected to someone who is gone
- Learning to let go
- Accepting help from someone
- Moving on with your life

Cast: Patrick Swayze, Demi Moore, Whoopi Goldberg, Tony Goldwyn, Vincent Schiavelli. Director, Jerry Zucker. Writer, Bruce Joe Robin.

Synopsis: Sam Wheat, a young man killed during a robbery, contacts his devastated love, Molly, through a medium. He learns Molly is in danger from the one who arranged his murder. Sam is able to stop the murderer, say good-bye to Molly, and move on in the afterlife.

Comments: We may experience our greatest loss when we lose a loved one. For some the grieving is so painful they hold on to their memory of them to the point where they lose themselves to those memories. But when the memories get in the way of our moving on and living life, we must work to heal ourselves and go on. *Ghost* offers us an opportunity to be enlightened by the rich images given to us through Sam' and Molly's own healings. Belief in the afterlife may offer some consolation in their grief. Like *Flat Liners*, *Ghost* offers us an image of what it might be like to be caught between the real world and the afterlife. For some people belief in the afterlife is so strong that they live and wait for death. *Rapture* deals, in part, with that concept. In *Ghost* we are given an image of a pure relationship. Let yourself feel the healing when Sam is able to say good-bye and Molly is able to let go. Your tears are part of the healing. Note: If you are interested in mediums or channeling you may gain something from the role that Whoopi Goldberg plays. However, mediums and channelers have been under heavy scrutiny. Before you spend any money on this type of healing do some investigating and consider what you're getting yourself into. Remember, the goal is to be healed not hurt.

Year: 1990
Length: 127 min
Rating: PG-13
Color

The Good Mother

Healing Themes:

- When your attempts to be a good parent backfire on you
- Being accused of sexual misconduct
- Feeling betrayed by someone you trusted
- Losing your child in a divorce

Cast: Diane Keaton, Liam Neeson, Jason Robards, Jr., Ralph Bellamy, James Naughton, Teresa Wright. Director, Michael Bortman. Writer, Michael Bortman.

Synopsis: Anne, a divorced mother, falls in love with Leo, and is taken to court by her ex-husband for custody of their young daughter, Molly, because of his views on Anne and Leo's sexual conduct. In the end Anne looses her daughter and Leo, and is left to go it alone.

Comments: I have testified in court regarding the custody of a child. Often it's a matter of opinion with respect to who will be the better parent. But I have seen one partner punishing the other by trying to take the children away. I can assure you one of the most damaging things a parent can do to a child is to use that child to get back at an ex-partner. What about this case? *The Good Mother* gives an excellent portrayal of how our views of child abuse and neglect can run amuck; creating a problem where there is none. We cannot help but be mad at the system for controlling the mother's life yet the story also brings up some key points about appropriate behavior between adults and children. What becomes so distressing in this movie is how the mother has to put her life on hold after working so hard to create a good life for herself and her child. Note how it is automatically assumed that the boyfriend is guilty. Would that have been the case if it were a male child and a female girlfriend? It appears that men risk being accused of inappropriate activities simply because they are men. And what about the ex-husband? He steps in as soon as she brings a man into her life. It seems that his actions are really about jealousy and manipulation. If you are dealing with the loss of a child through a custody battle or you are experiencing being controlled by an ex-partner, you will get in touch with your true feelings as you deal with the issues in *The Good Mother*.

Year: 1988
Length: 104 min
Rating: R
Color

Grand Canyon

Healing Themes:

- Seeing yourself through the eyes of other people
- Feeling inspired to go on in life
- Realizing that we are all small parts of a very big picture
- Special Message: Life is unpredictable.

Cast: Danny Glover, Kevin Kline, Steve Martin, Mary McDonnell, Mary Louise Parker, Alfre Woodard. Director, Lawrence Kasdan. Writers, Lawrence and Meg Kasdan.

Synopsis: Mack, a Los Angeles lawyer, is confronted by gang members when his car breaks down. Simon, the tow-truck driver, arrives just in time. The movie weaves in and out of people's lives, flashing back and forth from chance event to chance event. They leave us standing at the edge of the Grand Canyon asking life's big question.

Comments: This is a movie, rich in images and events, that confronts us with the big question of why we are all here and shows us that we never know what tomorrow has in store for us. So many people think that life is set. Others see life as a series of bad events. There are constant messages delivered to us in this movie. The most dynamic moment comes at the end when we get to see ourselves standing at the edge of the Grand Canyon, when we are forced to realize that we are a small cog in an enormous wheel. I would like to suggest that you make a party out of this movie. Invite some friends over. Keep the alcohol use down to a minimum so you and your guests can stay sharp and in tune with the story. (No alcohol would be even better.) Pop some popcorn and let the movie roll. After the movie is over have a discussion about what you saw and felt. Talk about how you fit into "the big picture." Look at times in your life when you were taking one track and suddenly found yourself on another. You will find that you and your guests will become a little more emotionally intimate with one another. *The Big Chill, Over Forty, The Four Seasons,* and *The Joy Luck Club* offer similar experiences. You may want to save them for another night and another gathering of friends.

Year: 1991
Length: 134 min
Rating: R
Color

The Great Santini

Healing Themes:

- Living with an abusive parent
- Trying not to grow up to be like your parent
- Having to walk on eggshells for sustained periods
- When one parent looks the other way
- Accepting your feelings on the death of an abusive parent

Cast: Robert Duvall, Blythe Danner, Michael O'Keefe, Julie Ann Haddock, Lisa Jane Persky, David Keith. Director, Lewis John Carlino. Writer, Lewis John Carlino.

Synopsis: Lt. Col. Bull Meechum, a.k.a. The Great Santini, is a marine pilot who transfers his frustrations onto his family. Their worries about surviving with him are overshadowed when they learn that he has died in a plane crash.

Comments: I decided to read *The Great Santini* while I was writing my book. Without question, Santini is the most abusive character I have ever read about in a story. Pat Conroy, the author, created the ultimate story of an abusive husband and parent and victimized family. The movie allows the viewer to see how a man's repressed feelings of frustration and disenchantment are taken out on the world. Bull Meechum is a sick man and so is the family as they try to maneuver their way around him to avoid his abuse. However, doing the dance to avoid him does not always work. The movie will kick up a lot of emotion if you come from a family with a domineering, abusive parent. Do you find yourself having feelings about the abusive nature of Santini? What about the mother? Note how she takes the helpless victim role. How can she just stand by and let this all happen? Let yourself feel the fears of the family members as Santini abuses them verbally, emotionally, and physically. Use this movie to confront your feelings. You may experience the desire to get professional help or join a survivor's group for abused adult children. Do whatever it takes to let go of the past and move on with your life.

Year: 1980
Length: 118 min
Rating: PG
Color

The Great Sinner

Healing Themes:

- When gambling takes over your life
- Slipping deeper and deeper into an obsession
- Forfeiting your loved ones for your obsession
- Realizing that it can happen to you

Cast: Gregory Peck, Ava Gardner, Melvyn Douglas, Walter Huston, Ethel Barrymore. Director, Robert Siodmak. Writers, Ladislas Fodor and Christopher Isherwood

Synopsis: A young man tries to help a fellow human being stop gambling. He places a few bets himself just to prove that there's nothing to walking away from the gambling tables. In the process of proving his point he gets hooked.

Comments: I was in Las Vegas many years ago. I watched a man cash in his pay check for the week and start gambling (still in his work clothes). His pay check dissolved before my eyes. You would think that with the amount of people who have problems with gambling, there would be more movies on this subject. I could find but a few. In my opinion this one's the best of the group for its excellent portrayal of the addiction of gambling. As you will see, the addiction starts slowly, but when it takes hold there appears to be no way to stop the disease from taking over. (No wonder it's called "the gambling bug." How appropriate.) Notice how smug Peck is with the addicted man, how he thinks this man should just take charge of his life. If it were only that simple! People who are addicted to gambling experience the exact same feelings as those addicted to alcohol, sex, religion, etc. It consumes them to the point where they no longer have control over themselves. Do you find yourself relating to what happened to Peck? Maybe you were beyond being addicted one day and hooked the next. I have seen some people lose everything they own and a lot of what their friends and families own due to the disease of gambling. If you or someone you care about is being consumed by this disease, I support you in getting some help. Attend addiction support groups. Gamblers Anonymous meetings take place all over the world. Talk to your therapist, counselor, minister, etc.

Year: 1949
Length: 110 min
Rating: Unrated
B&W

Guess Who's Coming to Dinner

Healing Themes:

- When the significant person in your life is of a different race or color
- Asking your family to accept your life choices
- Learning to open up your heart and mind
- Letting go of old prejudices

Cast: Katherine Hepburn, Spencer Tracy, Sidney Poitier, Katherine Houghton, Cecil Kellaway. Director, Stanley Kramer. Writer, William Rose.

Synopsis: A young woman comes home from college with her fiancé, an African-American. While Christina and Matthew never imagined Joanna would make such a choice, they come to see John as a person their daughter loves and not a person of color.

Comments: We can always find some reason to decide that another person isn't good enough or equal to what we believe they should be. What would the world be like if we just accepted each other for who we are inside? *Guess Who's Coming to Dinner,* like *Jungle Fever,* confronts us with the race issue. What feelings did you have when Joanna's parents opened the door? Did you experience being neutral about John or did you pass judgment because he was African-American? Maybe you felt strong about her being white if you are African-American or of another race. Do you think John was more accepted because he was a well-educated man, a doctor? This is such a painful issue for many people, yet this healing story is for the world. It reminds us that we are hearts and souls, not the color of our skin. If I could, I would reach out to you to let you know that love is about being happy and comfortable with someone rather than being with someone for money, power, or to make your family happy. To be at peace with yourself, you must make your own life choices; you must work for the inner joy which will bring people into your life whom you might otherwise have turned away. Open your eyes and see beyond the exterior. Who knows, if you take the first step, people might follow and see the real you.

Year: 1967
Length: 108 min
Rating: G
Color

Harvey

Healing Themes:

- Living in a fantasy world
- If you drink a little too much
- Accepting people as they are
- When someone is trying to control your life
- Being happy and feeling free

Cast: James Stewart, Josephine Hull, Victoria Home, Peggy Dow, Cecil Kellaway, Charles Drake, Jesse White, Wallace Ford, Nana Bryant. Director, Henry Koster. Writers, Mary Chase and Oscar Brodney.

Synopsis: Harvey is a rather big rabbit, but Elwood is the only one who can see him. Elwood's sister wants to commit him to an institution. Elwood drinks too much, but neither he nor Harvey can see any reason why they should be in an insane asylum, nor can the judge.

Comments: In my original draft I stated that Harvey is an imaginary rabbit. The proofreader left me this note: "He's not imaginary, he's real, he's real." I used to be able to see lots of things when I was a child. Maybe, just maybe, Elwood sees that rabbit because he still has enough kid in him. Of course, in science we have to give Elwood a title. It makes everyone who can't see the rabbit feel so much better. He could be paranoid, delusional, schizophrenic, an alcoholic, or all of the above. (Now, don't you feel better?) You should be able to put imaginary friends behind if you've experienced a healthy, nurturing childhood. Elwood could be hiding in Harvey to avoid his real feelings. Notice the control Elwood's sister exerts over his life. When someone is a little different we tend to reject them until they conform to our own standards. One final point, our Elwood is an alcoholic. Maybe you know an Elwood. You figure because he's a happy drunk he's okay. Think again. Let's cut to the chase. Maybe we would all do ourselves well to be a little different from everyone else. And there's no question we need to live life clean and sober. How about giving both bits of healing a try? Who knows, Harvey and sobriety may make a visit before Easter. It's up to you.

Year: 1947
Length: 111 min
Rating: PG
B&W

He Said, She Said

Healing Themes:

- Realizing there are two sides to every story
- Putting aside your competitiveness and being open
- When you're having problems letting go of friends
- Meeting someone half way

Cast: Elizabeth Perkins, Kevin Bacon, Sharon Stone, Anthony LaPaglia, Charlaine Woodard, Phil Leeds. Directors, Ken Kwapis and Marisa Silver. Writer, Brian Hohlfield.

Synopsis: An editor forces two up-and-coming journalists to work together on the same news column. The story weaves its way in and out of their lives from each of their perspectives. In time they work through their differences and find their way to each other's heart.

Comments: I would say more than half of my appointments every day consist of "he said, she said" problems. That's what makes this movie such a gift. It was directed by a man and a woman who supply us with their views on love, life, and how to pursue a bit of happiness. Listen to how he has trouble expressing his thoughts. We know he has some feelings, but where is he hiding them? Is it only typically male to hold feelings inside? Are you someone who keeps everything all bottled up? Maybe your partner has no idea how you feel and you want him or her to read your mind. And what about her? Is she struggling with power, frustrated over the reality that he won't listen to what she wants from him? Maybe you feel like you're not being listened to, or even that you're being taken advantage of in your relationship. Each of them has a different way of viewing the same event, but they can't see each other's point of view. This is quite common. Learning how to deal with these problems is the key. Take time to let your partner into your life, your interests, your hopes, and your dreams. Learn to listen and to have open and honest communication with each other. When that happens you are on the road to having a true partnership with someone who can love and cherish you as much as you love and cherish them.

Year: 1990
Length: 115 min
Rating: R
Color

Hellraiser

Healing Themes:

- When you can't let go of your obsession
- Taking things too far
- Putting people at risk to meet your own needs
- Betraying trust
- The consequences of keeping your anger bottled up inside

Cast: Andrew Robinson, Clare Higgins, Ashley Laurence, Sean Chapman, Oliver Smith. Director, Clive Barker. Writer, Clive Barker.

Synopsis: A woman, manipulated by her dead lover, entices men into her home for their blood to bring her lover back to life. When he returns to life he has no use for her. Both are ultimately destroyed by the very force that rules their lives.

Comments: It is difficult to imagine how such a graphically gory film could offer a healing and enlightening message. Yet each of us must gain self-awareness in our own way. *Hellraiser* offers one more way to see that life cannot take a healthy course if all you do is search for that next "ultimate high." Let's look at a few parts of this movie. Notice his obsession with "The Box" and it's myth. Life has become boring and he wants experiences that will take him out of living in the here and now. Can you see that is exactly what happens? He leaves the here and now for a life of pain and misery. Yet he believes it will take him to a heightened state of pleasure. This is very similar to how people feel about drugs, alcohol, food, gambling, etc. They will do anything to have that moment of pleasure. She does the same thing when she becomes obsessed with him. It was the intent of this film to create a fantasy of what happens to the soul when we go too far and cease to live life as it was intended. Listen to the words of Pinhead when he deals with the concept of pleasure. He represents evil and its lure towards degradation. Trust your inner self, find "The Box" in your life, and get rid of it. Note: This film is very graphic. Those of you who are not use to seeing horror movies may want to think twice before watching this film. There are two other *Hellraiser* movies with the same message.

Year: 1987
Length: 94 min
Rating: R
Color

Hot Spell

Healing Themes:

- Living with a chaotic family
- When you are codependent
- If food is the only thing that loves you
- Trying to get your own identity
- Dealing with a death and going on
- Living in a fantasy that someone really loves you
- Trying to escape from an abusive home

Cast: Shirley Booth, Anthony Quinn, Shirley MacLaine, Earl Holliman, Eileen Heckart. Director, Daniel Mann.

Synopsis: A married housewife, the mother of three, works hard at keeping her family together. The father, unhappy about growing old, takes out his frustrations on his family. He dies in an auto accident while leaving town with his girlfriend. The family has to look at themselves and the future.

Comments: Sometimes I am just amazed at what was produced in the earlier movie-making years. It seems as if prior to the mid-seventies no one knew that dysfunctional families existed. What am I saying, for I didn't even know what a dysfunctional family was myself. Well, this writer knew exactly what he was doing. *Hot Spell* has everything: codependency, alcohol, emotional abuse, denial, you name it. It's a veritable feeding frenzy for those of you who want to heal from your family background. The key figure is Mom. Listen for the telling moment when she promises her husband she'll work harder if he will only stay. How painful that is to watch. Can you relate as she turns to food for comfort in times of emotional crises? Notice that the daughter supports her mother's codependency and in turn is codependent herself. Watch the eldest son try to hide his father's affair from his mother. After the death of his father, he picks up where Dad left off. And then there is the young son who just wants to be left alone. It all comes together on the night of the father's birthday. What a telling scene; the family meal, the sarcasm, the abuse, the chaos, etc. Be sure you're prepared to handle this moving experience. You're in for quite a ride.

Year: 1958
Length: 86 min
Rating: Unrated
B&W

I Know My First Name Is Steven

Healing Themes:

- Trying to start all over again
- Having a child return home
- Feelings of being held prisoner
- If you feel as if you were left behind
- When your life has been turned upside down

Cast: Cindy Pickett, John Ashton, Corin "Corky" Nemec, Ray Walston, Barry Corbin, Arliss Howard. Director, Larry Elikann. Writers, J. P. Miller and Cynthia Whitcomb.

Synopsis: Steven Staynor, kidnapped at the age of seven, is held captive by an emotionally ill man to meet his own sick needs. Steven believes he has been abandoned by his family, then escapes his captor seven years later. He works to fit back into the life he once knew.

Comments: It is very difficult for us to imagine what Steven must have experienced. For all practical purposes he was like a prisoner of war, taken from the world he knew and thrown into another world he never wanted. Most people cannot comprehend the healing people must go through to overcome something like this. So, having to do something against your will and being left behind is the focus of this healing story. What would it be like to be imprisoned by someone and at the same time have feelings of abandonment? Are you someone who lived with one parent and were not allowed to see the other? Maybe you wondered why the people who said they loved you didn't come for you. If you lived in a home where you were abused you may have had some similar feelings when your aunt or uncle or grandparents didn't stop the abuse or save you from what you were living through. Steven's case is different than most, but don't put your emotions aside. We can't help but become a little more compassionate for those who have feelings of abandonment. Let your feelings in and experience this movie on as many emotional levels as possible. Finally, there is a tragic ending to this story. In real life, Steven died in a motorcycle accident a few months after the movie was aired.

Year: 1989
Length: 200 min
Rating: Unrated
Color

I Never Sang for My Father

Healing Themes:

- Having to take care of a parent
- Realizing a parent is getting too old to take care of him or herself
- Relationships between fathers and sons
- Trying to have a family bond that you have never had before

Cast: Melvyn Douglas, Gene Hackman, Dorothy Stickney, Estelle Parsons, Elizabeth Hubbard, Lovelady Powell. Director, Gilbert Cates. Writer, Robert Anderson.

Synopsis: A young man, taking care of his aging father, does his best to cope with his father's idiosyncrasies and the demands that his father places on their relationship. Eventually the son comes to his own resolve and accepts the relationship for what it can be.

Comments: It seems most of the movies I come across that relate to parent/child issues focus on relationships between mothers and daughters. When I see men in my office, we eventually discuss their feelings about their fathers—the struggles in their childhood and their feelings over not being close. How difficult and painful these feelings are to deal with. We have some real inner healing for men in this movie. Notice how the son works at keeping his feelings inside. His emotions suddenly move to anger and frustration when he tries to deal with his father. Like *Dad*, with Ted Danson and Jack Lemmon, there is a point where they both begin to realize that their time with each other is limited. But how do we deal with the emotions that come with this realization? Reach out and communicate. Listen to each other. Talk to not at one another. Maybe you're afraid you will have to take care of your aging parents. Possibly you are terrified about the idea of losing them. It is also possible the reverse is true; you could be the aging parent. How are you coping with the idea you may need to be taken care of as you get older? How about your feelings and your worries about being a burden to your children? I can assure you that you must start by breaking through the barriers between you and bringing feelings to the surface. Watch *I Never Sang for My Father;* it may help you move toward a connectedness with a parent that you've always longed for.

Year: 1970
Length: 93 min
Rating: PG
Color

I'm Dancing as Fast as I Can

Healing Themes:

- Addiction to Valium
- Having to kick a habit
- When your family is not there for you
- If people want more from you than you can give
- If your lover turns his or her back on you

Cast: Jill Clayburgh, Nicol Williamson, Dianne Wiest, Daniel Stern, Joe Pesci, Geraldine Page, James Sutorius, Cordis Heard, Richard Masur, Ellen Greene, John Lithgow. Director, Jack Hofsiss. Writer, David Rabe.

Synopsis: Barbara Gordon stops taking Valium but has no idea what the effects will be on her mind and body. She struggles to get a foothold on reality. Barbara wins the battle over her addiction and gains control over her life.

Comments: *I'm Dancing as Fast as I Can* tells a true story about a specific drug, Valium. Notice how Barbara can't seem to focus or control herself. How can that be? Barbara's a high-powered editor? She's got it made. But the truth is she doesn't have it together. Her prescription drugs may have kept her from falling apart for a while but now it's all caught up with her. Watch how her family is in denial and doesn't want to believe their daughter would be so weak. Where's the love and understanding Barbara needs? And what about the boyfriend? Notice the way he tries to push her into being something she's not, and when she can't perform, he's gone. When the drug user starts to change, their friends often can't handle it. Maybe you know someone who is like Barbara. Are you having trouble accepting the new, emerging person, the real person inside? Let them know. It's not one-sided. This is an excellent movie to help you gain an understanding of this dangerous drug. WARNING: If you want to quit the use of Valium, I would recommend you do so under a doctor's supervision. Also, join a support group such as Narcotics Anonymous. The healing process can be a difficult, long road but well worth the journey.

Year: 1982
Length: 107 min
Rating: R
Color

Immediate Family

Healing Themes:

- If you are trying to adopt a child
- Giving your child away
- Knowing you have the right to change your mind
- Dealing with the consequences of a decision

Cast: Glenn Close, James Woods, Mary Stuart Masterson, Kevin Dillon, Linda Darlow, Jane Greer, Jessica James, Mimi Kennedy. Director, Jonathan Kaplan. Writer, Barbara Benedek.

Synopsis: Michael and Linda Spector, unable to conceive, enter into an open adoption arrangement. After having the baby, the mother changes her mind. With much soul searching the young girl and her boyfriend decide to go through with the adoption.

Comments: There are many hurdles in life. Some of those are by choice, others by divine circumstance. Healing can come when we accept the way things are in this world. Why can a couple who could care less about having a baby conceive while another couple who is desperate for a child be unable to conceive? There are so many different reasons. For those who are considering adopting and those who are thinking about being a surrogate mother or giving up their own baby, this is an important movie for you. You can feel both the pain and the joy for Michael and Barbara as they deal with their inability to have a child and subsequently finding someone who is willing to give up her child for adoption. The other side of the coin is the couple who deals with the pain of not wanting a child and the joy that comes with making the loving commitment to raise their child. But the roller coaster of emotions never stops. No matter who you are you must prepare yourself for the scenarios presented in this movie. You do not want to be in denial over the potential problems that come with the adoption process. Be sure you get counseling, the assistance of an attorney who has done adoptions before, and references on all the professionals who are working on the adoption. This is a decision for life. Try to make it the best decision it can be.

Year: 1989
Length: 95 min
Rating: PG-13
Color

In the Best Interest of the Child

Healing Themes:

- Losing control of your life
- Knowing when to let go
- Refusing to see things as they really are
- If you are hospitalized with a serious illness
- Having to take charge of someone else's children
- When it looks like family has turned their backs on you
- Memories of being left behind

Cast: Sally Struthers, Sarah Jessica Parker, Lexi Randall, Gary Graham, Susan Barnes, Jayne Atkinson, John Dennis Johnston, Tom Hodges.

Synopsis: A mother of five, abandoned by her boyfriend, ends up in a psychiatric institution, and the children are shifted from one home to the next. When she is capable of raising her children she realizes they need a place they can always call home and lets them go.

Comments: This movie is rich with messages for those who may be dealing with abuse and abandonment. We know the mother is sick, but at least she got help. We have medications today that can help people such as her lead relatively normal lives. Take special note of how the oldest child has become a caretaker for the other children. Did you lose your childhood by having to grow up too quickly to become the parent? Let yourself feel those memories. Don't be embarrassed to shed tears over a lost childhood. Your own wellness happens when you learn to heal through the self-expression that comes from letting go. How did you feel when you saw how well the foster parents were doing with the children and then they were taken away? Are these decisions really made in the best interest of the children or are they self-serving to the parents who simply want them back? If you have other siblings who are dealing with some of these issues, invite them over to watch the movie with you. Discuss your memories and work through your feelings. On the other side of the pain is an emotional wellness and freedom you may not have experienced. Give this one a try. I think you will be glad you did.

Year: 1994
Length: 100 min
Rating: PG
Color

Ironweed

Healing Themes:

- When you've hit rock bottom
- Living on the streets
- If alcohol has consumed your life
- Compromising yourself
- Overlooking someone's actions to meet your own needs

Cast: Jack Nicholson, Meryl Streep, Tom Waits, Carroll Baker, Michael O'Keefe, Fred Gwynne, Diane Venora, Margaret Whitton. Director, Hector Babenco. Writer, William Kennedy.

Synopsis: The movie weaves its way through the days and nights of two hopeless alcoholics, Francis and Helen, who are trying to survive during the depression in Albany, New York.

Comments: Sometimes it takes the experience of seeing negativity in someone else's life to help you get in touch with the way you don't want your life to turn out. It helps you come out of denial about what you or someone you care about might be doing to themselves. This is a very difficult movie to watch. If you or someone you know has issues with alcohol, this movie will kick up a lot of feelings. Can you imagine getting so disempowered you are forced to abandoned all your dreams? We all have a little fear founded on what might happen if we become so down and out that we have to live on the streets with no home, job, or family to turn to. Francis and Helen have hit absolute bottom. Notice how all sense of self-worth has left them yet they both cling to a piece of their past. Notice how Helen uses sex as part of her survival tool versus how her male counterpart survives. Will that role in our society ever change? If you find yourself relating to anything at all in this movie, reach out for some help. There are 12-step groups all over the world that can help you with issues of alcohol, drugs, gambling, sex, etc. All of these issues and more can lead you to a sad end if you don't deal with them now. You don't have to get to that point if you take action. You also may want to try *The Fisher King, Barfly,* and *The Boost* to help you get in touch with similar issues. There's healing in seeing the things in life we do not want to become.

Year: 1987
Length: 135 min
Rating: R
Color

It's a Wonderful Life

Healing Themes:

- What life might be without you
- Getting a second chance
- Be careful of what you wish for, you just might get it
- Learning you're more loved than you thought you were

Cast: James Stewart, Donna Reed, Lionel Barrymore, Thomas Mitchell, Henry Travers, Beulah Bondi, Frank Faylen, Ward Bond, Gloria Grahame, H. B. Warner, Frank Albertson, Todd Karns, Samuel S. Hinds, Mary Treen, Sheldon Leonard, Ellen Corby. Director, Frank Capra. Writers, Frank Capra, Frances Goodrich, Albert Hackett, and Jo Swerling.

Synopsis: George wants to see the world, but he falls in love and stays in his small town. His company comes under investigation and he tries to commit suicide. When an angel grants his wish that he was never born, he sees what life would have been like without him.

Comments: Hopefully, you will watch this movie well before the holidays. There are so many messages without trying to deal with all that holiday stuff. Pay attention to the small-town experience. It's a piece of Americana. Everybody knows everyone else. Do you even know your next-door neighbor? What of the reaction of the pharmacist when he learns he has lost his son? He hits George. Have you ever been upset and taken your anger and frustration out on someone else? Who does the old miser remind you of? He's everything that life is not intended to be—a metaphor for all that is sour in the world. Notice the way the love relationship between George and his wife grows. You know, I could go on about each message. But I want you to grasp the most important one of all. We can accept that we're here for a reason and do all the good we can in the process of living out our lives. Tell yourself you're a valuable person. Accept that you have a contribution to make and that you can fulfill the miracle of your dreams. Let your angel see you through this wonderful life.

Year: 1946
Length: 129 min
Rating: Unrated
B&W

Jason's Lyric

Healing Themes:

- If alcohol and drugs are tearing your family apart
- When memories of an abusive parent haunt you
- Escaping your past to have a better life
- Helping a child to get on the straight and narrow

Cast: Forest Whitaker, Allen Payne, Jada Pinkett, Bokeem Woodbine, Anthony "Treach" Criss, Eddie Griffin, Suzanne Douglas, Lisa Nicole Carson, Lahmard Tate. Director, Doug McHenry. Writer, Bobby Smith.

Synopsis: Jason carries around the guilt of shooting his abusive, alcoholic father. He meets Lyric, who is fighting the poverty, gangs, and violence in her surroundings. Together they plan an escape to a better life. Then Lyric is shot and their dream becomes that much more urgent.

Comments: There are many reasons people want to experience healing. Some need to deal with memories from their past; others because of what's happening in the present; and still others for fear of what the future will bring. But what happens if it is all coming down at once? Jason has memories of an abusive parent, sees the frustrations of a brother who can't get his life together, and has the desire/fear of moving beyond a dead end world. Some of you will be able to relate strongly to Jason's flashbacks, hiding in the closet to avoid being hit. Can you see how Josh is following in the footsteps of the father, keeping the family in chaos? Notice how Jason is the codependent person in the family, putting himself and his needs second to everyone else. He wants to break away yet he feels responsible for what happens to everyone but himself. Do you put yourself in second place? Are there things you want to do with your life but don't because you feel like you would be abandoning your family? There are support groups such as Alanon to help you learn to let go of those who need to take responsibility for their own actions. *Jason's Lyric* takes you on a healing journey to show you the way through this type of crisis.

Year: 1994
Length: 119 min
Rating: R
Color

Jo Jo Dancer, Your Life Is Calling

Healing Themes:

- When drugs are all that you live for
- Refusing to see what you are doing to yourself
- Being forced to look at your destructive behavior
- Looking at how you got to where you are
- Dealing with memories of an abusive childhood

Cast: Richard Pryor, Debbie Allen, Art Evans, Gay Hauser, Barbara Williams, Paula Kelly, Wings Hauser, Carmen McRae, Dianne Abbot, Scoey Mitchell, Billy Eckstine. Director, Richard Pryor. Writer, Rocco Urbisci.

Synopsis: Jo Jo Dancer is a man who makes little sense to people as he increases his drug and alcohol use. It all comes tumbling down when the device he is using to heat his crack blows up in his face. Jo Jo makes a journey from hospital recovery to re-examining his chaotic life.

Comments: Richard Pryor has said *Jo Jo Dancer* is not the story about his past involvement with drugs. He once made front-page news when his crack preparation device blew up in his face. He literally crashed through his front room window and ran down the street on fire. This incident, he reports, changed his life. That's what makes this one of the great movies to help you or a friend on your healing journey. After his accident, Jo Jo makes an honest statement about his life and his use of drugs, which anyone with an addiction can relate to. Can you see this is the first step out of denial? He forces us to see the chaos in his life that is caused, in part, by his drug addiction, the chaos that acts as a catalyst to keep up the self-destructive behavior. I really like the reflective experience when Jo Jo lets us into his life. I doubt if many of you had a parent who made a living as a prostitute, but don't be so quick to turn your back on his history. Again, look for the chaotic upbringing, the instability, the lack of love and nurturing. In your past was there a parent who drank and was not emotionally available for you? Did your family offer little or no support? Use the movie as a guiding light. When you're ready, reach out to those who can help: therapists, groups, teachers, ministers, and others. Let them in for that second chance to live life with dignity, one day at a time.

Year: 1986
Length: 97 min
Rating: R
Color

The Joy Luck Club

Healing Themes:
- Going back to your roots
- When relationships are strained
- Understanding why you are what you are
- Listening to stories from the past
- Hearing the wisdom from those who are older

Cast: Tsai Chin, Kieu Chinn, Ming-ha Wen, Tamlyn Tomita, Frances Nugyen, Lauren Tom, Lisa Lu, Rosalind Chao, Andrew McCarthy. Director, Wayne Wang. Writers, Amy Tan and Ronald Bass.

Synopsis: Four San Francisco women, all immigrants from China, gather weekly to play Mah Jong and brag about their daughters. When one woman dies, the others realize that their daughters really don't know them. One by one the mothers reveal their pasts to their daughters.

Comments: This wonderful movie gives you an opportunity to see how the past life of a parent affects the present and future of the child. This is a perfect example of why I believe movies are so important to our healing. Movies help us move through the process more quickly because we get to see ourselves through someone else's experiences. Our own memories can be selective and not allow us to deal with the truth. And the truth is what these women are coping with. Is it so surprising that they would have lives laced with abuse, sadness, disappointment, chaos, and affairs? Look at where they came from and listen to the messages these women got. "You're just a servant." "You have no value." Don't avoid hearing and seeing the messages simply because you didn't have the same set of circumstances. When you're feeling emotional about what's happening to them, you can be assured you're really getting in touch with yourself. And here's the big pay-off. One of the daughters makes the journey back to her roots because she needs to know where she came from before she can know where she's going. Invite some close friends over to watch *The Joy Luck Club*. After it's done spend the time reflecting on the movie and sharing your experiences. If you're like me, this movie will be with you for a long time.

Year: 1993
Length: 136 min
Rating: R
Color

Jungle Fever

Healing Themes:

- Falling in love with someone of another race
- If you're thinking about having an affair
- Staying close to your children
- When someone in the family uses drugs

Cast: Wesley Snipes, Annabella Sciorro, Spike Lee, Ossie Davis, Ruby Dee, Samuel L. Jackson, John Turturro, Lonette McKee, Anthony Quinn. Director, Spike Lee. Writer, Spike Lee.

Synopsis: Flipper is a happily married man who finds he is attracted to Angie, a temp in the office. Flipper's wife kicks him out of the house and Angie's dad beats her. Outside prejudice forces the two to separate and return to their former lives.

Comments: Sometimes I am surprised at the number of different issues that can be packed into a single movie. I found this one a little overwhelming. I haven't the time to watch movies twice, but I've seen *Jungle Fever* three times. First, there's Flipper's affair and the effect that has on his child. Most people don't get that idea. They think the only people being affected are the adults. But what about the children, the employers, the friends? Pay particular attention to the way men and women talk about each other. There seems to be a constant battle taking place between the sexes. Did you agree with what they were saying? Did you find yourself taking sides? Do you think an affair is ever justifiable? Many people won't see the issue of the affair through their feelings about black/white relationships. People get in the way of each other's lives because of religion, race, color, and sex. Did you see that the father's prejudice was no different than the prejudice between the men and women? Did you react to the drug use in the family? Do you think part of the problem began with the religious fanaticism of the father? Look, there's much too much going on in this movie to get onto one page. Gather some friends together and watch it, then spend some time in an open, honest discussion. There's a lot to learn about you and your friends.

Year: 1991
length: 132 min
Rating: R
Color

The Karen Carpenter Story

Healing Themes:

- Losing control and taking a destructive path in life
- Growing up feeling as if you were second best
- If food rules your life
- Refusing to see what you are doing to yourself

Cast: Cynthia Gibb, Mitchell Anderson, Peter Michael Goetz, Michael McGuire, Lise Hilboldt, Louise Fletcher. Director, Joseph Sargent. Writer, Barry Morrow.

Synopsis: Karen Carpenter grew up in the shadow of her brother Richard. After they start a band, a recording company discovered Karen's beautiful voice. She developed an eating disorder and lost her health. Anorexia eventually lead to her death at a very young age.

Comments: I'm really pleased the movie industry makes movies about this terribly destructive problem. This story is for those who are struggling with this issue and for those who are trying to understand why this is happening to a loved one or friend. So what has caused Karen to do this to herself? Notice how the family sends messages to Karen that it is Richard who is the one with the talent. Even when she is a successful singer her family tells her she isn't good enough. It could be that, like Karen, your efforts at self-achievement were overshadowed by another family member. How did you get attention? Maybe you acted out in school or caused problems at home. Could it be you took control of your life by taking control of your body? That's what this disease is all about, taking control when you feel as if you have no control at all. Notice that Richard has his own problems and begins taking drugs. Why? Could it be he does not know how to handle his success? We can begin to be healed by watching them and learning to let go of those old, destructive messages. Remember, this is a family-based disease. There can be no healing unless you confront yourself and move towards family resolve. Groups like Overeaters Anonymous are ready to receive you with open arms. Why not also give *Eating, Kate's Secret,* and *For the Love of Nancy* a try?

Year: 1989
Length: 100 min
Rating: Unrated
Color

Kate's Secret

Healing Themes:

- Keeping secrets from your family
- When food becomes your only friend
- Feeling like you need to keep up a front
- Destroying yourself with your own addiction
- Getting help before it is too late
- Living through the recovery process

Cast: Meredith Baxter Birney, Edward Asner. Director, Joseph Sargent. Writer, Barry Morrow.

Synopsis: Everyone thinks Kate is perfect, but she has a secret; she's bulimic—she consumes large quantities of food and then gets rid of it by throwing up. When her body can no longer take the abuse, she is forced into recovery and gets in touch with what's causing her to be so self-abusive.

Comments: It's difficult for most people to understand how someone can be so driven to eat food. Yet, like alcohol, drugs, gambling, etc., food is a substance that can be abused. If you have an eating disorder, tell yourself you will stay with your feelings and not try to avoid the difficult and painful scenes with which Kate confronts us. If you are trying to learn why someone in your life has this eating disorder, watch with an open, nonjudgmental attitude. The most important kind of healing support you can give to someone with this problem is lots of love and understanding. That's the kind of healing that will last a lifetime. Kate's emotional problems have come out in the form of bulimia; she eats her food like everyone else and then induces reverse peristalsis, or throwing up. As time goes on she does it more often, suffers physically, and yet is unable to quit. Can you see how her behavior is similar to an alcoholic or drug addict in that they all increase substance abuse over time while learning ways to hide what they're doing? Possibly you or someone you know abuses food. There are places for help and support such as Overeaters Anonymous or eating disorder treatment centers. Eating disorders kill, but self-awareness heals. Also try *What's Eating Gilbert Grape* and *Eating*, two more wonderful healing stories.

Year: 1986
Length: 100 min
Rating: PG
Color

Kramer vs. Kramer

Healing Themes:

- Fighting for the custody of your child
- When you are being judged because you're a man
- Learning to take care of your child
- Realizing you were unhappy in your relationship

Cast: Dustin Hoffman, Meryl Streep, Jane Alexander, Justin Henry, Howard Duff, JoBeth Williams. Director, Robert Benton. Writer, Robert Benton.

Synopsis: After his wife, Joanna, leaves, Ted struggles as a working single parent. Joanna returns to fight for custody of their son. Ted's career falls apart, courtroom battles ensue, and in the end, Joanna realizes Ted is the one who is prepared to give their son what he needs.

Comments: Are you someone who thought life was set, only to find that it fell or is falling apart? It takes a tremendous amount of healing to get over a separation or divorce. And it's even worse when there's a child involved. And what if you are the father who is struggling to put your life back together only to be confronted with the question of who will gain custody of your child? *Kramer vs. Kramer* begs us to look at these most difficult issues. As we deal more and more with divorce and parents' and childrens' rights we must also deal with the emotional effects on the family. Ted and Joanna appear to be the perfect couple, but looks are deceiving. Notice that the child becomes an innocent victim of his mother's decision. Should she be made to give up her rights because she wants to follow her dream? What about the effects her decision has on her husband? He can't work, he must take care of his son, and he has his own emotions to deal with. It's simply overwhelming. Children often go away feeling that it's something they did that caused the divorce. Have you been carrying around feelings of anger or hopelessness because of your parents' divorce? Give *Kramer vs. Kramer* a try. You will get in touch with some of the feelings you've avoided. It's time to deal with your emotions and put those hurtful memories behind you.

Year: 1979
Length: 105 min
Rating: PG
Color

Lady Sings the Blues

Healing Themes:

- Being consumed by drugs
- Making a success and then losing it all
- When you make a living at something that you hate yourself for
- Getting a big break in life and blowing it
- Falling in love but not being able to handle it

Cast: Diana Ross, Billy Dee Williams, Richard Pryor, James Callahan, Paul Hampton, Sid Melton. Director, Sidney J. Furie. Writers, Terence McCloy, Chris Clark, and Suzanne de Passe.

Synopsis: Billie Holiday was a jazz singer who rose to fame in the mid-twenties and thirties. Born into poverty and abuse, Billie ends up prostituting until she has an opportunity to sing. As she gains popularity she begins to use drugs and alcohol to get through her chaotic days and nights. Her life and substance abuse catch up with her, ultimately causing her death.

Comments: Sometimes it helps to see a story about someone's real-life struggle. And Billie Holiday definitely epitomizes the rise and fall from grace. Like *Sid and Nancy* you see what happened to those who turned to drugs and alcohol in the process of living life. There is a tendency for many people to believe entertainers become involved with alcohol and drugs because it's a part of the profession. Entertainers are no different than you or me. They have the same fears, joys, and backgrounds as we do. You will see some clues to Billie's life course of self-destruction: broken home, molestation, prostitution, pressures to perform, etc. No matter how famous Billie becomes, she still tries to fill that empty hole inside. Is that what you're dealing with? Are you searching for some missing piece, but you don't know what you're searching for? Maybe you are experiencing success in your life and at the same time can't get off your path of self-destruction. Possibly you have a friend or relative who is on the road to self-destruction. Whichever is the case, there are people out there who are willing to open their arms and their hearts to anyone who wants to work on their recovery. Give this one a try; take life one step at a time and tell yourself you don't have to sing the blues any more.

Year: 1972
Length: 144 min
Rating: R
Color

Less Than Zero

Healing Themes:

- Falling into the wrong crowd
- Being pressured into doing something you don't want to do
- Getting addicted to drugs and alcohol
- Doing anything for money
- Seeing what you're doing to yourself before it's too late

Cast: Andrew McCarthy, Jami Gertz, Robert Downey, Jr., James Spader. Director, Mark Kanievska. Writer, Harley Peyton.

Synopsis: An in-group of upper-class young people go to sex, drug, and alcohol parties. Julian is forced to pay his drug debt by prostituting himself. Clay and Blair try to help him, but he dies from an overdose. Julian's death changes the lives of Clay and Blair forever.

Comments: The fall into drug and alcohol abuse doesn't happen overnight. It's a slow decent into addiction. When I work with young people who are addicted or on the road to being addicted, my heart aches for them. They're so sure they've beat the system, so confident they're in control. *Less Than Zero* gives us some real insight into this young, hip, slick, and cool group. Clay is the one on the outside who is looking to get involved, maybe. He wants to be with Blair but she's a few steps ahead of him. She's a tempting invitation. Did you compromise who you thought you were just to be accepted into the "in crowd." Think back, is that why you picked up your first cigarette? Did you start drinking because your friends were drinking and that's what it took to still be their friend? Maybe, like Julian, it took the drugs and alcohol to relax and feel okay with yourself. Can you see he's lost all sense of himself. And all of this comes at a terribly high price. What a dramatic, telling scene when Julian turns to selling his body to pay for his drugs. Clay and Blair get a second chance and you can too. Here's an idea, invite some of your friends over, pop this one in the VCR, and let'er roll. Have some meaningful discussion about how this movie made you feel. Talk about the pressures you have experienced to get involved in the drug lifestyle. You will see a better way to grow in your life and enjoy the future that awaits you.

Year: 1987
Length: 98 min
Rating: R
Color

Life of the Party: The Story of Beatrice

Healing Themes:

- If your drinking is out of control
- Seeing yourself for who you are
- Reaching out to help those who are like yourself
- Making the world a better place in which to live

Cast: Lamont Johnson, Carol Burnett, Lloyd Bridges, Marian Mercer, Geoffrey Lewis, Conchata Ferrell, Gail Strickland. Director, Lamont Johnson. Writers, Carrol Burnett, Ken Welch, and Mitzi Welch.

Synopsis: Beatrice is truly the life of the party, but she has a problem. In time she realizes she is sick and needs to stop drinking. She decides she wants to do more than not drink; she wants to reach others who have the same problem and help them recover from their alcoholism.

Comments: How much more perfect can a title be than *The Life of the Party*? Beatrice is a real person and this is the story of her recovery. When I come across movies about real people, I include them in my book. The incidents in the movie give you a clear picture of what alcoholic behavior is really like. Notice how people love the Beatrice who drinks and the way they encourage her. You can see she has lots of reinforcement to keep drinking. Watch as she goes through the courageous process of letting the alcohol addiction go. That's a pretty scary thing to do. Beatrice could always count on her alcohol being there for her. And that's no different for the compulsive overeater, gambler, smoker, etc. So one of the first steps in recovery is saying good-bye to your old friend and hello to your real friends in recovery. It's the most difficult part of recovery. Most people slip into the old patterns because they are still hanging out with their drinking buddies. Beatrice did more than stop drinking. She was the founder of the L. A. recovery house for alcoholics. Part of the healing process is giving the gift of recovery to others once you've found it yourself. *The Life of the Party* is a good movie to show to a friend or a group who is on the road to recovery. Try using it as the focus of an AA meeting. You'll be the life of the meeting.

Year: 1982
Length: 100 min
Rating: Unrated
Color

A Long Way Home

Healing Themes:

- Looking for lost brothers and sisters
- If you were adopted
- Going on a journey into your past
- Having to deal with an uncaring bureaucracy
- Finding your family

Cast: Timothy Hutton, Brenda Vaccaro, Rosanna Arquette, Paul Regina, George Dzundza, John Lehne, Bonnie Bartlett. Director, Robert Markowitz.

Synopsis: Three children are separated and sent to live with foster parents. When one of the brothers grows up, he realizes he must look for his lost siblings. He goes through bureaucratic frustrations to find his brother and sister. When he finds them he knows he's finally home.

Comments: Over the last ten years, many people have become very outspoken about wanting to find their real parents and/or siblings. *A Long Way Home* asks us to deal with some of the issues that surround families being torn apart and the trials of finding those family members who are lost to an uncaring system. Notice how the young man experiences emotional pain over needing to find his family. Can you relate to his pain? What did you think of the kind of support he got from his family and friends when he decided he wanted to find his siblings? We need to know where we have come from to know where we're going in life. Maybe you were adopted or you've never taken the time to learn about your roots. Why not pick up your family album and learn about your family's past. Ask a parent or grandparent about your family history. Put together a family tree. There are even computer programs to help you. For those who are searching for family members, there are now national organizations to help you. The end of the journey is not always joyful. But no matter if you find them or not, it's the attempt that is important. And as you will see, the end of the journey can be tremendously healing. Start to organize your family information and begin putting the pieces of your past together. What a wonderful way to become whole again.

Year: 1981
Length: 97 min
Rating: Unrated
Color

The Longest Runner

Healing Themes:

- Realizing that your children are not in control of wetting the bed
- Trying to be like everyone else
- Looking at different ways a parent can be abusive
- Turning a bad thing into a good thing

Cast: Michael Landon, Lance Kerwin, DeAnn Mears, Brian Keith, Melissa Sue Anderson.

Synopsis: The parents of a teenager refuse to believe that their son can't control his bed wetting, so his mother hangs his sheets out of the window to punish him. Each day he runs home from school to take down the sheets before anyone can see them. He eventually gets over his bed wetting and becomes a world-class runner.

Comments: *The Longest Runner* is semi-autobiographical. Among other things it deals with a problem known as enuresis, or bed wetting. Some children wet their beds nightly while others never do. In some rare cases it can be due to a physical problem, but usually it means there is something going on with the child emotionally. Maybe they're afraid to get up in the middle of the night. Possibly they are emotionally upset because of family arguments or something going on at school. It's important to talk with your children and let them know you're there for them. But punishing them for wetting the bed is never the answer. How did you feel about the way his mother treated him? I was so angry at her. What an unloving, uncaring way to treat her son. I felt as if he got no support from his father. Maybe that was part of the problem. But isn't it interesting that because he constantly ran home to remove the sheets from the window he became a runner. While bad can become good, it is you who must make that good happen. His healing came from running. My healing came from my music. I would practice the clarinet for hours to drown out the family fights. Find your own way to heal your negative childhood experience. If you are a parent, treat each child with love, understanding, and lots of patience. Your reward will come in the form of a child who will remember your support and is capable of giving you love and joy in return.

Year: 1976
Length: 74 min
Rating: Unrated
Color

Looking for Mister Goodbar

Healing Themes:

- When pursuing sex gets you into trouble
- Looking for love in all the wrong places
- Leading a double life
- Getting involved with people you really don't know
- Using alcohol to be someone you're not

Cast: Diane Keaton, Tuesday Weld, Richard Gere, Tom Berenger, William Atherton, Richard Kiley. Director, Richard Brooks. Writer, Richard Brooks.

Synopsis: Theresa Dunn is a lonely, young teacher who cruises the bars at night, using alcohol to open up her personality. She allows a stream of men into her life in a series of one-night stands and meets Tony. Disaster occurs; Theresa is murdered.

Comments: Maybe you feel a little lonely for someone, anyone to spend time with. What do you do? Have you ever spent time with someone who took you down a dangerous path? Have you done things you regret in the name of love? This movie reminds us there is a price to pay for looking for love in all the wrong places. For those who enjoy watching talk shows, this is a fairly common theme. Do you find yourself relating to Theresa? Are you someone who leads a double life like she does? Watch Teresa's behavior. Notice how drugs and alcohol weave their way in and out of one bad relationship after another. Do you need to numb yourself to cope with work and to relax enough to be social? There are other choices you can make. If you're trying to fill that empty hole, why not join a support group and start talking about that emptiness? If you feel as if your life is not turning out the way you had hoped and you're feeling lonely and left out, get into action. Take some night classes, join a health spa, go to book readings. Meet people who want the same things as you. Theresa gives us a chance to see ourselves and heal our spirit through her mistakes. What a wonderful way to have a better chance at life without having to look for Mr. or Ms. Goodbar.

Year: 1977
Length: 136 min
Rating: R
Color

The Lost Weekend

Healing Themes:

- If you are not seeing addicts for who they are
- Turning to alcohol to avoid living life or to hide your fears
- Living a lie
- When it's finally time to get your act together

Cast: Ray Milland, Jane Wyman, Phillip Terry, Howard da Silva, Doris Dowling, Frank Faylen. Director, Billy Wilder. Writers, Charles Brackett and Billy Wilder.

Synopsis: A writer experiencing a writer's block turns to alcohol. He refuses the help of his brother who attempts to reach out to him to get him sober. A woman who falls in love with him becomes part of his denial, refusing to see the problem. Eventually, he accepts responsibility, stops drinking, and starts to write again.

Comments: *The Lost Weekend* is one of the best movies ever made dealing with one man's addiction to alcohol. No matter what is going on in his life, alcohol is all that is important to him. He is willing to give up everything—a new love, his work, his family, etc.—just to have his alcohol. Notice how hard he works to avoid dealing with the problem. Watch how he hides his bottle. You can't help but be somewhat amazed at the scene were he pulls his secret stash in from the window. Do you have a secret hiding place for your alcohol, cigarettes, food, drugs, etc.? Listen to him make promises and then break them. You will get a chance to see how codependency works as his brother and his girl-friend choose to deny the truth about his addiction. Do you see how they make excuses each time he slips or lies? Notice how they keep giving him one more chance. When do you think you would have had enough of his lies? What is especially unique about *The Lost Weekend* is that it was made long before alcoholism was the hot topic it is today. I would strongly recommend giving this one a try. Spend some time reviewing your own behavior. When you come out of denial you can finally see the truth about yourself. And living in the truth is a big step towards recovery. The beauty of it all is knowing you needn't have any more lost weekends.

Year: 1945
Length: 100 min
Rating: Unrated
B&W

M.A.D.D.: Mothers Against Drunk Driving

Healing Themes:

- Realizing that driving under the influence can kill innocent people
- If you have been a victim of someone else's alcohol problem
- Grieving the loss of a child
- Working to make a difference in the world
- Making sure your child's death was not in vain

Cast: Mariette Hartley, Paula Prentiss, Bert Remsen.

Synopsis: When her daughter is killed, Candy Lightner is so outraged at the apathetic attitude society has toward drunk driving that she campaigns for more strict laws and forms a nationwide organization, M.A.D.D., that fights against drunk drivers and for better laws.

Comments: *M.A.D.D.* lets us into the life of one woman's struggle over the loss of her child and her refusal to let her daughter's life go unacknowleged. Have you lost a family member in an automobile accident caused by someone who was drunk? How did you feel when you watched this movie? Could you get in touch with Candy's anger at the man who murdered her daughter? What about the way he was treated? Did it seem as if his rights were more protected than Candy's daughter's rights? Maybe you're someone who can't stop drinking. Did you feel anything when you saw this movie? Many people don't have any idea about how impaired their driving is after they've been drinking. Do you promise yourself you won't drive and then wake up the next day knowing you drove while you were under the influence of alcohol or drugs? Candy Lightner did not want to see one more family lose their child to a drunk driver. She turned her pain into a triumph over adversity, as in the movie *Adam*, where a father turned the loss of his son into a national campaign. After watching this movie look around you to see if you know anyone who drinks and drives. Do what you can to stop them from driving under the influence: take their keys, drive them home, call a taxi, or let them sleep it off at your house. I would like to believe this movie will stop you and/or a friend from ever drinking and driving again. How about not disappointing either of us. There are lots of support groups to help you. Get into action, TODAY!

Year: 1983
Length: 97 min
Rating: Unrated
Color

Made in Heaven

Healing Themes:

- Having a second chance
- Searching for that one true love
- Seeing what life after death might be like
- Following your heart and listening to your inner voice

Cast: Timothy Hutton, Kelly McGillis, Maureen Stapleton, Don Murray, Marj Dusay, Ray Bideon, Amanda Plummer, Mare Winningham, Timothy Daly. Director, Alan Rudolph.

Synopsis: A romantic story on the theme of reincarnation. A boy and girl fall in love in heaven and are committed to finding one another when they are reborn, committing to find one another even though they know they won't remember having met. Their lives go in separate directions; still, they find their way into each other's arms.

Comments: *Made in Heaven* is for those of you who are interested in the images and ideas about the afterlife. As in *Defending Your Life* and *Flat Liners,* in this movie we have an opportunity to see someone's notion of what happens if once we die we end up being recycled back to earth. Now, for those of you who think this is hogwash, this movie is nothing more than entertainment. What do you think? Is it possible that we find our soul mate even before we're born? Do you think there are messages given to us before we're born that bring us to certain events in our lives? Many people believe that if we don't listen to the messages we're born with we end up going down false paths in life. Do you have trouble listening to your inner voice, the one that tells you not to get involved with something or someone? Maybe you turn your inner voice off when you tell a lie or eat that piece of cake you know you shouldn't eat. I felt terribly frustrated when they kept missing each other. How about you? Who knows, maybe there is a soul mate out there who will make their way back to you after watching this movie. Have a little fun and give this one a try.

Year: 1987
Length: 103 min
Rating: PG
Color

The Man With the Golden Arm

Healing Themes:

- Turning your back on your addiction
- Getting a second chance to follow your dream
- Trying to break away from old relationships
- Turning to someone for help

Cast: Frank Sinatra, Eleanor Parker, Kim Novak, Arnold Stang, Darren McGavin, Robert Strauss. Director, Otto Preminger.

Synopsis: A recovered heroin addict just released from prison wants to return to being a drummer. he tries to avoid his old haunts, but eventually falls back into old havits and gets hooked again. There's a woman in his life who loves him. She struggles to get him off heroin.

Comments: Every once in a while I get lucky and come across an older movie that's perfect for the book because it doesn't glamorize an addiction. *The Man With the Golden Arm* shows the devastating effects addictions can have on our lives. Some people have actual physical symptoms when they try to stop their substance abuse. How did you feel when he started to go through the withdrawals from his heroin use? What a terrifying experience. It takes a great deal of courage to do what he did. Listen as he sets up the rules for his own healing process, telling her not to give him his drugs no matter what he says. Maybe you have experienced a friend coming to you and promising you anything if you will just loan them the money for some drugs or their next bet. Did they try the old, "I'd do it for you"? That's part of what codependency is all about. Did you notice how strong she had to be with herself to stand back and let him go through the withdrawals. She was in pain herself, the pain of not being able to fix him. Do you have a friend or relative who can't set boundaries, who's constantly rescuing someone from one disaster after another? If you're supporting the behavior of someone who has an addiction, STOP! You're enabling them to extend their addictive cycle. Both the dependent and the codependent have to go down the path of recovery to experience real healing. Dig deep for the courage and join one of the many support groups that can help you.

Year: 1955
Length: 119 min
Rating: Unrated
B&W

The Man Without a Face

Healing Themes:

- When the past haunts you
- What comes from listening to rumors
- If you can't accept people for who they are
- Realizing that it's what's inside that counts
- Making friends for life

Cast: Mel Gibson, Margaret Whitton, Fay Masterson, Gaby Hoffman, Geoffrey Lewis, Richard Masur, Nick Stahl. Director, Mel Gibson. Writer, Malcom MacRury.

Synopsis: Young Chuck Norstad strikes up a relationship with Justin McLeod, the man without a face, based on trust and respect. When rumors surface suggesting Justin molested a former student, they are forced to end their friendship. As Chuck graduates from school he remembers Justin.

Comments: *The Man Without a Face* confronts us with the way we deal with rumors and prejudice. Justin McLeod is a man who has learned to live his life in isolation because of the way people deal with his deformity. Chuck is able to look beyond Justin's facial scars to see the man inside. Listen to how rumors affect their relationship. How many times in your life have you passed judgment without truly knowing the facts? Do you take the time to confirm rumors or do you simply accept what you hear? As you can see, rumors are really amplified in this small town. And when we add the issue of molestation, Justin is prejudged as guilty. *The Man Without a Face* offers us some consciousness raising. The truth is that we have all been prejudged in one way or another. Through Justin we can get in touch with our feelings and begin to heal from the hurtful memories that come with being rejected or overlooked for superficial reasons. Watch this one with your children and listen to what they have to say. Talk with them and give them some good, solid ways of dealing with prejudice and rumors. You'll be amazed at how they can get to the core of some of the real issues. Let them know that it's kinder and healthier to not be a party to unreasonable rumors. For more real growth for the family watch *Mask* and *To Kill a Mockingbird*.

Year: 1993
Length: 115 min
Rating: PG-13
Color

Memories of Me

Healing Themes:

- If you can't say "I love you"
- Learning how to communicate
- Getting in touch with a father/son relationship
- Learning to let go
- Accepting a parent or child for who they are

Cast: Billy Crystal, Alan King, JoBeth Williams, Janet Carrol, David Ackroyd, Phil Fondacaro, Robert Pastorelli, Sidney Miller. Director, Henry Winkler. Writers, Robert Collector, Dana Olsen, and William Goldman.

Synopsis: Abbie decides to take a vacation from his medical practice to go see his father, Abe. Abe is glad to see him, but they can't seem to get close to each other. After Abbie and Abe struggle at their relationship they come to realize they have something special.

Comments: I believe the reason that so few movies are made about men dealing with men's issues is that men have a much more difficult time opening up to their emotions than women do. My experience in working with men in my practice is that I have to spend a long time breaking through that tough male, macho stuff. But I find that when men give themselves a chance to let go, they enjoy some wonderful healing. *Memories of Me*, like *Dad*, allows you to look at a father and son trying to make their way through years of emotional unrest. Do you have a strained relationship with a parent you can't seem to deal with? What things do Abbie and Abe do that remind you of your behavior? Do you make jokes to avoid your real feelings? There is one scene I would really like you to pay special attention to. At one point Abbie confronts his father about his never truly acknowledging Abbie's accomplishments. It's a powerful turning point in their relationship. Many people have this issue with their parents. Make this father and son night. Pop some popcorn, leave the beer in the refrigerator, and start up the VCR. When it's all over have that talk you've wanted to have your whole life. Take this wonderful healing journey with someone you love. What great memories you will have to keep forever.

Year: 1981
Length: 117 min
Rating: Unrated
Color

Memory of Us

Healing Themes:

- Questioning what life is all about
- Looking at your role as a parent
- Reflecting on your past
- When you think you've done it all wrong

Cast: Ellen Geer, Jon Cypher, Barbara Colby, Peter Brown, Robert Hogan, Rose Marie, Will Geer. Director, H. Kaye Dyal. Writer, Ellen Geer.

Synopsis: After years of marriage, a mother and housewife starts to question why she is on this earth; she starts to examine her purpose in life. The family sees the changes in her as she questions her life and finally learns to be at peace with herself.

Comments: We all want to know why we are here. There are no simple answers. We must each find our way. Some never truly live their life because they're lost in the question about the meaning of life. Can you relate? Do you get depressed because you question the meaning of life so much? We can see her struggle as she attempts to find herself. If you are a woman you can identify with the way she questions her role in life. Do you ask the same questions? Have your ever fantasized about running away, changing your name, and starting all over again? Maybe you have given up a long-term relationship because you wanted to find yourself. This is when having outside support is so important to help fill the emptiness you may feel. You may have a friend or relative who seems lost and could use help. Look for others who feel the same way you do and start talking with them about how they're coping. Get your family involved. Let them know how you're feeling. Don't hold it inside one more day. You don't have to go through these blue periods by yourself. You can experience healing when you reach out and take charge of your life. Join a group, volunteer your time to an organization that can use your talents, or start those classes to get that degree you've always dreamed about. It's okay to take a new course and still hold onto the things in your life that you care about. I would suggest that you watch *The Trip to Bountiful* and *A Duet for One* to help you with issues about feeling lost.

Year: 1974
Length: 93 min
Rating: PG
Color

Men Don't Tell

Healing Themes:

- Being in an abusive relationship
- If you are a man who is living with someone who is violent
- Trying to survive with someone who drinks
- Avoiding the truth about your partner

Cast: Judith Light, Peter Strauss, James Gammon, Noble Willingham, Stephen Lee, Mary Kane, Richard Grant, Reni Santoni, Carol Baker. Director, Harry Winer. Writers, Selma Thompson and Jeff Andrus.

Synopsis: A couple marry, have two children, and he has a successful career. But something goes terribly wrong. She is very abusive towards him and he is forced to defend himself. He deals with his embarrassment when he exposes the truth about their relationship.

Comments: To the best of my knowledge *Men Don't Tell* is the only movie made that deals with spousal abuse against the male. We do not hear about men being abused because they are embarrassed to report it. And this is exactly the point this movie brings to the surface. Men have gotten the message that it's not acceptable to fight back because they are physically stronger than women. If the men don't leave they are often physically hurt. What kinds of feelings were brought up when you watched what he was going through? Listen to the verbal abuse he endures. This is just as devastating as the physical abuse. Are you in a verbally abusive relationship? Is your partner loving one minute and attacking the next? Do you find yourself unwilling to fight back? What keeps you in the relationship? Watch as alcohol plays a big role in her abuse towards him. He can never seem to do anything right. What about the children? The movie didn't deal with this problem very much, but children are deeply affected when they experience spousal abuse. No matter if you are a man or a woman there are spousal abuse support groups that can give you tools to manage your life and relationships. Therapists, counselors, and religious counselors can also see you through this time in your life. Tell yourself you deserve all the good that life has to offer. Stop the abuse, NOW!

Year: 1993
Length: 100 min
Rating: Unrated
Color

The Men's Club

Healing Themes:
- When men gather to deal with their feelings
- Learning to open up and air your feelings
- Avoiding who you really are
- Finding out who you really are

Cast: David Dukes, Richard Jordan, Harvey Keitel, Frank Langella, Roy Scheider, Craig Wasson, Treat Williams, Stockard Channing, Cindy Pickett, Gwen Welles, Ann Dusenberry, Jennifer Jason Leigh, Ann Wedgeworth. Director, Peter Medak. Writer, Leonard Michaels.

Synopsis: Seven men decide they want to get together at one of their homes to start dealing with this "feelings thing" they keep hearing about. Moving farther and farther off track, they eventually end up with a hooker. By the end of the evening they learn what listening and talking are all about.

Comments: *The Men's Club* is a real find. Both men and women will grow as they listen to this all-male group. Try to find yourself in their behavior and words. Which one are you: the leader, the shy guy who rarely speaks, the one who never agrees with anything, or the one who is along for the ride? Notice how one man always writes off his feelings and rationalizes everything that's said. If someone feels something he thinks it away. Is that what you do? Do you have a logical explanation for everything? I hear a lot of women complain about that one. Are you uncomfortable in a setting where people deal with their feelings and not their thoughts? Notice the level of sarcasm and cynicism, especially as it relates to women. I find this is true of both men and women; they speak in the same negative way about the opposite sex. It seems we are at war with each other. Why waste the time? Pay special attention to what they do to avoid their feelings; their interests turn them to a hooker. No matter how hard they try, their attention is on women and sex. Do you turn to sex to avoid dealing with your emotions? Are you in a relationship where the only way you can show your feelings is by having sex? Try watching this one with a mixed group. Talk about what you got from the movie, put aside your differences, and learn to open up to each other.

Year: 1986
Length: 100 min
Rating: R
Color

The Miracle Worker

Healing Themes:

- Seeing what courage is really all about
- If you're holding your child back from growing
- Finding someone who can give you the support you need
- Learning that love can mean saying no
- Being patient with another human being

Cast: Anne Bancroft, Patty Duke, Victor Jory, Inga Swenson, Andrew Prine, Beah Richards. Director, Arthur Penn. Writer, William Gibson.

Synopsis: Helen Keller, born deaf and blind into a well-to-do family, was a wild child. In desperation the parents hire Annie Sullivan to teach Helen how to communicate and how to respond to a world she can neither see nor hear. After much effort, Annie reaches Helen.

Comments: *The Miracle Worker* helps us get in touch with our past and allows us to heal from some of the scars and experiences we had as children and still may be experiencing to this day. It's also about hope and inspiration in the eyes of adversity. The story is true, and both women went on to do important work in improving conditions for those born blind and/or deaf. Notice how the family becomes codependent to Helen, giving her anything she wants because of her physical disability. They won't let her grow. Annie Sullivan is the consummate teacher, guiding, assisting, and able to say no to Helen. You can't help but be inspired by Annie's patience. That's what it's all about, having the patience to stand back and let someone grow to their potential yet guiding them with love and kindness through their learning and healing journey. We can all learn something from Helen and Annie: Be patient, take charge, and move forward against all the odds. You will emerge triumphant in your success, feeling good from knowing you've made it to your potential just like Helen. Give *Wildflower, Rocky,* and *Lorenzo's Oil* a try. They're three more inspirational healing stories. Note: There are two versions of this movie. The second was released in 1979. What is interesting is that Patty Duke played the role of Annie in the 1979 version. Both versions are good. I prefer the 1962 version.

Year: 1962
Length: 97 min
Rating: Unrated
B&W

The Mission

Healing Themes:

- Carrying around the burden of guilt
- Turning your life around
- Fighting for what you believe in
- Grieving the loss of a loved one

Cast: Robert De Niro, Jeremy Irons, Ray McAnally, Aidan Quinn, Cherie Lunghi, Ronald Pickup, Chuck Low, Liam Neeson, Daniel Berrigan. Director, Ronald Joffe. Writer, Robert Bolt.

Synopsis: The jungles of Brazil are home to natives, Jesuit priests, and merchants who are out to rob the land of its wealth. The central character is a self-centered man who kills his brother for a woman. He changes his life to make amends and dies at the hands of those who were once his comrades.

Comments: Some movies have a healing message in only a few scenes, but it is so strong I have to recommend it. Every time I would ask a client to watch *The Mission*, they would look at me as if I had truly lost it. Well, pay close attention to what the central character does after he kills his brother. He becomes overwhelmed with grief and guilt. As penance he puts his brother's armor in a net and drags it through the jungle. Can you see that this is symbolic of the baggage you carry around with you? Do you have something you have done that you simply can't or won't let go of? Listen to what the two priests say as he lays before them exhausted from dragging his past with him. "Should we cut the rope?" one of them asks. "When he is ready he will let it go himself," the other replies. This is exactly what happens in recovery. People come to my office exhausted from the issues they have been holding on to. While I can't cut the rope for them, I can help them get to the point where they can release it themselves. Many people come to therapy to be fixed by their therapist. This merely keeps the client tied to the therapist. Recovery is a process. The healing happens when you can see your path, let go of the chains that hold you back in your life, and go forward on your own. The 12-step programs have a wonderful expression: "Drop the rock," which means, let it go. So, cut the rope, drop the rock, and get on with your life.

Year: 1986
Length: 125 min
Rating: PG
Color

Mommie Dearest

Healing Themes:

- Facing memories from your past
- Confronting the pain of an abusive childhood
- Realizing you never really had a childhood
- If you're someone who was adopted and felt like you had no control

Cast: Faye Dunaway, Diana Scarwid, Steve Forrest, Howard da Silva, Mara Hobel, Rutanay Alda, Harry Goz. Director, Frank Perry. Writers, Frank Yablans, Frank Perry, Tracy Hotchner, and Robert Getchell.

Synopsis: Christina, adopted by movie star Joan Crawford, recounts an abusive, chaotic, and unpredictable life. Joan is seen as an obsessive/compulsive mother whose tyrannical behavior is directed toward the children. Christina keeps the secret until her mother dies.

Comments: *Mommie Dearest*, an autobiography made into a movie, received a tremendous response from the public. I think we all have a tendency to believe that because someone is in the public eye they could not or would not do what Joan Crawford did to Christina. Yet we can see very clearly that fame, power, or money does not exclude anyone from being abusive. Notice how Joan acts out her emotional instability on her children. Christina never knew when or how she was going to be abused. You will also see that the people around Joan are oblivious to her behavior. Possibly you are someone who has fought with denial over the abuse you experienced as a child. How did you feel when Joan woke up her children and made them work? What was it like for you to hide your abuse from your friends and teachers? Possibly you asked for help but no one would listen. Maybe you were too afraid to tell anyone. Do you use things to numb the memories? Many people have problems with substance abuse because of their past. If you are carrying on the tradition of your abusive childhood by abusing your children, this movie will help you out of denial about your behavior. *Radio Flyer, Frances,* and *The Prince of Tides* touch on more issues of abuse.

Year: 1981
Length: 129 min
Rating: R
Color

The Morning After

Healing Themes:

- Reaching out to someone who needs help
- Learning there is more to life than the next drink
- Getting in touch with why you turned to alcohol in the first place
- Facing the fact you are a drunk

Cast: Jane Fonda, Jeff Bridges, Raoul Julia. Director, Richard Heffron. Writer, Richard Heffron.

Synopsis: One morning, Alex, an actress and a drunk, wakes up in a dead man's bed. Thinking she killed him, she runs away and meets Turner, an ex-cop who helps her work out what happened to her that night. Turner and Alex solve the murder and Alex gets a shot at sobriety.

Comments: I have seen a number of women in my office for issues relating to drinking and drugs. Because alcohol and drug addictions are usually associated with male behavior, women keep these addictions in the closet and suffer isolation. But when *The Morning After* was released, the closet doors were swung open. Then *When a Man Loves a Woman* took the door off the hinges. A number of clients have told me they can't remember what they do after they drink. Alex has no memory of the night before. Notice how Alex's personality changes as she goes from being sober to being drunk. Have people told you that you're a different person when you drink? That's a pretty good indication that you have a problem. Maybe you're not the one with the problem. Are you in a relationship with someone who goes too far with alcohol and drugs? What attracts you to them? I wonder if you and Turner have something in common. Maybe you're both codependent and love to be around people who need you for all the wrong reasons. But Alex gets her act together and so can you. She confronts herself with the reality that she has a serious illness, alcoholism. Are you ready to admit that to yourself? There are some great support groups to help. All you have to do is pick up the phone. There are wonderful books, tapes, and more movies to help in your recovery. Why not experience the joy of a beautiful morning after a sober night before.

Year: 1986
Length: 104 min
Rating: R
Color

Mr. Destiny

Healing Themes:

- Getting a chance to see what your life might have been like
- Not appreciating what you have
- Making changes for the better
- Learning that your life is truly wonderful just the way it is

Cast: James Belushi, Linda Hamilton, Michael Caine, Jon Lovitz, Hart Bochner, Rene Russo, Bill McCutchenor, Pat Corley, Courteney Cox, Kathy Ireland. Director, James Orr. Writer, James Orr.

Synopsis: Larry Burrows wants so much more than the average, everyday existence he lives. Getting his wish Larry sees what would have happened if, as a teenager, he had hit the winning run in a baseball game. He comes to realize that his life has turned out just the way he wanted it to.

Comments: If you've seen *It's a Wonderful Life,* you have an idea of what's in store for you. What if you had a chance to lead a whole new life? Would you do it? Here are the rules. You have to give up your job and all your bills. Sounds okay so far? But you would also have to give up your family, friends, and everything you know and love. How does it sound now? Starting all over is a fantasy for a lot of people. Well, *Mr. Destiny* gives us a chance to explore that fantasy through one man's life. Pay attention to the way people treat Larry in his new life. It can be very lonely at the top. Watch as he tries to deal with the love of his life. She doesn't even know who he is. Larry hadn't counted on that one. Ask yourself what's missing from your life that makes you want to have a fresh start. Why aren't you letting yourself live your dream? Are you using other people or things as an excuse to avoid self-accomplishments? If you are unhappy with your life, do something about it. Getting into action is your destiny; you're just not following your path in life. Remember, success only follows action. And success is a reflection of the healing work you've done in your life. You don't need an angel to change your destiny. You have all the answers, you must simply go on your journey to understand what they mean. Live life to the fullest!

Year: 1990
Length: 110 min
Rating: PG-13
Color

Mr. Jones

Healing Themes:

- If you know someone who is depressed
- Coping with a serious mental illness
- Crossing the boundaries in a therapeutic relationship
- When you're up one moment and down the next
- Being confronted by your peers for your actions

Cast: Richard Gere, Lena Olin, Anne Bancroft, Tom Irwin, Delroy Lindo, Lauren Tom, Bruce Altman, Lisa Malkiewicz. Director, Mike Figgis. Writer, Eric Roth.

Synopsis: Mr. Jones has a serious mental disorder, spending half the time high on life and the other half in a dark hole of despair. His psychiatrist becomes emotionally and physically involved with him. Mr. Jones gets a shot at a better life while the psychiatrist deals with her unprofessional behavior.

Comments: Have you ever known anyone whose behavior was so erratic that one moment they're the life of the party and the next they're down in the dumps? Maybe you are in a relationship with someone like Mr. Jones or it's you who experiences these highs and lows. Are you still going from day to day not knowing when the cycle of depression will hit? Well, *Mr. Jones* will be a real eye opener for you. Notice how convincing he is with his up, manic mood. But he's unable to stay focused for any period of time. A good example of this is when he closes his bank account after having opened it a week earlier. Today there is healing power both through therapy and medications. You or someone you know can live a happy, rich life with the proper treatment. We also see the effects of an intimate therapist/patient relationship. It is never, under any circumstances, acceptable for a therapist to get involved with a client/patient. As is the case of Mr. Jones, the damage can be irreparable. If you are involved with a patient or you are a patient who is involved with your therapist, seek help. It can be very difficult to trust anyone after this kind of boundary has been crossed, but it is important that you take another chance and reach out for help as soon as possible.

Year: 1993
Length: 118 min
Rating: R
Color

My Breast

Healing Themes:

- If you are concerned about breast cancer
- Refusing to see that you're putting yourself at risk
- Finding out you have a serious illness
- Being in a non-supportive relationship

Cast: Meredith Baxter, James Sherdian, Jamie Sutorius, Sara Botsford, R. H. Thompson, Barbara Barrie.

Synopsis: Joyce Wadler is a journalist on her way up when she finds out she has breast cancer. Joyce turns to her new boyfriend for support. He's suddenly too busy to give her any of his time. Joyce wins her battle against cancer and moves on to seek a more nurturing relationship.

Comments: The fact that a woman may die from cancer can become secondary to the fear, pain, and embarrassment that may accompany losing one or both breasts. Oftentimes a woman's identity and self-worth are tied to her breasts. Some women will actually chance losing their lives before they will lose a breast to surgery. Joyce Wadler shares the denial and turmoil she went through with the news of breast cancer. Listen to Joyce when she says she gets a check-up once a year and that she is healthy. What's she really trying to avoid? One major issue that comes with breast cancer is the relationship between men and women. Some men can't handle this. And some women don't feel like women once the surgery is done. The man Joyce loves abandons her and is untruthful about his real reason for leaving. Are you a male struggling with the thought of your significant other losing a breast? Can you see she is the same person inside and that's the most important thing of all? It's paramount for both the man and the woman to acknowledge the emotional loss of the breast(s) in order to continue living full, intimate lives. I would strongly suggest watching this movie as a couple; embrace the knowledge that you have each other. At the time of this writing one out of nine women will develop breast cancer and some 46,000 die each year. Let's not be in denial about this any longer. Make arrangements for a check-up, TODAY!

Year: 1994
Length: 100 min
Rating: R
Color

My Name Is Bill W.

Healing Themes:

- When your whole life is hostage to addiction
- Finally finding the solution to the problem
- Making a difference in your life and the lives around you
- Helping yourself by helping others
- Not taking a drink one day at a time

Cast: James Woods, James Garner, JoBeth Williams, Fritz Weaver, Robert Harper, Gary Sinise, George Coe. Director, Daniel Petrie. Writer, William G. Borchert.

Synopsis: Bill Wilson and Dr. Robert Smith keep each other sober by talking about their problem and the solution to the problem. They look for other alcoholics and begin to organize the meetings that eventually become Alcoholics Anonymous.

Comments: Bill Wilson and Robert Smith, who are more often referred to as Bill W. and Doctor Bob, are an inspiration to anyone who has ever gone to a recovery meeting. Their names are synonymous with the process of healing. It's difficult to imagine that there is anyone who is not aware of the 12-step programs fostered by the efforts of these two men. Some of these programs are: Alcoholics Anonymous, Overeaters Anonymous, Narcotics Anonymous, Gamblers Anonymous, and Sex Anonymous, just to name a few. All of these groups operate on one concept: Gather together all of those with similar problems and allow them to support each other in their recovery. Addiction is an equal opportunity problem that keeps on giving and giving to the next generation. As you watch the movie you may see yourself or your friends in their behavior. There is a special moment in the movie when Doctor Bob and Bill W. have truly come to understand they have found the answer to their own recovery. And you can find the same answer. Reach out to those who have the same problems as you. So many addictions are caused by isolation problems. Get to meetings. Purchase 12-step reading materials to get yourself on the road to recovery. Accept that you have a problem, and know there is help. Trust that you are a good person and that you deserve a chance at a happy, healthy life.

Year: 1989
Length: 100 min
Rating: Unrated
Color

Naked Lunch

Healing Themes:

- When you're consumed by drugs
- Lost in a world that terrorizes you
- Realizing you don't want to lose yourself to your addiction
- Living in an illusion

Cast: Peter Weller, Judy Davis, Ian Holm, Julian Sands, Roy Scheider, Monique Mercure, Nicholas Campbell, Michael Zelniker, Robert A. Silverman, Joseph Scorsiani. Director, David Cronenberg. Writer, David Cronenberg.

Synopsis: A would-be writer supports himself by being a bug exterminator. When his drug-addicted wife leaves, he hunts for her through a dream-like nightmare, going from one illusion to the next on an inner quest for peace to learn that life is better without chaos.

Comments: I've said it before: we each experience recovery in different ways. I have tried to find a healing story for everyone. This may be the most surrealistic healing experience of your life—a combination of a Salvador Dali painting, *The Wizard of Oz*, and *The Adventures of Buckaroo Banzai* (not in the book). And Peter Weller invites each and every one of us to dine with him. I could spend time analyzing each scene, but you'll get the point. Try not to get caught up in the surrealism. You don't have to see the images he sees to relate to your own experiences. The bottom line is, Peter is no longer himself. Like all drug, alcohol, food, smoking, and any other mind-altering experiences, he has become someone else. Many therapists won't see someone who is still feeding their disease. They feel it's like stealing money, because trying to reach someone under the influence is virtually impossible. But there are ways out of the world Peter lives in. Treatment facilities will help you get over the initial hump of withdrawal. Support groups and halfway houses get you on the other side of your addictive behavior. Once you've reached that point you're in recovery and out of your addictive cycle. Note: Young people might see many of the movie's images as fascinating. If you are getting this movie for someone who is young, you may want to watch it first or check with a professional who has some background in youth counseling.

Year: 1991
Length: 115 min
Rating: R
Color

'Night, Mother

Healing Themes:

- If you're thinking about committing suicide
- Saying good-bye
- Making changes before it's too late
- Trying to save someone who doesn't think they can hold on one more day

Cast: Sissy Spacek, Anne Bancroft. Director, Tom Moore. Writer, Marsha Norman.

Synopsis: One evening a young woman tells her mother she will commit suicide. The mother tries to talk her daughter out of killing herself. They debate, laugh, and reminisce throughout the night. Then the daughter goes to her room, locks the door, and takes her life.

Comments: Stories such as this one can be overwhelming to those who are going through a painful time. If this is the case I strongly suggest that you seek support and guidance before viewing *'Night, Mother*. This is an incredible look inside the troubled mind of someone who has made the conscious decision to take her own life. You may see yourself in these two women who share their innermost thoughts with you. Notice the on-again, off-again relationship between them. Listen to the young woman talk about how she has decided to stop dealing with life's pain. Some choose suicide. Others choose food, violence, alcohol, etc. They're all the same, just different tools to use on the way out. And what of the mother? Can you feel her frustration? She's about to lose her daughter. What could you do to stop someone who wanted to take his or her own life? Should people have the right to end their lives or should we prevent suicide at all costs? What's important is that you know it never has to get to that point. As we listen we hear that many of the issues have been building up for years. If they had been in some kind of supportive counseling, they could have learned skills for the very problems that brought them to this crisis. Give *'Night, Mother* your utmost attention. After watching, go to those who need your support or seek help for the healing experience of your life. Suicide is a permanent solution to a temporary problem.

Year: 1986
Length: 97 min
Rating: PG-13
Color

9 1/2 Weeks

Healing Themes:

- When a relationship is based only on sex
- Being obsessed with someone
- Making bad choices in life
- Getting out before it's too late
- When it's an addiction and not a relationship

Cast: Mickey Rourke, Kim Basinger, Margaret Whitton, Karen Yahng, David Margulies. Director, Adrian Lyne. Writers, Patricia Knop and Zalman King.

Synopsis: Elizabeth and John meet and their relationship grows. Their encounters, mainly sexual, become obsessive, what some would call perverse. John takes things too far and Elizabeth runs from the relationship.

Comments: Being creative in sexual activity is a healthy part of any good relationship, but when it becomes obsession there is no relationship. Like *Rapture*, *9 1/2 Weeks* looks at what happens when sex and sexual fantasy begins to rule our lives. This movie is not for everyone. Many will be uncomfortable with the sexual scenes, but if you can accept this movie as an eye-opening message you will learn about yourself and those who fall into this trap. Elizabeth is a real victim in John's hands, right? WRONG! Let's not slip into denial. She's a willing participant. She was bored. We got that message over and over again. John offered her some excitement and Elizabeth was as much a part of those experiences as he was. The good news is she was able to draw a boundary and get out. It's not your job to do anything, sexual or otherwise, just because it's what your partner wants. Healing is learning to take care of yourself. Strong relationships are grounded in respecting each other's boundaries. For those of you who have sexual issues I would like to suggest going to Sex Anonymous. Seek therapists and counselors who specialize in treating sexual addictions. Finally, if you are both interested in venturing into some creative sexual experiences, why not give *9 1/2 Weeks* a try. But remember, that for this to be a healthy exercise, you both must consent to the journey.

Year: 1986
Length: 114 min
Rating: R
Color

Not My Kid

Healing Themes:
- Getting help for your addicted child
- Realizing that you weren't communicating when you thought you were
- Putting the pieces of your family back together
- Facing the truth about your problems

Cast: George Segal, Stockard Channing, Andrew Robinson, Gary Bayer, Nancy Cartwright, Tate Donovan, Viveka Davis. Director, Michael Tuckner. Writer, Christopher Knopf.

Synopsis: Life turns upside down when Segal and Channing find out their daughter is addicted to drugs. They seek support and help from a treatment facility. Each family member is forced to look at him or herself. One by one the family is put back together.

Comments: Most people tend to believe that young people become addicted to food or drugs or alcohol, etc., because they're hanging around the wrong crowd or they just have a weak character. Not necessarily so. The truth is people who become addicted to something or someone are attempting to hide from their true feelings. There are a number of ways to become addicted, some of which might be modeling (learning the behavior) from the family, child abuse, peer pressure, sibling pressure, etc. What comes to mind when you watch this movie? First you will notice the denial on the part of the parents. The title of this movie is pretty appropriate, don't you think? Then comes anger, as if the child were doing it to punish the parents. Maybe she is punishing her parents. What do you think? How do you feel about their solution? Would you have kicked her out? Maybe that's what happened to you. Clearly they came up with a solution. But some families remain in the problem. As a parent, you can learn to listen more, spend time with your children, and let them know how much you care. It's the best prevention in the world. Give this one a try. You will come together as a family and create a bond that no drug can pry apart.

Year: 1985
Length: 100 min
Rating: Unrated
Color

Nuts

Healing Themes:

- Keeping family secrets
- Feeling abandoned by your family
- Being sexually abused
- Realizing your parents turned their backs on you
- Dealing with the rage from your past

Cast: Barbra Streisand, Richard Dreyfuss, Maureen Stapleton, Eli Wallach, Robert Webber, James Whitmore, Karl Malden. Director, Martin Ritt. Writers, Tom Topor, Darryl Ponicsan, and Alvin Sargent.

Synopsis: The family of a high-priced prostitute charged with murder wants Claudia committed to an asylum. She refuses to discuss her family with her attorney. Claudia's lawyer discovers she was sexually abused by her father and she is acquitted of all charges.

Comments: The focus of *Nuts* is sexual abuse. You will feel a great deal of anger and sadness for someone who was a victim as a child and is now a victim of society. What did you feel about the father? Notice his facial expression. Does he seem honest and real to you or is he going through the motions of being concerned for Claudia? Her mother turned her back and chose not to see what went on in their home. You can see to what lengths her parents will go to keep the family secret. They were willing to have her put into an institution. Did you grow up in a home where outsiders weren't allowed in so that the family secret would not escape the confines of the four walls of your home. Make no mistake, this is a family in denial, sick with inappropriate behavior. For those who have experienced abuse I support you in watching this movie and dealing with the emotional memories that will come to the surface. You will grow from understanding what happened in your childhood and how you may have been driven to some of the behaviors you have as an adult. There are wonderful support groups for incest survivors. If this is happening to you now, seek the help of the police or a shelter. You must tell yourself you do not deserve to be abused. You have the right to a rich, full life, bountiful in healthy, self-nurturing experiences.

Year: 1987
Length: 116 min
Rating: R
Color

The Nutty Professor

Healing Themes:

- Finding your inner self
- Thinking you've found a magic potion to make you something you are not
- Learning to just be yourself
- Realizing there are no quick fixes

Cast: Jerry Lewis, Stella Stevens, Howard Morris, Kathleen Freeman. Director, Jerry Lewis. Writers, Jerry Lewis and Bill Richmond.

Synopsis: A college chemistry professor, the campus nerd, discovers a potion that turns him into a handsome, macho playboy. He is a real hit on the night club scene. He attracts one of his students; she eventually figures out who he is and accepts him anyway—well almost.

Comments: Well, you may think I have truly lost it. Why in the world would I choose this movie, you ask? This is a lighter way of dealing with the issue of our inner self. Like *Dr. Jekyll and Mr. Hyde* and *The Portrait of Dorian Gray*, *The Nutty Professor* shows us there is a part of us inside that is dying to get out. However, this movie tells us to accept ourselves for who we are. I'm sure most of you at one time or another have wished you were someone else. There's nothing wrong with a little fantasizing, but when you start living in that dream, you're not living in the here and now. You're giving up the special moments of your life to live someone else's life. Many people get caught up in drugs and alcohol so they can be something they're not. We see this when the professor decides to take his magic potion: drugs. Although he thinks he has become a "super stud," in truth he's merely altered the way he sees and thinks about himself. Do you find you drink or take drugs to become the person you wish you were? The bottom line is this: If you are using any substance or activity to change yourself, you are giving yourself a temporary fix to a temporary problem. And just like the professor, you will wake up to find you have returned to being who you really are. Enjoy who you are and people will accept you just as you are. Even though *The Nutty Professor* is a comedy you will see the healing that comes from self-acceptance and living in the moment.

Year: 1963
Length: 107 min
Rating: Unrated
Color

On Golden Pond

Healing Themes:

- Aging gracefully
- Knowing you only have a short time to be together
- Trying to gain acceptance
- Feelings of being neglected and unloved
- Working to communicate with the parent who never listened

Cast: Katharine Hepburn, Henry Fonda, Jane Fonda, Doug McKeon, Dabney Coleman, William Lanteau. Director, Mark Rydell. Writer, Ernest Thompson.

Synopsis: Chelsea has never been close to her father, Norman. She knows he is not getting any younger and if they're going to work things out, now's the time. With a little help from Ethel, her mother, they grow to understand each other.

Comments: Movies like *On Golden Pond* are a real gift. From beginning to end, the scenes are rich in healing messages. Before watching, make a commitment to stay with your feelings. I know this can be difficult for men especially, but give yourself permission to really feel your emotions as they come up. Who are you in *On Golden Pond?* Are you like Chelsea, a son or daughter of a parent whom you could never get close to? Maybe you're Ethel, pushing those in the family who are not talking to be closer to one another. You might be Norman, the one who can't seem to reach out to his children. Watch Chelsea as she performs for her father and dives off the pier. Is there someone whose attention you are trying to get? It may be that you fear your parents haven't got much longer to live. Are there some things that need to be said? Please don't wait. So many people ask me how to handle the pain that comes with losing a family member before they've had a chance to talk. Here's an idea. Watch *On Golden Pond* by yourself. Focus on the scenes that bring up some feelings and issues for you. When you're all done have a family gathering. Replay the movie and talk about what you're experiencing through the movie. Get the idea? The movie can bring up discussions you have always wanted to have.

Year: 1981
Length: 109 min
Rating: PG
Color

One Flew Over the Cuckoo's Nest

Healing Themes:

- Escaping from reality
- Coping with an abusive caretaker
- Finding friends in the strangest places
- Learning that you are not as together as you thought you were

Cast: Jack Nicholson, Brad Dourit, Louise Fletcher, Will Sampson, William Redfield, Danny DeVito, Christopher Lloyd, Scatman Crothers. Director, Milos Forman. Writers, Lawrence Hauben and Bo Goldman.

Synopsis: McMurphy avoids a jail sentence by faking that he is crazy and is sent to a mental institution where he has to deal with the tyrannical Nurse Ratchet. He rallies the patients to protest their treatment and then to escape. Oddly enough, McMurphy stays behind.

Comments: I thought you might like to see a somewhat realistic picture of what it might be like inside "a joint" like this. Soon after you start watching I want you to notice that all the inmates are like a family. Oh, it may be a little large with a few more parents—keepers—than your own family, but they work together as a family. Do you see how each person takes on a role: McMurphy, who's all talk and no action; the "silent ones"; the strong one who lies back; the caretaker. Are you beginning to wonder how your family ever made it in the real world? And what about Nurse Ratchet's role in the family? Do her actions seem abusive to you? How can they not? Watch how McMurphy falls prey to the very system he is trying to manipulate. Pay special attention when McMurphy decides to stay and the one you thought was crazy ends up leaving. Maybe McMurphy really knew that he belonged there all the time. So you've watched the movie and you've looked for yourself in the characters. Where's the healing? It's helpful to know that you're not alone in being pushed to the edge sometimes and you won't need to escape into alcohol, or food, or drugs, or...you get the point. There's no need to take the same route as McMurphy. Try support groups, therapists, a close friend, someone who will listen and not tell you how to lead your life. Gather a group of friends to watch this one. I'll bet you have discussions that you would never have expected.

Year: 1975
Length: 129 min
Rating: R
Color

Ordinary People

Healing Themes:

- Learning not to feel guilty for being the only survivor
- Dealing with the rage of losing a child
- Living with a parent who is in denial
- Feeling left behind and abandoned

Cast: Mary Tyler Moore, Donald Sutherland, Timothy Hutton, Judd Hirsh, M. Emmet Walsh, Elizabeth McGovern, Adam Baldwin, Dinah Manoff, James B. Sikking. Director, Robert Redford. Writer, Alvin Sargent.

Synopsis: Calvin and Beth lost one son in an accident. Conrad, their other son, feels guilt-ridden and was hospitalized when he became suicidal. He comes home to a domineering mother and a father who is emotionally unavailable. Beth leaves Calvin and Conrad to heal on their own.

Comments: I saw this movie in my early thirties. What an incredible effect it had on me. Everything I grew up with was happening right before my eyes. They made a movie of my life. Other people said the same thing. Then I realized that's why it's called *Ordinary People*, because to some lesser or greater degree this movie is about all of us, about a family in crises, a family that can no longer hide from their dysfunction. Do you want to lash out at Beth for her cold, abusive behavior or at Calvin because of his passive denial? Look at their body language. I call this "body oozing." You get mixed messages about what's really going on when they speak to each other through their bodies instead of their words. Does your heart go out to Conrad? Did you want him to just get out of that house? Isn't that what he did when he was sent to the hospital? Notice that Conrad is really never allowed to express his feelings and be heard. There are so many scenes to focus on, but don't miss the family picture-taking or the conversation on the lawn between Beth and Conrad. Stay in touch with your feelings. You may become overwhelmed, but don't stuff anything. Healing happens when you journey back to where it all began. *Ordinary People* will be your guide.

Year: 1980
Length: 124 min
Rating: R
Color

Our Very Own

Healing Themes:

- Searching for your birth parents
- Learning that you were adopted
- When your adopted child seeks his or her birth parents
- Appreciating the life you have

Cast: Ann Blyth, Farley Granger, Jane Wyman. Director, David Miller.

Synopsis: A high school senior learns she was adopted. Her happy family life is thrown into turmoil when she decides to find her birth parents. Rejected by her birth mother, she comes to realize how wonderful her life is with the family she's always known.

Comments: There I was, exercising at the gym. The volume to the television wasn't on, so all I could do was watch the actors. I investigated the movie later and found it has a beautiful healing message: Take a look at your past, then move forward. *Our Very Own* shows all the feelings a family goes through when their adoptive daughter/sister wants to find her birth mother and the emotional conflicts that arise when she learns she is adopted. Were you adopted? What was it like when you found out? Did you have a sense of emptiness or were you content knowing you had parents who loved you? Maybe you are parents who have adopted a child. Are you prepared to tell your child he or she was adopted? This movie shows us the torment these parents experience at the thought of losing their daughter to someone she's never known. Of particular interest is when she turns to her best friend for support and learns her friend's life has not been that good. The fact that you were adopted does not make your problems any worse or any better than anyone else's. Finally, note how the birth mother responds. How painful that her birth child means so little to her! But there is some real healing in this movie. She is able to let go of her past and move on with the only real parents she's ever known. This movie may be difficult to find. However, you can catch it from time to time on television channels showing older movies.

Year: 1950
Length: 133 min
Rating: Unrated
B&W

Over Forty

Healing Themes:

- Being reunited with old friends
- Uncovering some unanswered questions
- Growing older and moving on
- Recalling the past

Cast: Roger Blay, Monique Mercure, Pierre Theriault, Patricia Nolin, Jacques Godin, Luce Guilbeaut. Director, Anne Claire.

Synopsis: Friends in their forties reunite after thirty years. Each of them is struck with the revelations about things they never knew from their younger years. By the end of the gathering they learn to let go of the past and live in the present.

Comments: I don't know about you, but I grew up listening to "Life is over at forty" and "Enjoy it while you're young." Sound familiar? People come to see me feeling down and depressed because they've hit this imaginary wall called "forty." Come on! It's not over, you're just getting started. Now, I have already recommended *The Big Chill* and *The Breakfast Club*, which have a similar theme. What makes this movie a little different is the age group. First, try to find one or more of the characters you most directly identify with. Also, look for a relationship that reminds you of one from your past. As you listen to them talk to each other, try to get in touch with how these people make you feel. Are you envious of their accomplishments or are you satisfied with what you've done so far in life? Do you have any sadness for someone special you left behind? Does getting older worry you or are you at peace? Can you see that getting older is only a state of mind? As they move into middle age their interests have changed, at least for some of them. Notice how their maturity levels are different. Some of them simply never grew up. I think it's important to spend some time reflecting on the past with old friends. Invite some friends over, play the movie, and make a night of it. Spend the time sharing each other's past. Take the chance on sharing your feelings openly. And when you do, you will have grown—not by years but through your own inner awareness.

Year: 1982
Length: 105 min
Rating: Unrated
Color

Parenthood

Healing Themes:

- Learning for the first time about being a parent
- Dealing with family members in day-to-day situations
- Confronting your fears of being a parent
- Starting a family again

Cast: Steve Martin, Mary Steenburgen, Dianne Wiest, Martha Plimpton, Keanu Reeves, Tom Hulce, Jason Robards, Jr., Rick Moranis, Harley Kozak, Leaf Phoenix. Director, Ron Howard. Writers, Lowell Ganz and Babaloo Mandel.

Synopsis: Gil and Mary are already raising what they think is all the children they will have, dealing with the everyday problems of parents in the 1980s. When Gil gets the word that Mary is pregnant again, he just about goes over the edge. But somehow it all works out when the family gathers at the hospital to welcome their newest member.

Comments: My heart goes out to those of you who are simply overwhelmed with parenthood. So, I've included this one because there's healing from learning you're not alone. That's all there is to it. And, if you are thinking about becoming parents, *Parenthood* is a wonderful teaching tool. It does an excellent job of accurately portraying life's problems and it's a movie the whole family can watch together. You might also find you gain a better understanding of each other's needs and what each family member is going through. Also, let's not forget the message we get about wisdom. Take special note of the grandmother. Older people can have a wonderful and clear perspective on life. Often it is philosophical and profound. There is a tendency to write off the older generation too quickly. Take some time to listen to what they have to say. Because they've already been on the journey they have a pretty good idea about how to make it through life with the least amount of skinned knees. Make this movie the family entertainment for the evening.

Year: 1989
Length: 124 min
Rating: PG-13
Color

Paris Is Burning

Healing Themes:

- Living the gay lifestyle
- Appreciating our differences
- Accepting people for who they are
- We all have a place in this world

Cast: Documentary with Carmen and Brooke, Andre Christian, Dorian Corey, Paris Dupree, Willi Ninja, Pepper Labeija, Junior Labeija. Director, Jennie Livingston.

Synopsis: A view of the underground world in New York City where a group of people who are gay enter into fashion/dance shows to earn money. They spend their days getting ready for the shows and their nights going from contest to contest. Each one has a story and each story has a different ending.

Comments: I struggled with myself about putting this movie in the book. It's one of two documentaries I felt had some healing messages. The other one is *Dialogues with Madwomen*. So, given the documentary style, what do I think you can gain from this movie? Two things: It's okay to be different. It's all right to live in this world and do what you believe in. Secondly, for those of you who are gay and live the gay lifestyle, you may see something of yourself in this group. You may get in touch with something that will make you happy about who and what you are and something that makes you unhappy. Now, I really don't want to say much about this movie or what to look for, but I can assure you at the very least you will be entertained. But please let's all capture one idea. We have arrived on the earth for a purpose, though we may not know what that purpose is yet. Let's accept each other for who and what we are. Let's not waste our energy or our spirit in focusing on the lives of others and condemning them for who they are. When we point our fingers at someone else, we're merely avoiding looking at ourselves. I know I can experience my own healing when I embrace the idea of acceptance and take my own life journey. Enjoy the party. You'll have fun with this one.

Year: 1990
Length: 78 min
Rating: Unrated
Color

Philadelphia

Healing Themes:

- Dealing with the prejudice related to AIDS
- Accepting the inevitability of death
- Feeling abandoned by family, friends, and co-workers
- Gathering all your inspirational strength

Cast: Tom Hanks, Denzel Washington, Jason Robards, Jr., Mary Steenburgen, Antonio Banderas. Directer, Jonathan Demme. Writer, Ron Nyswaner.

Synopsis: Tom Hanks plays a successful young lawyer, a member of a prestigious law firm, whose life is turned upside down when he is fired for having AIDS. With the help of another attorney he sues the firm and wins his case. All his friends gather to mourn the loss of this very special man.

Comments: *Philadelphia* is an extraordinary piece of work. There is really no other movie like it. Here is an opportunity to explore your feelings about AIDS and how fear and ignorance manifest themselves in the form of prejudice. You do not have to be suffering from AIDS to understand the true dynamics in this movie. Isn't the need to find a cure for AIDS just a metaphor for the healing we must all go through as we journey through life? We all must live with the reality that we ourselves are going to die and that we are going to grieve the loss of a loved one. *Philadelphia* confronts us with the giant life messages about our own fear and grief. Or are they one and the same? Notice the stages of denial. At first he chooses to ignore the truth. Then he seeks anything to avoid dealing with the truth. As he moves into sadness can you feel his pain when he listens to the opera. Finally, he reaches acceptance. But there is something he must do. He must confront all of us about our fears and prejudices shown by his own group of professionals who turn their backs on him, making who he is into something ugly, not to be dealt with. How corrupt! How immoral! Have you ever been the victim of prejudice because you were ill, another color, another sex, or…? Have you lost a job or been forced to move because of what you are, not who you are? Maybe you have been a party to an act of prejudice. Let this movie inside your soul.

Year: 1994
Length: 125 min
Rating: R
Color

The Picture of Dorian Gray

Healing Themes:

- Trying to hide your evil self
- Living life at other people's expense
- Being spiritually corrupt
- When you can't see yourself for who you really are
- Getting the real picture

Cast: George Sanders, Hurd Hatfield, Donna Reed, Angela Lansbury, Peter Lawford. Director, Albert Lewin. Writer, Albert Lewin.

Synopsis: Dorian Gray stays perpetually young while a portrait of himself, painted in his early twenties, continues to age. As Dorian goes through life, the painting becomes more and more corrupt. His life comes to a tragic close and the portrait returns to its original image.

Comments: I have some all-time favorite movies from my childhood that have had a lasting effect on me. *The Portrait of Dorian Gray* is one. When I was growing up there was a television station that would play the same movie five days in a row. After I saw this the first time I would rush home each day to see it. I was too young to know what it truly meant. Now that I'm older I understand. *The Portrait of Dorian Gray* shows us what happens when we bottle up secrets inside, what we turn into when our character becomes corrupt and out of sync with the world. Like *Dr. Jekyll and Mr. Hyde* and *Alien* it also looks at our inner self and the evil side we may keep hidden. Are you honest with your feelings? Or are you acting one way and feeling another? Possibly you're keeping a secret: a marriage, money you owe, a child you have not acknowledged, or someone you've cheated. Hiding the secret may come out in alcoholism, eating, smoking, violence, and other addictions. What secrets are you keeping inside you? Can you see them slowly making their way to the surface, in anger, pain, sleeplessness, depression? When we watch Dorian we see what we must do to stop our own inner portrait from turning ugly and grotesque. We must be true to ourselves and our feelings, experience life with honesty and respect. When that begins to happens we experience the healing. The colors of our portrait are rich and true. Note: *Dorian Gray* is the title of a 1970 version. It's okay, but go for this one.

Year: 1945
Length: 110 min
Rating: Unrated
Color

Play Misty for Me

Healing Themes:

- Feeling helpless
- Seeing people for who they really are
- Fear of being stalked
- Sex for all the wrong reasons

Cast: Clint Eastwood, Jessica Walters, Donna Mills, Don Siegel, John Larch, Jack Ging. Director, Clint Eastwood. Writers, Jo Heims and Dean Reisner.

Synopsis: A caller's request to play a record on the radio leads to a sexual encounter with the disc jockey. The relationship turns to obsession as she stalks him. When he tells her it's over, she turns violent. In the process of defending himself, he kills her.

Comments: *Play Misty for Me* is the forerunner to *Fatal Attraction*. Both these movies have the same basic theme: obsession that leads to insanity and death. Over the years I have worked with a number of people who became obsessed with someone. There are lots of theories about why people become obsessed: too much love, not enough love, a drunken parent, etc. The truth is we really are not sure. But it happens. Did you realize she was obsessed when she first called? "Play Misty for me," she whispers. She had built up a fantasy image of him and she didn't even know him. Maybe you've found yourself sitting in front of someone else's apartment spying on their every move. That's stalking. Or maybe you call and hang up as soon as they answer. Just checking to see if they're home. That's stalking. How about following someone from class to class? You get the point. People are stalked and murdered every day because of hate, lust, envy, etc. You don't have to be a victim of someone else's or of your own obsession. This movie will help you get in touch with your behavior. There are support groups, counseling centers, and therapists who specialize in treating people suffering from the emotional effects of a stalker or because of an obsession. It's critical that you get close to your fear or terror which comes from this most serious problem.

Year: 1971
Length: 102 min
Rating: R
Color

Postcards From the Edge

Healing Themes:

- When your mother is driving you crazy
- Taking drugs to make you feel good
- Relationships that never go right
- When alcohol is your best friend

Cast: Meryl Streep, Shirley MacLaine, Dennis Quaid, Gene Hackman, Richard Dreyfuss, Rob Reiner, May Wickes, Conrad Bain, Annette Bening, Michael Ontkean. Director, Mike Nichols. Writer, Carrie Fisher.

Synopsis: Suzzane Vale is an actress on a downward spiral. To make matters worse she has an overbearing mother who was a famous actress. She gives up on the idea of recovering from her addictions by herself and checks herself into a hospital, much to the dismay of her mother.

Comments: If you can get on the other side of the comedy in this movie, you have a lot to gain. Notice the chaos in Suzzane's life. Most of it's brought on by herself. Notice how it's always someone else who causes the problem. Suzzane does a wonderful job of showing us the effects of alcohol in our life. When the alcohol is mixed with the chaos, life becomes one trauma after another. No getting around that one! Watch the scene where her boyfriend breaks up with her. Look familiar? Oh, maybe you didn't have a gun, but boy I'll bet you could relate. Listen to the people around her as they try to get her back on track. They eventually throw up their hands in pure frustration. Have you gotten to that point with anyone you know? Are you fed up with their dramatics and antics? Take care of yourself first. It's healing to leave the chaos behind and get on solid footing. Sometimes that means saying good-bye to an old friend or relationship that continues to drag you down. Try to get in touch with your feelings—mostly anger I'll bet—whenever her mother talks to her. No matter what Suzzane does it's just...not...good...enough. Now I know you can feel that one. Try watching this with your significant other. Talk over the parts that you relate to. It's also good for a group session. It's a wonderful opportunity to cut through the denial and step into reality.

Year: 1990
Length: 101 min
Rating: R
Color

Pretty in Pink

Healing Themes:

- When you meet someone and fall in love
- Being left by someone you care about
- Having the strength to be your own person regardless of what people say
- We are all the same no matter how much money we have

Cast: Molly Ringwald, Andrew McCarthy, Jon Crier, Harry Dean Stanton, James Spader, Annie Potts, Andrew "Dice" Clay, Dweezil Zappa, Margaret Colin, Alexa Kenin, Gina Gershon. Director, Howard Deutch. Writer, John Hughes.

Synopsis: The high school snobs break up a relationship between their friend, Blane, and Andie, a girl from the "other side of the tracks." Andie has a best friend, Duckie, who, if it were up to him, would be her boyfriend and protector. Blane finally realizes he loves Andie.

Comments: *Pretty in Pink* is simply a wonderful movie to help you get in touch with your high school years. Look for a character with whom you identify. You may find yourself in more than one of the characters. Personally, I liked Duckie. My favorite scene is in the record store. You can't miss it. I wish I was as uninhibited as Duckie. He just feels free to be who he is no matter what. Was there a piece of him in you? And what about the hip, slick, and cool group? Lots of money and no ability to feel any kindness, gentleness, or empathy for anyone, including themselves. Do you recall that group in school? Follow along as the movie progresses and stay with your feelings. Do you feel embarrassed, sad, happy, angry, left out, lonely, etc.? Each of us had different experiences in school and we all have a few wounds that never quite healed. Here's one way to deal with some of those old high school memories. This movie will lend a hand at helping you get in touch with some of your buried feelings and it may motivate you to get to your high school reunion. Don't be afraid to watch this one with a friend, lover, or even a group of people. At the very least you and whomever you watch this movie with will have a great time reminiscing. What a great opportunity to let those who you care about today into bits and pieces of your yesterday.

Year: 1986
Length: 96
Rating: PG-13
Color

Pretty Woman

Healing Themes:

- Fairy tales can come true
- Meeting people in the strangest ways
- There is nothing that can stand in the way of love
- Learning that you can be a good partner in your relationships

Cast: Richard Gere, Julia Roberts, Ralph Bellamy, Jason Alexander, Laura San Giacomo, Hector Elizondo. Director, Gary Marshall. Writer, J. F. Lawton.

Synopsis: Edward Lewis, a high-powered businessman, needs a woman on his arm for appearance' sake. He picks up Vivian, a Hollywood prostitute, and makes her over. The business relationship between them gets serious. He faces the dilemma of leaving her behind or marrying her.

Comments: After *Pretty Woman* was released therapists reported seeing some clients who where fantasizing about either meeting and marrying prostitutes or becoming a prostitute and meeting and marrying a rich businessman. This is a little like what happened when *Love Story* was released. Some people were dreaming of falling in love and dying in the arms of their husband or having the love of their life die. Sound strange? Not really. We're all looking for that special someone. Some of us have been lucky enough to find that person. *Pretty Woman* is really another version of the Cinderella story. The most important lesson we gain from this movie is that love can happen to us any time, any place, or any where. You must simply open your heart and your eyes to the possibility. Many people have just given up on finding that someone special. Give yourself a chance to really meet people who you have turned your back on because they don't have some surface quality. Look for kindness, a gentle nature, honesty, trust, morality, and so on. These are the qualities which make up a long-lasting, loving relationship.

Year: 1989
Length: 117 min
Rating: R
Color

The Prince of Tides

Healing Themes:

- Dealing with skeletons in your family's closet
- Growing up with abuse from a parent
- Helping a family member in a time of crisis
- When a therapist has crossed a boundary

Cast: Barbra Streisand, Nick Nolte, Blythe Danner, Kate Nelligan, Jeroen Krabbe, Melinda Dillion, Jason Gould. Director, Barbra Streisand. Writers, Pat Conroy and Becky Johnston.

Synopsis: When his suicidal sister is hospitalized, Tom Wingo meets with her psychiatrist, Susan Lowenstein. Together they uncover buried memories from the family's past. Although Tom and the psychiatrist have a love relationship, Tom returns to his wife, healed.

Comments: *The Prince of Tides* brings up issues relating to family dysfunction, including physical and emotional abuse, alcohol, rape, and mental illness, to name a few. There is so much going on that it's impossible to deal with all the issues in the write up. Here are some of the key points I'd like you to focus on. Watch for the mother's manipulation of the children, the father's constant abuse and testing of the family, and the sister's ability to remove herself from reality through her writing. How do you feel inside when you listen to the father speak to the children? Possibly you are a parent who is treating your family in this manner. How did you feel when Tom finally let go of his secret? Have you a secret that you keep stuffing inside of you? Do you find you have to work harder and harder to hide your secret? Use Tom as an example. Turn to someone you trust and start the healing that comes from letting go. You will see that alcoholism is present in both Tom's and Susan's families. Isn't it interesting that they're attracted to each other? You're going to feel pain, sadness, and rage. Use the movie as a way to grow from the experience. One final note: It is never acceptable for a therapist to become involved with a patient or client. This kind of involvement is a form of abuse and is destructive to the healing process. If you are experiencing this, I support you in ending the relationship and seeking more appropriate help.

Year: 1991
Length: 132 min
Rating: R
Color

Radio Flyer

Healing Themes:

- Escaping from an abusive stepparent
- Turning to a sibling for support and help
- Getting away from the alcohol and abuse
- When a parent can't see their spouse for who they really are

Cast: Elijah Wood, Joseph Mazzello, Lorraine Bracco, Adam Baldwin, John Heard, Ben Johnson. Director, Richard Donner. Writer, David Mickey Lewis.

Synopsis: Life suddenly changes for Mike and Bobby when their mom decides to marry a man who is an abusive alcoholic. Bobby and Mike realize that they've got to escape. They turn their Radio Flyer into an airplane as one of them escapes to safety.

Comments: What a wonderful film. I had no idea what the title meant until I saw the movie. Radio Flyer is the name of a wagon. You know, the kind you see little kids pulling behind them, full of toys or even other kids. Mike and Bobby need their Radio Flyer to escape from the abuse in their home. If you've experienced abuse then you can understand how important it was for them that they had something; some way to escape. We all find different ways to escape painful situations. You can't help but see the terrible effects of alcohol on the family. The denial on the part of the mother is even worse when the stepfather's abuse finally puts Bobby in the hospital. She turns her husband into the authorities and then turns right around and takes him back, abuse, alcohol and all. Now that's denial. Mike and Bobby show us how fantasy is used to escape the reality of child abuse. Look for the covert and overt forms of abuse: physical as well as verbal abuse. Notice how the children try to insulate their mother from the reality of the abuse and how they remain loyal to her throughout their stepfather's attacks. This is how children will sometimes protect their parents from being parents. When you're all done, sit back, get in touch with how you feel and start the process of grieving over lost childhood years and any abuse that accompanied those years. Leave the denial behind and take on a fresh look at life.

Year: 1991
Length: 114 min
Rating: PG-13
Color

Rain Man

Healing Themes:

- Finding a lost relative
- Learning compassion
- When you've learned that a parent has abandoned you
- Taking advantage of someone for all the wrong reasons

Cast: Dustin Hoffman, Tom Cruise, Valeria Golino, Jerry Molden, Jack Murdock, Michael D. Roberts. Director, Barry Levinson. Writers, Ronald Bass and Barry Morrow.

Synopsis: Charlie Babbitt learns he has been removed from his father's will. He also discovers he has a brother named Raymond, who lives in an institution. Charlie decides he wants his share of the money from the will and removes Raymond from the care of the institution to prove his point. Raymond is an idiot savant with extraordinary talents. Charlie tries to exploit him to get his fare share of their father's will. He realizes his brother means more to him than money and returns Raymond to the place he calls home.

Comments: If you are curious about the character Raymond, he is a real person. He is alive and well as of the publication of this book. And yes, he is an idiot savant with the special talents portrayed in the movie. However, the rest of the story is fiction. Charlie thought he wrote his father off years ago. Obviously not, or he wouldn't be so angry. How would you feel if you found out you had a brother you never knew about? Some families keep secrets that eventually come to light, leaving those who are still alive to deal with the legacy of the family lies. There's no room for secrets in a loving relationship. What about the way Charlie tries to manipulate Raymond? Can you see he was taking his anger out on Raymond when he was really feeling hurt and sad over his father's abandoning him? The healing comes when they bond as brothers; Charlie teaches Raymond to dance and Raymond teaches Charlie the meaning of family love. Sometimes it takes a special life moment to open the doors for us. We experience the pain of learning the truth about our past, then embrace the healing from letting go of resentments and moving on with our lives.

Year: 1988
Length: 104 min
Rating: R
Color

Rape and Marriage: The Rideout Case

Healing Themes:
- Living in a relationship with no boundaries
- When you've been sexually violated
- Having the courage to stick with your decisions
- Leaving someone you love who is sick

Cast: Mickey Rourke, Linda Hamilton, Rip Torn, Eugene Roche, Conchata Ferrell, Gail Strickland, Bonnie Barlett, Alley Mills, Gerald McRaney, Rita Taggart. Director, Peter Levin.

Synopsis: A married couple from Oregon realize they have personal problems to work through. She begins to feel less sexually attracted to him. He decides to take away her right to choose to have sex with him; he rapes her. She takes him to court on rape charges.

Comments: Rape is a horribly violent act. I can assure you the act of rape has nothing to do with love and marriage. In a marriage it is normal for each person to have different sexual interests and drives. Demanding sex is an unacceptable way to meet your needs. And that is at least one of the important messages we can gain from this movie. In this case, we experience one woman's struggle to maintain her rights and her dignity after she is raped by her husband. Use this movie to ask some very fundamental questions: Do you have the right to touch a person, in any way, when they do not want to be touched? Isn't that what we teach our children? Why then is unwanted sexual contact any different? Notice the indignation and the denial he goes through as he attempts to defend his actions. Most of this kind of defense is done in the spirit of, "But she's my wife. That's my right. It's her job to give me sex when I want it." Not so. The right to have or not have sex lies solely in the hands of the individual. Watch this movie as a couple. If you have been, or are being perpetrated against, no matter who the perpetrator is, consider exercising your rights. We heal ourselves when we take back the control over our lives. And we continue the healing when we enter into relationships which embrace the awareness that love and marriage do not give us a license to take someone's dignity away from them.

Year: 1980
Length: 96 min
Rating: Unrated
Color

The Rape of Richard Beck

Healing Themes:
- Turning the tables and feeling vengeful
- Coping with the embarrassment of being sexually violated
- Becoming a new person from a traumatic event
- Learning a new respect for others

Cast: Richard Crenna, Meredith Baxter Birney, Pat Hingle, Frances Lee McCain, Cotter Smith, George Dzundza, Joanna Kerns. Director, Karen Arthur. Writer, James B. Hirsch.

Synopsis: Richard Beck, a big city cop, takes the hard line towards women as rape victims. Things change when he experiences being raped. He feels embarrassed and humiliated telling others what has happened. The legal process changes his perspective on women and rape.

Comments: When you hear the word rape, do you automatically associate the act with women and children? Most people do. But it happens to men and men are far less likely to report a rape than women. To the best of my knowledge this is the only movie made that deals with the rape of a man. For the first time we see an adult male coping with this most painful issue. Rape is something women have dealt with for centuries, often without the aid, support, or sympathy of men. First, what do you think of our Mr. Beck? The people who wrote this script did a great job of putting every male stereotype into this tough, non-caring cop, who sees women as second-class citizens who do nothing but cry their way through life. Notice how he is treated differently; how he is different. Do you find yourself being sympathetic or do you feel like he's getting what's coming to him? I think some people believe this is what men must go through to understand and be empathetic towards women who have been raped. What do you think? If you are someone who is carrying around the burden of molestation or rape, reach out for help and work to resolve your pain. Also, treat this movie as an opportunity to open the doors of understanding and being empathetic to those who have experienced the hideous act of rape to the human body and spirit. **Note:** This movie may also be found under the title *The Broken Badge*.

Year: 1985
Length: 100 min
Rating: Unrated
Color

The Rapture

Healing Themes:

- Being sexually promiscuous
- Not seeing life for what it is
- Using alcohol to numb your feelings
- Switching from one addiction to another
- Living in an obsession
- Slipping over the edge

Cast: Mimi Rogers, David Duchovny, Patrick Bauchau, Will Patton. Director, Michael Tolkin. Writer, Michael Tolkin.

Synopsis: Sharon, once a swinger, becomes an evangelical Christian. She marries and has a child. Her husband is killed. God becomes an obsession; she believes they will be taken by God to a better place. Fantasies motivate her to kill her daughter and the world comes crashing down around her.

Comments: First, *Rapture* may not be easy for some of you to watch. It moves rather quickly from problems about sex to issues about religion. Each of these issues is portrayed in a straightforward, no-nonsense manner. Let's look at the overall problem. Can you see Sharon tried to fix herself by replacing one obsession, sex, with another, religion? Maybe you can relate to what she has done. Did you stop smoking only to gain fifty pounds? Do you know someone who quit drinking and now spends all their time working? And what about Sharon's sexual escapes? Some people are addicted to sex the same way that other people are addicted to gambling, shopping, alcohol, etc. How about her switch from sex to religion? (This is known as religiosity.) She is as absorbed in religion as she was in sex. Same thing. Different fix. Don't misunderstand me. People receive wonderful, spiritual healing through religion, but too much of any one thing takes us over the edge and into avoiding our lives as they were intended to be lived. I think you'll get the message. Start the healing now. There are support groups such as Sex Anonymous to help you through to a more fulfilling life. If religion is the problem try going to a minister, priest, or therapist. There are answers out there; you must simply open your eyes to see them.

Year: 1991
Length: 100 min
Rating: R
Color

Regarding Henry

Healing Themes:

- Having to start all over again
- Learning the real meaning of life
- Finding out who your friends really are
- Realizing that money and power aren't everything

Cast: Harrison Ford, Annette Bening, Bill Nunn, Mikki Allen, Donald Moffat, Nancy Marchand, Elizabeth Wilson, Robin Bartlett, John Leguizamo. Director, Mike Nichols. Writer, Jeffrey Abrams.

Synopsis: Henry, a successful, high powered lawyer, doesn't have much time for his family, but he does have time for an affair. Henry is shot in the head, loses his memory, and has to start over again. He learns what life is really about and rediscovers his loving family.

Comments: Sometimes we just get lost on our journey through life and forget what life is all about. For some, money and power get in the way. Like *The Closer*, *Regarding Henry* shows us life is not about money and power. Life is family, people we love and who love us. It's easy to see Henry is a man who is enamored with his power, lost in what he does and who he is in his profession. It's startling what happens when people have to accept that wake-up call. You will get that message loud and clear. Notice Henry has problems when he is forced to take time off. Old friends can't accept the new Henry. Business people don't want him around. The point is that with the self-awareness comes healing, whether it is a physical or emotional healing, there are many changes that follow. You will experience losing old friends and gaining new ones. You will struggle with how to have a healthy relationship and learn to get rid of your old, self-absorbed ways. When you watch this movie, try to set aside the reality that he is suffering from some brain damage and amnesia. Use the movie as a metaphor for the idea of being "hit over the head" to get a better life. You'll learn that children can often teach us the very lessons we forgot, but knew when we were once children. This is a great movie to watch as a couple. Use it as an opportunity to remind yourselves what life is really all about and rediscover the relationship you once had before it's too late.

Year: 1991
Length: 107 min
Rating: PG-13
Color

Rocket Gibraltar

Healing Themes:

- Saying good-bye to your family
- Reminiscing over the past
- Seeing ourselves through other people's relationships
- Learning from our children
- Accepting the death of a loved one
- Learning life's lessons from those who have come before us

Cast: Burt Lancaster, Bill Pullman, John Glover, Suzy Amis, Macauley Culkin. Director, Daniel Petrie. Writer, Amos Poe.

Synopsis: Grandpa wants everyone at his birthday party. His children and grandchildren get into conflicts with each other and while everyone is off worrying about their own problems he dies peacefully in his sleep. His grandchildren lay him to rest where they believe he would be happy.

Comments: Rocket Gibraltar is an absolutely beautiful movie. The healing messages are simply extraordinary. When you watch the ending you can't help but come full circle in your life. In many ways this movie is *The Big Chill, Grand Canyon,* and *The Trip to Bountiful* all rolled into one. It brings us into their family gathering and begs us to look at our lives. Did you notice that while each member of the family brought his or her own children to the gathering, they still returned to the role they had when they were growing up? Do you tend to return to your childhood roles once you have contact with your parents? Do you have a sense of powerlessness, intimidation, resentment, etc.? Which character or characters do you identify with: the complainer, the debater, the organizer, the quiet one, the one who's always acted out? There is also a great deal to be learned from Grandpa. He knows it is time to say good-bye and wants to leave with grace and dignity. I loved the way he stood back and let us see the family through his eyes. This man teaches us a little about how to die. He certainly teaches his grandchildren, who can see beyond the family's petty arguing. We get the payoff when the family gathers by the sea to watch him off to another life. What a wonderful healing moment as they all come together as one.

Year: 1988
Length: 118 min
Rating: R
Color

Rocky

Healing Themes:

- Digging deep inside for all you've got
- Confronting life's biggest challenge
- Meeting your soul mate
- Feeling good about who you are
- Being rewarded for your efforts

Cast: Sylvester Stallone, Burgess Meredith, Talia Shire, Burt Young, Carl Weathers. Director, John G. Avilsen. Writer, Sylvester Stallone.

Synopsis: Rocky Balboa is a has-been boxer who makes his living collecting on bad debts. What he wants most in life is a shot at the big time. Rocky goes the distance in spite of everyone betting against him. Along the way he meets a woman and triumphs in love, life, and boxing.

Comments: So you're wondering what *Rocky* has to do with healing stories. Sometimes movies give us a special moment; a visual experience we will never forget. I never forgot the way *Rocky* made me feel and I never forgot the scene that made me feel that way. Let me point it out to you. Rocky starts training for the big fight. He does everything from chasing chickens to doing one handed push-ups. (I tried that one and fell flat on my face.) Anyway, Rocky starts to run. And as he does the *Rocky* theme begins to play. (If you've seen *Rocky* I know you can hear it playing in your mind right now.) At the end of his run, he reaches a pinnacle moment, a moment of triumph. Rocky climbs the stairs of a majestic state building, stands beside a statue, and overlooks the city he knows he's conquered. He has arrived and you know what? Every one in the audience felt themselves arrive with him. That's the moment I want you to experience. I want you to feel Rocky's energy when he climbs those stairs. Get in touch with your own feelings when he raises his hands above his head. Tell yourself you can do anything you want in life. You can get that diploma, open your own business, have a nurturing relationship, confront your fears. What greater healing than the triumph that comes from telling yourself you can do anything and then doing it? Take charge of your future and make every dream in your life come true.

Year: 1976
Length: 119 min
Rating: PG
Color

Roe vs. Wade

Healing Themes:

- Standing up for what you believe in
- If you feel abortion is the only way out
- Being confronted with your moral and ethical beliefs
- Fighting the legal system for what you believe
- Helping make history

Cast: Holly Hunter, Amy Madigan, Terry O'Quinn, Kathy Bates, James Gammon. Director, Gregory Hobit. Writer, Alison Cross.

Synopsis: This is based on the experiences of the Texas woman whom the courts called Roe in the Supreme Court case of Roe vs. Wade, which decided that women have a constitutional right to abortion.

Comments: Roe vs. Wade is a landmark case which gives women control over their own bodies; it gives them the right to have an abortion. Some of you who are anti-abortion may feel this is an inappropriate movie to have in a book on healing stories. But *Roe vs. Wade*, the movie, is about more than abortion rights; it's about having the courage to stand up for what you believe in. As you watch this movie try and stay with your feelings about what Roe went through to achieve her goals. I have worked very hard at not passing judgments on issues such as abortion and adoption. I want you to take your own stand about this most sensitive and difficult personal decision. Try to watch this movie with an open mind. Does Roe have the right to have an abortion? Is she killing a living child? Do people have the right to control your body? Should they have the right to stop her from having an abortion? This is a wonderful movie to help you answer some very personal, moral, and ethical questions for yourself. Let's talk about Roe's courage to fight for what she believes. Have you ever fought for something when other people hated you for what you believed? Maybe you wanted the right to wear certain clothes, listen to a different style of music, or go out with someone whom other people didn't like. Look, I'm not trying to trivialize what Roe did. I am simply letting you know it's important to stand up for what you believe in.

Year: 1989
Length: 100 min
Rating: Unrated
Color

The Ryan White Story

Healing Themes:

- Coping with people's prejudices about AIDS
- Accepting that someone you love is going to die
- Being abused due to ignorance
- The importance of education

Cast: Judith Light, Lukas Haas, George C. Scott, Michael Bowen, George Dzundza, Valerie Landsburg, Sarah Jessica Parker, Mitchell Ryan, Peter Scolari, Grace Zabriskie.

Synopsis: From a routine blood transfusion used in treating hemophilia, young Ryan White contacts AIDS. The community reacts and tries to get him kicked out of school. Ryan and his mother campaign for human rights. Ryan becomes a hero in the fight for understanding the disease and AIDS prevention.

Comments: I don't think there is a person on the face of the earth who has not been affected by AIDS in one way or another. Lives lost to this horrible worldwide epidemic include friends, relatives, entertainers, writers, and AIDS researchers. But none has touched our hearts more than Ryan White. He made his way from place to place telling all the townspeople not be afraid of him or others with AIDS; but rather to see him as a way to learn and understand more about AIDS. He made us listen. And he helped us heal some of our wounds of ignorance and fear. Additionally, what makes this movie important is the concept of human rights and the way people choose to ignore those rights; specifically Ryan's rights. People can become irrational and so incredibly cruel when confronted with their fear of the disease. Some people seem to make a game out of treating Ryan and his family as if they have the plague. However, I would also ask you to see there are those who were able to rally around Ryan to offer him support and hope. In many ways Ryan died as a symbol for AIDS. The world focused on Ryan and his incredibly mature fight for life. How about showing this movie in a junior high or high school classroom? Ryan made life better for those who have the fear of acquiring AIDS and those who are still living with the disease.

Year: 1989
Length: 100 min
Rating: Unrated
Color

Same Time Next Year

Healing Themes:

- Feeling like you're getting away with something
- Accepting that life changes
- Getting in touch with growing older
- Saying good-bye

Cast: Alan Alda, Ellen Burstyn. Director, Robert Mulligan. Writer, Bernard Slade.

Synopsis: An accountant and a housewife, both married but not to each other, rendezvous once a year at the same location With each passing year their affair takes a new turn as they share experiences and watch each other change. After twenty-five years they realize it's time to say good-bye.

Comments: *Same Time Next Year* is a great movie to help you get in touch with your past. You have a wonderful opportunity to see bits and pieces of yourself in these two characters. For those who were born in the early fifties you will experience lots of flash backs as the two of them display clothing and personality changes you probably went through. When you watch the movie, do you have any sadness or a sense of loss over days gone by? Maybe you are able to watch the movie and be grateful that those years are behind you. For some, the past is something to be left behind. Is there an old friend or relationship that was important to you? Why have you lost contact with them? Here's an idea, why not pick up the phone and call someone you used to be close to? Get reconnected. You will be amazed at how energized you become with this kind of experience. You have a terrific opportunity to reminisce with your past and rekindle a relationship which you've forgotten about or didn't feel like you had the time to continue. Also notice the stages each of them goes through. These stages are typical—albeit stereotypical—of the changes we all experience in life. Sit back and let yourself enjoy the emotions and memories this movie brings to the surface. Why not try this one with a group? Gather some friends together, watch the movie, then take some time to talk about each other's past. It's a great way to get in touch with yourself and with some of your current friendships.

Year: 1978
Length: 119 min
Rating: Unrated
Color

Sarah T: Portrait of a Teenage Alcoholic

Healing Themes:

- Realizing your teenager is an alcoholic
- Remembering growing up with alcohol in the family
- Trying to recover from an addiction
- How to go about helping your children

Cast: Linda Blair, Verna Bloom, Larry Hagman, William Daniels, Mark Hamill, Laurette Spang. Director, Richard Donner.

Synopsis: Sarah realizes she can escape her family problems by drinking. When her parents see what is happening, they reach out for help. Sarah is given treatment for her alcoholism. She learns to confront her family and communicate the feelings she's been keeping bottled-up inside.

Comments: Prior to starting work on my book I was on staff at a treatment facility for children and adolescents. In between appointments I would leave my office and go to the facility to see some of the kids who were admitted for alcohol and drug abuse, among other things. Some were not any older than ten and eleven years old. Some of these kids looked as if they had lived through a war. So why do they do that to themselves? Where does all this destructive behavior come from? Sarah does an excellent job of helping us see how and why a teenager begins to drink and use drugs. Often families simply don't realize how their children are coping with the stress of the family's dysfunction. Notice how Sarah slowly begins her alcohol use. She learns over time she can hide from her feelings whenever there are family problems. Observe how she uses her parent's behavior as a reason to drink. Listen to how the family focuses on the alcohol to avoid dealing with their feelings; the issue becomes the alcohol, not why she started to drink. Can you see this is denial? Sarah is merely a product of the family chaos no one wants to see. She learns it's much easier to drown her feelings with alcohol than it is to deal with them. There's no one around who will listen to her. That's where support groups can be so valuable. Alateen, Alcoholics Anonymous, and Alanon are all out there to see you on your journey.

Year: 1975
Length: 100 min
Rating: Unrated
Color

The Secret Life of Walter Mitty

Healing Themes:

- Feeling dominated by other people
- Living up to your potential
- Realizing that you can be anything that you want

Special Message: Get into action. Don't live your life in a daydream.

Cast: Danny Kaye, Virginia Mayo, Boris Karloff, Fay Bainter, Ann Rutherford, Florence Bates, Thurston Hall. Director, Norman Z. McLeod. Writers, Ken Englund and Everett Freeman.

Synopsis: Walter Mitty has a doting mother and a fiancé who will follow in her footsteps. Walter's fantasies get him into trouble. Suddenly he's more like the characters he fantasizes about then he is himself. He eventually finds himself and a woman who loves the real Walter Mitty.

Comments: We all have a little Walter Mitty in us. I know I do. Using your imagination to get away can be a lot of fun; there is nothing wrong with a little fantasy. In fact, fantasy can be a healthy thing to do to relieve stress and tension. However, some people spend their lives living in fantasy. They spend so much time in fantasy that nothing gets done. But why? Are they escaping their own life because it's unsatisfying and boring? Are you like Walter, living your life through someone else's adventures? Notice that Walter goes from place to place, but actually accomplishes nothing. Instead of just thinking about going to school...send for the application, fill it out, and send it back. Don't simply wish you had another job, get your resume together and send it out. Stop sitting in front of your television watching the same old thing over and over again, join a health club or draft some plans to open that business you've been talking about. You get the idea. Go inside yourself and get in touch with the reasons you're living a fantasy life. Work on living in the here and now. If you have some Walter Mitty in you, this movie is a great motivator. Remember, fantasy is good, but too much fantasy will hold you back and stop you from accomplishing all your dreams. As you can see, when Walter finally got into action in his life, he took charge and became the person he always dreamed he could be. Now it's your turn. Go for it.

Year: 1947
Length: 105 min
Rating: Unrated
B&W

She Said No

Healing Themes:

- Taking a chance on someone
- Being betrayed
- Having others call you a liar
- Fighting for what you believe in
- Self-doubt
- Dealing with rape and abuse
- Emerging triumphant from life's battle

Cast: Veronica Hamel, Judd Hirsch, Lee Grant, Ray Baker, Mariclare Costello, Arthur Rosenberg, Rae Allen, Stan Ivar.

Synopsis: A young woman accuses a man of date rape. He turns the tables and sues her for defamation of character. Her employer, friends, and neighbors turn their backs on her. She finds a lawyer who agrees to help her. Eventually the truth comes out and he is held responsible for his actions.

Comments: It takes tremendous spirit of the heart and soul to heal from the pain of rape. For some years I saw both women and men in my office who were struggling with those memories. When I discovered I could help them by having them watch movies which dealt with rape, I found a way to reach those who could not otherwise break out of their devastating memories. It is estimated that one in ten women will be raped in their lifetime. The statistics are staggering. This movie also takes a look at the problems associated with making a claim of rape. How did you feel hearing the lies of the rapist as he makes himself out to be the victim and her the perpetrator? Watch how people reject her over the possibility that her actions may disrupt their lives and their businesses. How does she make you feel when she refuses to back down? Notice the scenes showing that this man maintains a normal presence during his working life. Make no mistake, this is a sick man who needs psychological help. I think there is a tendency for most people to believe that because a person is a professional or is highly educated that person wouldn't or couldn't do such a heinous act. Not so. Movies such as *She Said No* can give you the courage to do the healing you need to get your life back.

Year: 1991
Length: 100 min
Rating: PG
Color

Shirley Valentine

Healing Themes:

- Breaking out of old patterns
- Realizing that you are a special person
- Discovering that other people see you as attractive or sexy
- Setting limits with your significant other

Cast: Pauline Collins, Tom Conti, Alison Steadman, Julia McKenzie. Director, Lewis Gilbert. Writer, Willy Russell.

Synopsis: Fed up with being ignored, Shirley goes on vacation by herself to a romantic island in Greece. She meets a man who helps her find the real Shirley Valentine. Her husband hunts her down and begs her to come back. But Shirley's a new woman now.

Comments: Are you someone who feels like life is passing you by? Do you want more but don't know how to make things better? Maybe you're caught in a routine and you want to escape, change your name, and move to an island where no one knows you. Well, have I got a movie with a healing message for you. *Shirley Valentine* is a movie for women who feel like they're caught in a rut. And it's for men who have forgotten it's important to love and cherish the woman in their life. Shirley is every woman from anywhere. Look into her life and listen to her talk. One of my favorite moments is when she makes the decision to get out of the house and be on her own. Shirley takes charge. She goes from quiet desperation to being motivated and decisive. Have you gotten to that point in your life? Do you feel like all you're doing is going from day to day with no acknowledgment by anyone of how hard you are working and the contribution you're making to the family? What about her husband? His sole purpose for living is to work, come home, watch television, and "pop" Shirley. Any of this strike a cord? I want you to feel how Shirley felt when she dives off that boat. What a special moment. Suddenly she knows she is free. Stay with all of your feelings when you watch *Shirley Valentine*. Break out of the mold you've created as a couple and begin to do things you talked about when you first met. Let Shirley be a metaphor for your own courage to break the chains that hold you back.

Year: 1989
Length: 108 min
Rating: Unrated
Color

Sid and Nancy

Healing Themes:
- Falling into sick relationships
- Losing touch with reality
- Like attracts like
- Giving it all away for drugs and alcohol

Cast: Gary Oldman, Chloe Webb, David Hayman, Debbie Bishop. Director, Alex Cox. Writers, Alex Cox and Abbe Wool.

Synopsis: Sid Vicious, former lead singer of the Sex Pistols, meets American groupie Nancy Spungen. Sid and Nancy become entrenched in drugs and alcohol until one night during one of their drug parties Sid kills Nancy. There is an investigation but not much happens to Sid.

Comments: Sometimes it is difficult for young people to hear or see the message about the effects of drugs and alcohol. So I'm hoping that *Sid and Nancy* will drive you to explore this issue. What makes it a little easier is that Sid and Nancy were real people and this is a true story. Somehow that makes the journey more realistic. This movie takes a look at the effects that drugs and alcohol have on our body, our spirit and our soul. Here are some things I would like you to notice: First and foremost you will see the effects the drugs and alcohol had on their ability to function. Sid was on his way to stardom. But his addiction got to the point where he couldn't even perform any longer. Notice the physical and mental brutality which is linked with taking drugs. And what of the relationship between Sid and Nancy? Can you see they were attracted to each other's chaos? Do you know a couple who have that same chaotic existence, day in and day out? Are you in that kind of relationship? *Sid and Nancy* really makes us look at ourselves and see the things about who and what we are that we don't want to see. So here's the good news. You don't have to continue on that path any longer. They gave you their life story so you won't have to live it yourself. Reach out. Get some help. Go to support groups like Alateen and Alcoholics and Narcotics Anonymous. Reach out to a school teacher or counselor. Let them know you need help. If you are a parent, try to guide your children along a healing path.

Year: 1986
Length: 111 min
Rating: R
Color

Silence of the Lambs

Healing Themes:

- Uncovering frightening mysteries of the mind
- Realizing your own uniqueness
- Pushing yourself to the edge of madness
- Feeling like you are being held captive
- Emerging triumphant

Cast: Jodie Foster, Anthony Hopkins, Scott Glenn, Ted Levine, Brooke Smith, Charles Napier, Roger Corman, Anthony Heald, Diane Baker, Chris Isaak. Director, Jonathan Demme. Writer, Ted Tally.

Synopsis: The FBI believes Hannibal Lector, a psychiatrist who is in prison for killing and cannibalizing his victims, can help them on a case. While Clarice Starling has a degree in psychology, she is no match for Lector, who invades her psyche. The FBI solve their case, but not without great cost.

Comments: Therapists play the role of detective, uncovering the mysteries in your mind. I often feel I am going on an expedition with you to uncover the real truth about who you are. I would like you to listen to Mr. Hannibal Lector—more affectionately known as Hannibal the Cannibal. While Clarice is trying to go on her own fact-finding mission, Hannibal draws her into his web of psychodrama. Listen to him work his words so as to bring her in. Feel the tension as he manipulates his speech to get from her everything he wants. How do you feel? Scared, afraid of the process of getting to the bottom of who you really are beneath your tough exterior? What is it like for you when you finally uncover that hidden, dark secret? Do you want to run and hide like Clarice? I know it's real easy to get caught up in this most unusual story line. But stay with me here. Although Hannibal is sick, and that's putting it mildly, he does a beautiful job of forcing us to look at our fears. Where are we going in our lives and what drives us to get there? We must work to reach inside ourselves, heal what's stopping us from moving on, and begin living healthy lives beyond the solid, cold bars which hold Hannibal in his cell. This movie is not for everyone. Some scenes are more than graphic. For some, this movie may be more detrimental than helpful. You have lots of options in my book.

Year: 1991
Length: 118 min
Rating: R
Color

Six Weeks

Healing Themes:

- Realizing how precious life is
- Coping with a terminal illness
- Abandoning one relationship for another
- Dealing with the loss of a child

Cast: Dudley Moore, Mary Tyler Moore, Katherine Healy, Shannon Wilcox, Bill Calvert, Joe Regalbuto. Director, Tony Bill.

Synopsis: A politician leaves his wife when he meets a woman whose little girl, Niki, is dying of leukemia. Niki squeezes every inch of living into a few short months. Patrick and Charlotte separate and go their separate ways when they're left with just the memory of Niki and all her dreams.

Comments: What a wonderful, touching movie. *Six Weeks* is the movie I like people to watch when they're feeling a little blue about their own lives. We hear Niki tell us not to waste one moment, to embrace every minute of every hour. So sit back with someone you care about and watch this one together. Niki handles her inevitable death by making the most of what time is left. She plays out many of her fantasies and experiences life to its fullest: being part of Patrick's campaign, seeing her mother married, dancing in the ballet. What a bright, healthy way to handle it, yet most people get caught in the fear of dying. What about the relationship between Patrick and his wife? Was he honest with her? In truth he was falling in love with Charlotte. The more involved he became with her the more he focused on Niki as the reason for that involvement. And for that reason he was not honest. He could not admit to his wife and family that he wanted to be with someone else. Finally, let yourself feel the grief over the loss of Niki. Charlotte needed to be alone. Patrick needed to be with Charlotte. It is at this point that he is betrayed by his own dishonesty. Can you see that he now has twice the grieving to do? There can never be any healing, any going on with your life unless you allow yourself to grieve. Some of you have problems letting yourself go, especially the men. But try. Just let yourself experience your emotions and you will feel the healing that comes from your own tears.

Year: 1982
Length: 107 min
Rating: PG
Color

Sleeping With the Enemy

Healing Themes:

- Living with someone who is obsessed with control
- Dealing with an abusive partner
- Escaping from a bad relationship
- Finding someone who is healthy who cares

Cast: Julia Roberts, Kevin Anderson, Patrick Bergin, Elizabeth Lawrence, Kyle Secor, Claudette Nevins. Director, Joseph Rubin. Writer, Ronald Bass.

Synopsis: Sara is married to Martin, a violent man who is obsessed with everything in his life, especially her. She fakes her death to start life all over again. She is just learning to trust again, beginning a new relationship when Martin tracks them down and Sara has to fight for their lives.

Comments: A good marriage is based on love, trust, and respect for each other. Without these three fundamental ideas a marriage, or any relationship, will not survive. Sometimes a couple remains together if one of them is holding the other hostage. That's exactly what you will see in *Sleeping With the Enemy*, an abusive man holding his wife hostage through threats and violence. So why do I want you to watch this movie? Because Sara overcame many of her fears to finally break away. Many women each year attempt to get away from their abusive husbands. Some are successful, some return out of fear for their lives or the lives of their children, and some fear they can't make it on their own. Are you someone who is terrified of your spouse or partner? Do you feel you or your child are always at risk for violence if you don't do things just right? Have you tried to get away but are afraid because you have no place to go? If so, it's time to get your life back. What did you feel when he stalked Sara? I found this to be a difficult part to watch. That's why this movie is well titled. There is no question that Martin is the enemy. Use this movie as a way to get in touch with your fears, then move towards solution. Take action to stop those who would try and control you. There are support groups, shelters, and victim hotlines where you live. Make some calls.

Year: 1991
Length: 99 min
Rating: R
Color

Sleepless in Seattle

Healing Themes:

- Losing the love of your life and learning to start over and move on
- Through the eyes of babes
- Not knowing there is someone out there who is listening
- When that magical moment happens

Cast: Meg Ryan, Tom Hanks, Bill Pullman, Rosie O'Donnell, Rob Reiner. Director, Nora Ephron. Writers, Nora Ephron, David Ward, and Jeff Arch.

Synopsis: Sam Baldwin, recently widowed, moves to Seattle with his son to start a new life. Annie Reed hears his story on a radio talk show and becomes infatuated. Sam and Annie have their separate experiences, but ultimately they get together at the Empire State Building.

Comments: This story is similar to *An Affair to Remember.* Both movies offer us wonderful healing messages about love, romance, and finding that very special someone. Now, you might feel like this one is pure fantasy. Well, each of us has a fantasy about meeting and having that special someone in our lives, true? Absolutely! In this movie you get to experience that fantasy romance; that chance meeting with someone who might be your soul mate. Take pleasure in their chance meeting; the serendipitous events which finally brought them together. There are some other important messages this movie has to offer. You may get in touch with losing a spouse or significant other. Listen to Sam talk about this most painful experience. Did you think Sam just gave up on love? And what about his son? He seems to have gotten lost in the shuffle. He was also in pain and yet he felt he needed to help his father. But I would suggest the needs of this little boy were unattended. I know it is difficult, but you must look out for your children if you have lost someone. They've lost them too. Children learn how to grieve from adults, usually their parents. If they don't grieve they can become stuck for the rest of their lives, unable to get in touch with feelings buried long ago. I know you men have a difficult time with your emotions. Watch it alone if you need to. What a delightful way to heal when you experience someone else's joy.

Year: 1993
Length: 105 min
Rating: PG
Color

Something About Amelia

Healing Themes:

- When a parent sexually abuses a child
- Refusing to see the truth
- Learning to take care of yourself
- Getting support from those you can trust

Cast: Ted Danson, Glenn Close. Director, Randa Haines. Writer, William Hanley.

Synopsis: There is something wrong with the relationship between a father and his daughter, Amelia. When it is discovered that he is having an incestuous relationship with her, Amelia is taken out of the home and he is arrested. The family seeks help to heal and put all the pieces together.

Comments: There is a tendency for many people to believe this type of abuse occurs in families from low socio-economic groups. This is simply not the case. The movie does a great job of pulling us out of denial about that misconception. Incest can occur in the family next door. Some of you may already know that because it may have happened to you. Notice how Amelia's father manipulates her so he can get what he wants—a physical relationship with his daughter. You hear his child-like jealousy when he found out there was a boy who was interested in her. In one of their conversations he says, "There must be another boy." How telling of the role he has for himself in Amelia's life. He sees her as cheating on him. He's lost all sense of his role as a father. The mother seems to have no idea of what's going on. Ask yourself if she is truly oblivious or does she choose not to see what he's doing to Amelia? You will also notice that Amelia is both avoidant and submissive to maintain peace. How awful it must have been for Amelia to have her mother call her a liar and not even listen to what she had to say. When I choose movies, I select them knowing they may be quite painful for some of you to watch. Healing happens when you let the old, haunting pains out to allow for the magnificence of your own rebirth. Don't stop with this movie. Continue your work with *Ultimate Betrayal* and *Closet Land*, two more movies that deal with incest.

Year: 1984
Length: 100 min (approx)
Rating: R
Color

Sophie's Choice

Healing Themes:

- When memories of past choices haunt you
- Being involved with someone who is emotionally unstable
- If sex is what drives your relationship
- Accepting death and moving on

Cast: Meryl Streep, Kevin Kline, Peter MacNicol, Rita Karin, Stephen D. Newman, Josh Mostel. Director, Alan Pakula. Writer, Alan Pakula.

Synopsis: Stingo, a young writer living in a boarding house, attempts to rescue Sophie from the abusive clutches of Nathan's manic treatment of her. It all comes to a tragic end as Nathan dies, leaving Sophie on her own.

Comments: I can still remember the time and place when I first saw this move. It may have a stunning effect on you, as well. There is so much going on I suggest you watch it a couple of times. Look at the desperate relationship that exists between Sophie and Nathan. Can you see how her experiences in the Nazi concentration camps are mirrored in a relationship that abuses her both physically and mentally? You see, she has become attracted to the thing she believes she deserves in her life. She is like someone who grew up in a violent alcoholic home and later in life marries an alcoholic who abuses her. Can you see the pattern? We tend to refer to her behavior as being codependent: whenever he does something erratic she tries to adjust and take on part of the responsibility for his actions. Does that hit home? Are you someone who avoids dealing with the reality that the person you are with is not owning their own behavior so you take it on? Stingo is right in there with the same codependent behavior as Sophie. Watch how he plays the knight in shining armor. And what about Nathan? He is suffering from a serious mental disorder, marked by depression and extreme manic behavior. If the person you're with will not help themselves I can assure you they're not ready for you to help them. I would like you to use this movie as a way to emotional awareness. Healing comes when you choose to see your own way.

Year: 1982
Length: 157 min
Rating: R
Color

St. Elmo's Fire

Healing Themes:

- Dealing with the fear of moving on
- Having friends to support you through a crisis
- Handling life transitions
- Realizing that the people in your life are moving on
- Feeling too attached to others to see them for who they really are

Cast: Emillio Estevez, Rob Lowe, Andrew McCarthy, Demi Moore, Judd Nelson, Ally Sheedy, Mare Winningham, Jenny Wright, Andie MacDowell. Director, Joel Schumacher. Writers, Joel Shumacher and Carl Kurlander.

Synopsis: Seven students who recently graduated from college celebrate their new found freedom and share their fears about the future. Relationships become rocky when life pushes them in different directions. In the end they come to realize how important they are to one another.

Comments: When you watch this group you can't help but feel like they're all part of the same team; each of them is looking out for the other. You may feel a great sense of loss in not having had that kind of bond with friends, or it may bring warm memories, make you appreciative of the friendships you have. Was there a special group of friends who were there for you? Possibly by looking back you can see how this kind of friendship is missing in your life. *St. Elmo's Fire* may serve those who have had difficulty transitioning out of college or a programmed lifestyle such as the armed services or long-term employment. People often have a sense of emptiness when they leave places where they worked or went to school. Why not make a party out of this one? It's a great way to open up some communication and hear about the lives and friendship of those who are part of your life today. You will experience a sense of growth and freedom and at the same time reopen some doors you thought were locked forever. If you tend to isolate, try joining support groups, clubs, or organizations designed to help you meet others who would like a chance to meet you. Give it try. Tell yourself that you're worth the effort.

Year: 1985
Length: 110 min
Rating: R
Color

Stanley and Iris

Healing Themes:

- Meeting that special someone
- Falling in love later in life
- When family members take advantage of you
- Revealing the truth that you can't read or write
- Learning to learn all over again
- Being accepted for who you are
- When you feel like you've been left behind

Cast: Jane Fonda, Robert De Niro, Swoosie Kurtz, Martha Plimpton, Harley Cross, Jamey Sheridan, Feodor Chaliapin, Zohra Lampet. Director, Martin Ritt. Writers, Harriet Frank, Jr. and Irving Ravetch.

Synopsis: Iris, a widowed mom, is robbed and Stanley, a co-worker, comes to her defense. They begin a relationship. In time he discloses that he can't read. Iris tutors him and he leaves town to find a better job. Much to her surprise he does not forget her and returns to continue their relationship.

Comments: This movie offers us an opportunity to get in touch with some real feelings about how relationships grow over time, the struggles relationships go through, and the happiness that comes with making it work. They're inspirational in many ways. Notice how angry you become over the sister and brother-in-law. How could Iris put up with that from them? Yet, how many times have you felt obligated to someone? Also, is there a handicap that you have in your life that you have not talked about, one that embarrasses you? It took a lot of courage for Stanley to tell Iris he couldn't read. I know. I didn't learn to read, write, or spell until I was twelve. I still struggle with the problem. I consider myself lucky to be in a relationship with someone who understands my handicap. I think opening up brought the relationship closer. Finally, let yourself feel Iris's sense of abandonment when he leaves. No matter whether it is a lover, friend, or parent, abandonment is a feeling that is important to allow yourself to own. Watch this movie with someone you trust and care about. You may find that it helps you open up to them.

Year: 1990
Length: 107 min
Rating: PG-13
Color

Star Wars

Healing Themes:

- Looking for the hidden meaning
- Fighting the forces that hold you back
- Reaching deep inside for your inner strength
- Not succumbing to outside forces

Cast: Mark Hamill, Carrie Fisher, Harrison Ford, Alec Guinness, Peter Cushing, Kenny Baker, James Earl Jones, David Prowse. Director, George Lucas. Writer, George Lucas.

Synopsis: Luke Skywalker's life changes when he is sent on a mission to fight the villains from the Galactic Empire led by the evil Darth Vader. He meets Hans Solo, a hotshot space pilot who knows how to get out of any jam. With some help from a very special force, Luke saves Princess Leia and defeats the Galactic Empire.

Comments: Why am I recommending this movie? What could a futuristic fantasy have to do with healing stories? *Star Wars*, like *Aliens* and *Dr. Jekyll and Mr. Hyde*, reaches us in different ways. Horror, fantasy, and science fiction movies are rich in symbolic messages about life, success, and freedom. They also contain messages about good and evil. In fact, this movie sends all of those messages. Expressions such as "May the force be with you" speak to an inner being or inner self. There is a sense of spiritualism and having the strength to win out over desires that hold us back in life: alcohol, drugs, gambling, obsessive relationships, over spending, etc. "The dark side" is in all of us. It begs us to avoid our own challenges in life and let others win out over us. I could write for pages about each area of symbolism, but I want to leave this up to you. Here's why. Symbolism, as is the case with dreams, has different meanings for each of us. My interpretation and what I think is important may be different, and more importantly, may overlook what you think is important. This is a great movie to watch in a group. It's just fun to hear what meaning it has for others. There are two other movies, *The Empire Strikes Back* and *The Return of the Jedi*, that form a trilogy. Go for them all; have fun with this healing approach.

Year: 1977
Length: 121 min
Rating: PG
Color

Steel Magnolias

Healing Themes:

- Refusing to accept your limitations
- Coping with the death of a child
- Learning to accept the choices that your children make
- When friends force you to deal with difficult issues

Cast: Sally Field, Dolly Parton, Shirley MacLaine, Darryl Hannah, Olympia Dukakis, Julia Roberts, Tom Skerritt, Sam Shepard, Dylan McDermott, Kevin J. O'Connor, Bill McCutcheon, Ann Wedgeworth. Director, Herbert Ross. Writer, Robert Harling.

Synopsis: A group of women gather at a beauty shop to get ready for Shelby's wedding. Shelby has diabetes and in spite of the protests from M'Lynn, her mother, she has a baby. Shelby dies and the women mourn the loss of a daughter and friend.

Comments: *Steel Magnolias* gives us an opportunity to find ourselves in one or more of the characters. It also gives a beautiful portrayal of the intimate relationship between mother and daughter. Did you get in touch with any feelings when the two of them were together? Ask yourself if their relationship was anything like the one you had with your parent(s). One of the important issues this movie deals with comes out when the daughter dies. Grieving is a part of life. We must grieve if we are to experience our own freedom to live the rest of our lives. What feelings come to the surface when you experience the anger, pain, and loss that M'Lynn goes through? Notice how the friends rally around M'Lynn to support her in her loss. This kind of support does not seem to exist nor is it directed to the men. Why? Where is the father? Are men excluded from the grieving? I don't think so. Men hurt just like women. This is why I would especially like the men to sit and experience the feelings between the women. This is a touching movie that will reach inside of you. Breathe and let yourself feel the emotions this movie will evoke. You might also like to give *The Joy Luck Club* and *Chantilly Lace* a try—these are also touching journeys.

Year: 1989
Length: 118 min
Rating: PG
Color

Stella

Healing Themes:

- Feeling that your children need more in their lives
- Facing your limitations
- When your whole life is in chaos
- If drinking is affecting your life
- Thinking that all there is is money

Cast: Bette Midler, John Goodman, Stephen Colins, Eileen Brennan, Ben Stiller, Trini Alvarado, Marsha Mason. Director, John Erman. Writer, Robert Getchall.

Synopsis: Stella wants her daughter, Jenny, to have the chances in life that she herself didn't have. In spite of her daughter's protests, Stella sends Jenny to live with her father and makes an exit from Jenny's life for Jenny's own good.

Comments: You can use this movie to get in touch with some of the emotions that go with memories about lost dreams and just not feeling good enough about yourself. I was the kid who always wished I came from the other side of the tracks. I know now those fantasies merely drained me of the energy I could have used to obtain my own dreams. Yes, the experience made me promise I was going to make things better in my life. But what do you do when you think your life is slipping away and you haven't accomplished what you wanted? Like Stella, you may decide to send your child away to be with those who can fulfill your dream. Can you see those were Stella's dreams, not her daughter's? Her daughter was content with her life, but her mother did not let her have her own choices. What of Stella's relationship with her alcoholic friend? Can you see that alcohol was always a part of her life, and her drinking buddy is merely a reflection of her own alcoholism? Do you think it was her abuse of alcohol that made her believe she wasn't good enough? We have all experienced being pressured by our parent's dreams. Live your own dreams, not someone else's. Let your children be the best they can become because that's what they want for their lives, not yours. Let go of who you are *not* and accept who you *are* with the knowledge you have the power to be anything you want in this world.

Year: 1989
Length: 109 min
Rating: PG-13
Color

Stranger in the Family

Healing Themes:

- Coping with a horrible accident
- Dealing with the pain and fear that you might lose your child
- Accepting that your child is not the same as he or she was before
- Asking to be accepted for who you are

Cast: Teri Garr, Neil Patrick Harris, Randle Mell, Sierra Samuel, Kathryn Dowling, Cully Fredricksen, Mag Ruffman, Kris Hefan, Jeff Bryant.

Synopsis: While out driving with a friend, Steven is struck by a drunken driver. He is injured and loses his memory. He tries to regain his identity but it's no use, for his memory is completely gone. In time the family comes to accept the new Steven and let the old one go.

Comments: Whenever possible I have made a practice of introducing movies that deal with various issues relating to the physically or emotionally challenged. This movie focuses on a condition known as retrograde amnesia. I'm sure most of you are familiar with the condition known as amnesia. As you will see, Steven has no memory whatsoever. He has to relearn everything. One of the first things I would like you to observe is the patronizing way the doctor treats the family. The same experience seems to happen when the school tries to turn its back on Steven's reeducation needs. Also, you will feel some frustration as the person who caused the crash suffers little repercussion for her wrongdoing. Follow the family as they share the trials of having to live with someone who has the needs of a baby. You will also feel some anxiety when his parents lose their patience with him. It was clear that Steven's mom was angry because he could no longer live up to her expectations. As observers we wonder why they can't be more patient with him. The truth is, if you are in the middle of having to deal with someone who has been traumatized it's not easy to remain patient. Most important is to learn to accept anyone for what they are, not what they were. *Regarding Henry* gives us the adult version of this story.

Year: 1991
Length: 100 min
Rating: Unrated
Color

The Summer of '42

Healing Themes:

- Looking back at your childhood
- Losing your virginity
- Feeling lost from the death of a loved one
- Coming of age

Cast: Robert Mulligan, Jennifer O'Neill, Gary Grimes, Jerry Houser, Oliver Conant, Katherine Allentuck, Christopher Norris, Lou Frizell. Director, Robert Mulligan. Writer, Herman Raucher.

Synopsis: Hermie becomes infatuated with a married woman who is a summer visitor at a small island off the coast of New England in 1942. When her husband is killed in the war, she becomes intimate with the teenage boy for one night. Hermie returns to see her, but she has gone.

Comments: I remember I was in college when I saw *The Summer of '42*. I was deeply moved. (Of course I couldn't show my feelings. I needed to be macho. Nonsense.) I doubt many teenagers would watch this movie. I'm even a little concerned they would get the wrong idea. As was the case with me, it's a chance for men to get in touch with their youth and their own coming of age. As you watch the movie you will experience a little embarrassment over some of the things you used to do and say in your youth. Most young boys and girls do become infatuated with an older person at some point in their young life. All of those experiences are pretty normal. Who do you remember from your past—a teacher, a friend of your parents, or maybe your coach? I want to point out that what takes place sexually between the woman and the boy is molestation. Irrespective of the circumstances, he is still under age. Oddly enough, we tend to overlook this issue if the boy is under age, but if the girl is under age it's a whole other story. Most men don't want to deal with this issue, but it's there for all of you to look at. I would suggest you watch this movie alone. Allow your mind to be free and simply experience the feelings that come rushing back as the memories of the past take shape.

Year: 1971
Length: 102 min
Rating: R
Color

Sybil

Healing Themes:

- Uncovering an abusive past
- Putting all the pieces together
- Working through a mental illness
- Dealing with sexual abuse

Cast: Sally Field, Joanne Woodward, Brad Davis, Martine Barlett, Jane Hoffman. Director, Daniel Petrie. Writer, Stewart Stern.

Synopsis: In the process of a woman's therapy all sixteen of her personalities emerge along with flashbacks of her childhood and the memories of abuse that took place. Sybil and her psychiatrist work to put all the pieces of her life back together.

Comments: Every once in a while I come across a movie that is so extraordinary I suggest that everyone watch it. *Sybil* is more than just a movie; it is an account of a young woman's struggle to heal herself from a horribly abusive childhood. The movie has some similarities to *The Three Faces of Eve*. However, the similarity ends with the graphic display of family abuse. Let me get some technical stuff out of the way before we get into this movie. Sybil suffers from what is known as multiple personality disorder (MPD). Simply stated, she has more than one personality. Have you ever been around someone who switches personalities just like that? Well, what Sybil has is quite different. Just watching what Sybil goes through to put all the pieces of her life together is very healing. Notice the way the therapist gently nurtures their relationship. She becomes the kind and patient parent Sybil never had. Watch how Sybil has learned to handle her abusive childhood. She literally becomes other people, sixteen of them, all of whom help her cope in her adult life. Stay with your feelings when you watch the scenes of Sybil's mother abusing her. These are some very painful moments to watch. Let me make a few recommendations. If you are in therapy, get the opinion of your therapist with respect to seeing this movie. Next, ask a close and trusted friend to watch *Sybil* with you. Sometimes we can all use a little help on the road to self-awareness and recovery.

Year: 1976
Length: 122 min
Rating: Unrated
Color

Taking Back My Life: The Nancy Ziegenmeyer Story

Healing Themes:

- If you've been raped
- Confronting your fears
- Standing up for your rights
- Working out problems in a relationship

Cast: Patricia Wettig, Stephen Lang, Shelly Heck, Joanna Cassidy, Gina Hecht, Eileen Brennan, Ellen Burstyn.

Synopsis: While on her way to take a real-estate exam, Nancy is raped. She is afraid to go after her attacker who has threatened her if she goes to the police. Nancy goes through a great deal of inner turmoil over how she should deal with both the legal and personal issues.

Comments: If you are someone who has experienced rape or any kind of abuse this is an important movie for you to watch. It is crucial that you take action in your life as Nancy does and not leave your emotions locked up inside. Observe what she has to go through at her medical examination. If you look closely you will see how she emotionally escapes the experience. What about her fear and pain? Can you relate to the terror that comes with a rape or molestation and the threats of retaliation? How did you feel when you learned more about the legal system and the rights of the victim versus the perpetrator? You may find yourself feeling hopeless or angry. Those emotions are part of the grieving process on the journey to self-healing. Nancy gets lost in the system. That's not uncommon. Rape victims often report feeling as if they are the criminal. Notice the terrible strain this puts on her relationship with her family. And what about her husband's mother? What do you feel about her role in the relationship? You may find that her character kicks up more feelings than just those related to the issue of rape. You have a tremendous amount to gain from experiencing all the feelings that will surface from watching this movie. If you are someone who has been victimized in any manner, join a support group, or seek a therapist, ministers, or a counselor. Support is a primary step in total recovery and the self-healing process.

Year: 1992
Length: 100 min
Rating: PG
Color

Tales of Manhattan

Healing Themes:

- Life is unpredictable
- Picking yourself up by your coattails
- Accepting life's gifts
- When you're too drunk to think
- Crime doesn't pay

Cast: Charles Boyer, Rita Hayworth, Henry Fonda, Ginger Rogers, Charles Laughton, Edward G. Robinson, Ethel Waters, Paul Robeson, Eddie Anderson, Thomas Mitchell, Cesar Romero, George Sanders. Director, Julien Duvivier.

Synopsis: A man's dress coat ends up in the lives of six different groups of people. As the coat passes from group to group we see all the lives that the coat touches: the actors, the financiers, the butlers, the homeless attorney, the thief, and finally a whole town struggling to survive.

Comments: Okay, I'm introducing you to one of my all-time favorite movies. It's like a little treasure. I found it one night, or should I say early one morning. I figured it was just another one of those old movies. Boy, was I wrong! It's really six movies in one, each with its own message. Now, normally I would point out certain areas that I would like you to look at. Not this time. I would like you to simply experience this movie and capture the inspirational messages that weave their way in and out of each story. Some of you will see some points where others do not, and vice versa. What's wonderful about this movie is that we follow a tail coat and not a person from story to story. I found that I was more easily absorbed into each story because I was focused on the tail coat and suddenly I was in the story. It's a great experience. There is one overall message I would like you to be sure to get from this movie: Life is unpredictable. You can make all the plans for the future that you want, but you must remember that there is a greater plan. Trust that there is a force that guides all of us and listen to your inner voice to put yourself in sync with the big plan.

Year: 1942
Length: 118 min
Rating: Unrated
B&W

Terms of Endearment

Healing Themes:

- Growing up with a domineering mother
- Finding love in middle age
- Being in a relationship with an alcoholic
- When communication is a problem
- Dealing with the death of a child
- If you're deceiving someone you love

Cast: Shirley MacLaine, Jack Nicholson, Debra Winger, John Lithgow, Jeff Daniels, Danny DeVito. Director, James L. Brooks. Writer, James L. Brooks.

Synopsis: Thirty years in a mother/daughter relationship is marked by their ups and downs in communicating with each other. They both take on outside relationships that do not meet the other's approval. When Emma's illness proves incurable she comes to terms with her mother and her life.

Comments: This movie is for those of you who are having problems communicating with other family members. It's also for those who are working at letting go of someone who has died. We cannot help but get invested in Emma or Aurora. Which of the characters do you relate to the most? Notice the way that Aurora discounts everything Emma says. This often takes place in families that do not know how to communicate. Can you hear that Aurora and Emma are talking at each other rather than to each other? How destructive. This is the primary reason people turn to counseling. Please hear this loud and clear: It is not possible to have a healthy, happy relationship with anyone without clear communication. Also, note the mid-life love relationship between Aurora and the astronaut. And some think that life is over at forty. By the way, is this man a drunk? Why do you think she's attracted to a drunk? Maybe his alcoholism is a metaphor for her own chaotic family. Because this movie takes place over time viewers have an opportunity to see themselves at different stages in their own life. Feel the pain and loss as Aurora learns that her daughter is dying. You're going to feel every scene in this movie. Sit back and let the tears flow.

Year: 1983
Length: 132 min
Rating: PG
Color

That's Life

Healing Themes:

- Growing old gracefully
- Exchanging your aches and pains for love
- Using sex to feel young again
- Handling everybody else's problems but your own
- When your children are having problems growing up

Cast: Jack Lemmon, Julie Andrews, Sally Kellerman, Chris Lemmon, Emma Walton, Rob Knepper, Robert Loggia, Jennifer Edwards. Director, Blake Edwards. Writer, Wilton Wexler.

Synopsis: An architect approaching his sixtieth birthday is becoming a neurotic about every ache and pain. He is not even aware that his wife may have cancer. When his wife confronts him about his behavior he comes to realize that his life is pretty darn good just the way it is.

Comments: Let me start with a little direction on this one. Try not to get caught up in the humor, or you may miss some of the key messages that this movie has to offer us. Some people do not handle aging and the fear of dying very well. Notice how the wife handles her pain; she chooses to keep everything inside. She deals with her fears alone as opposed to her husband who wants the world to feel for him. That's not the way to handle those problems. Learn to reach out. There's healing that comes from sharing with those who care. On the beach, she is comforted by someone who she never thought would take the time to listen. Who are you overlooking in your life? There is a bit of *Rocket Gibraltar* in this movie. Watch how the adult children revert back to being what they were like when they lived in the house. Although it is a bit overplayed, watch how the mother becomes the problem solver and caretaker for everyone and that no one ever asks how she is doing. It is a bit disturbing to me that his affairs are overlooked. We understand he is searching for his youth, but that's not a justification for having an affair. We continue to get the message that it's okay for men to find their identity in sexual escapades and conquests. This of course is nonsense. The healing comes when we learn to accept life on life's terms. There are no quick fixes. Learn to enjoy the time you have with the one who can love you in return.

Year: 1986
Length: 102 min
Rating: PG-13
Color

Thelma and Louise

Healing Themes:
- Breaking out of an abusive relationship
- Sowing your oats
- Having a fling
- If someone forces him or herself on you
- Loyalty to friends even though it is unhealthy

Cast: Susan Sarandon, Geena Davis, Harvey Keitel, Christopher McDonald, Michael Madsen, Brad Pitt, Timothy Carhart. Director, Ridley Scott. Writer, Callie Khouri.

Synopsis: Thelma, the dutiful housewife, and Louise, the rebel waitress, hit the road for a week of adventure. When one of them is almost raped, they go on the run from the law for defending themselves. When there is no place else to run, they call it quits, literally.

Comments: Some would say this movie is not the best example of a positive, healing message. I don't see it that way. But let me say this: I am not suggesting that you jump in a car and do what these two have done. Additionally, the answer to life's big questions will not be found by riding off the edge of a cliff. Instead, view their actions as a metaphor for freedom and self-liberation. I am suggesting that sometimes it's important to look at your life and decide whether or not you want to continue on with the way things are going. You can do it through Thelma or Louise or both for that matter, and you can do it in the safety of your own home, popcorn included. Who knows, after viewing the movie you may want to sit back and make some…well, some less dangerous decisions. One final note, as you watch the attempted rape, try to stay with your feelings. Maybe something like this happened to you. I am always amazed at the lack of boundaries that some people have. He had no right to go after her. I can assure you that the alcohol is no excuse. If you're someone who has experienced what these women went through you will enjoy the dignity that comes from standing up for what you believe in and not allowing others to rule your life.

Year: 1991
Length: 130 min
Rating: R
Color

This Boy's Life

Healing Themes:

- Trying to get your act together
- Growing up with an abusive stepparent
- If a parent looks the other way
- Being around an adult who is a poor role model

Cast: Robert De Niro, Ellen Barkin, Leonard DiCaprio, Jonah Blechman, Eliza Dushku, Chris Cooper, Carla Gugino, Zack Ansley, Tracey Ellis, Kathy Kinney, Gerrit Graham. Director, Michael Caton-Jones. Writer, Robert Getchell.

Synopsis: A single mother with one young son meets Dwight, who is nice to her and her son, Toby. They fall in love. All is well at first, but in time Dwight becomes more abusive to her and Toby. She almost loses her sense of self. When a final abusive act takes place, she takes Toby and hits the road.

Comments: Like *Radio Flyer, This Boy's Life* shows us both overt and covert abuse. Notice how Dwight starts making negative comments to the boy. Some of you will relate to his behavior immediately. Also notice how Toby's mother turns her head. She ignores her child to keep her life together. That's not what parents are supposed to do. Parents should protect you, not turn their backs on you. And what about the physical abuse? Dwight torments the boy with his adult strength, calling it, "Just teaching the boy a few things." His abuse of alcohol is apparent, a typical component of this kind of personality. Finally, listen to Dwight as he mimics Toby and torments him, which is another form of abuse. In spite of his actions the boy was not able to take on any other role but that of the victim. (You've sure got to give him credit for trying.) Whether you are a parent in denial or someone who is acting abusively in the family, try to use the movie as a tool to begin working through your own issues instead of transferring them to those around you. If you experienced this kind of abuse with your siblings, gather them together to watch the movie. Spend time discussing your feelings. This is a wonderful way to get out of denial and to begin the journey of self-healing.

Year: 1993
Length: 115 min
Rating: R
Color

The Three Faces of Eve

Healing Themes:

- Uncovering the secrets of a traumatic childhood experience
- Revealing all that you are
- Dealing with an insensitive spouse
- Finding your way home

Cast: Joanne Woodward, Lee J. Cobb, David Wayne, Vince Edwards. Director, Nunnally Johnson. Writer, Nunnally Johnson.

Synopsis: Eve, a woman in her early twenties, enters into therapy. After some time it becomes apparent to the therapist that Eve has three separate identities. After working with her for some time he is able to bring her three personalities into one and Eve begins living a normal life.

Comments: I can recall watching some old westerns on television. A dust bitin' cowboy turns to a sod buster—that's cowboy talk—and says, "You're nothing but a two faced, lyin' son of a...." Of course, that was his last observation. But what does that statement really mean? I've heard other people say—not about me of course—"You're showing another side of yourself." Well, the truth is each of us has a personality with many sides—strong, weak, happy, sad, passive, aggressive, and so on. Okay Doc, so what's your point? Simply, it is those sides that make up who we are in this world; they give us our identity, road maps to our character. And just because we see personality changes in people doesn't mean there is something wrong with them. But on rare occasion, as is the case with Eve, life can become overwhelming and the mind needs to protect itself. And when that happens we literally see another face (or in the case of Eve, her three faces). Eve suffered from a serious mental disorder known as multiple personality disorder. A traumatic event in her life was the foundation for her condition. View this movie as a way of getting in touch with the pieces of your true self. Then ask yourself a few questions: Am I one way to some people and another way to other people? Am I keeping secrets from people so that they will continue to like me? Have I buried my dreams to follow someone else's dream? We can all experience healing when we free up the energy we are using trying to be something in life that we're not.

Year: 1957
Length: 91 min
Rating: Unrated
Color

To Kill a Mockingbird

Healing Themes:
- Living with prejudice and racism
- Standing up for what you believe in
- Being a party to rumors
- Living in the fear of reprisal

Cast: Gregory Peck, Brock Peters, Phillip Alford, Mary Badham, Robert Duvall. Director, Robert Mulligan. Writer, Horton Foote.

Synopsis: An attorney in a small Southern town defends a local black man accused of raping a white woman. In a town of bigots and racists his family and law practice suffer because of his efforts to prove the woman a liar. He wins the case, but the town will not forgive him for defending a black man.

Comments: We get an opportunity to see this movie maker's perspective on what bigotry and racism looks like. Although the writer chose a small Southern town, a stereotype, we can see how the immoral acts of prejudice and racism can grow and engulf any community. Over the last ten years we have seen the number of people who belong to hate groups grow. What are your feelings on these issues? Childhood issues of lying come into play when a woman lies and falsely accuses a black man of rape. Take special note of the way the townspeople use irrational thinking to justify not giving the accused a fair trial. Have you ever been a party to doing something founded in prejudice against another person? Why? Do you really feel some people are better than others? Maybe you have suffered at the hands of racism and prejudice. How did you handle it? Also note the special family bond that exists between the father and his children. Even though this is an older movie we get a strong sense of the abuse between the accuser and her father. You can see how the family secrecy has affected her. Can you get in touch with her fear? Her terror? Also notice how rumor has ruled the town's thinking. We see how this type of thinking begins when the children respond to the rumor about their neighbor down the street. Do you see how what the children are doing is symbolic of what the whole town is doing? This movie can turn on the light to awareness.

Year: 1962
Length: 129 min
Rating: Unrated
B&W

Torch Song Trilogy

Healing Themes:

- If you are gay, accepting your sexual orientation
- Living with the death of a loved one
- Learning that one of your children is a homosexual
- Enjoying life to its fullest

Cast: Anne Bancroft, Matthew Broderick, Harvey Fierstein, Brian Kerwin, Karen Young, Charles Pierce. Director, Paul Bogart. Writer, Harvey Fierstein.

Synopsis: Two gay men, Arnold and Alan, struggle with telling their friends and family of their love for each other. When they feel they have finally made it to the point of feeling comfortable with their union, one of them is murdered in a senseless killing. Life seems as if it's all but over for the other.

Comments: For those of you who struggle with your sexual identity this movie offers support. However, this movie is not just for those who are gay or in question of their sexual identity; it's for anyone who's been in a relationship. The movie shows us the importance of being loved for who we are verses being loved conditionally. You may recall being in a relationship with someone whom your family did not approve of. What emotions did you experience as you tried to get them to accept your lover? Anger? Rage? Hurt? Pressure? Notice the mother-son relationship. How did you feel about the way they spoke with each other? I felt strained, as if I wanted him to get out of there. It didn't seem very real to me. On another note, how did you feel when you saw the two men being intimate? Did viewing this portion of the movie make you uncomfortable? Why is it not okay for people of the same sex to be intimate? Let yourself feel the pain associated with the death of one of the lovers. I am still amazed that people have to succumb to violence when they do not agree with another person's point of view or lifestyle choice. If you are a homosexual, you will grow from experiencing this couple's relationship. If you are not, you will grow by taking a step closer to accepting people for who and what they are.

Year: 1988
Length: 117 min
Rating: R
Color

Toughlove

Healing Themes:

- When your children are out of control
- Getting support from those with some experience
- Setting boundaries
- Loving your children enough to stop them from hurting themselves

Cast: Lee Remick, Bruce Dern, Piper Laurie, Eric Schiff, Dedee Pfeiffer, Dana Elcar, Beth Miller, Jason Patric. Director, Glenn Jordan. Writer, Karen Hall.

Synopsis: Jen and Rob Charters start having problems with their adolescent son. They try everything they can think of to keep him on track. Nothing seems to work until they find Toughlove, an organization that helps parents with difficult adolescents. They get their family back on course.

Comments: Sometimes parents get to the point where they feel as if they have no place to turn. They will read books, listen to tapes, and become imaginative in their attempts to get their children back on track. Some turn to counselors, ministers, and hospitals. The truth is, unless the parents take charge and the child starts working on what's bothering him or her, it's not possible to have a healthy, chaos-free family life. Toughlove, a self-help support organization, is based on the concept that if the parents lay down clear, solid guidelines and boundaries with consistent consequences and rewards that are handled in an appropriate manner, the parents can take back control of the family. I would like you to pay close attention to how the family got to where they are. Was the house run with clear boundaries? Did the children know or learn early on the difference between right and wrong? Could the parents have predicted their child's behavior given the past family history? Are the children acting out what they've been taught by the parents? Healing comes with consistency and predictability. It's the name of the game for a healthy, nurturing family. By the way, I'm not saying therapists and counselors can't help. There are many who are trained in this area. Be sure you find out what their expertise is before you get started.

Year: 1985
Length: 100 min
Rating: Unrated
Color

The Trip to Bountiful

Healing Themes:

- Living life to the fullest
- Growing old with grace and dignity
- Making that journey back to your past
- Realizing the beauty of all that you have
- Making sure you've left no stone unturned

Cast: Geraldine Page, John Heard, Carlin Glynn, Richard Bradford, Rebecca De Mornay, Kevin Cooney. Director, Peter Masterson. Writer, Horton Foote.

Synopsis: Carrie Watts is very unhappy and feels as if she is a burden to her son's family. She goes back home to Bountiful, Texas, for one last look at her roots. This woman experiences life in a way she never could have imagined. Carrie realizes she has truly come home.

Comments: All of us have a sense of growing old. For some, aging is a positive part of life, full of beautiful memories. For others, aging is a terrifying, often emotionally crippling experience. But it does not have to be that way. We can all enjoy getting older if our lives are rich and spiritual. When you watch this movie you will see Carrie's pain as she deals with the reality that her life is almost over. Notice how she feels useless and burdensome in her son's home. She recalls her younger days when she too had a life. She decides she doesn't have to live as if her life is done. And that is the point: live life to its fullest. Simply because you are not an elderly person does not mean you can't relate to what she is going through. You might recall driving by a school yard and noticing children at play. How did you feel? How about when you listen to music and you realize that you have not kept up with the times, or observe someone very young obtain a position in the office because of her or his youth? These feelings are with us all the time. What makes the difference is how we handle life's journey. Learn to be at peace with yourself and the life you've led. Watch this movie as a couple if you can. You may be able to take that bountiful trip together. If you are the children of elderly parents, support them in the process of taking their own personal journey. When the time comes, you will want your children to do the same.

Year: 1985
Length: 106 min
Rating: PG
Color

Ultimate Betrayal

Healing Themes:

- When memories of abuse rise to the surface
- Supporting family members through the tough times
- Dealing with those who want you to keep the family secret
- Confronting the abusive parent

Cast: Marlo Thomas, Ellen Harkett, Mel Harris.

Synopsis: A woman is haunted by her past when her sister decides to take legal action against their father for the molestation that took place in her childhood. Two other sisters get involved and a trial ensues. The sisters emerge triumphant in the bittersweet court decision.

Comments: This movie is based on a true story and court case. This is unquestionably the best movie to date dealing with the subject of incest and abuse. There is now a precedent for those who want to take legal action against an abusive parent. A number of courts have been found to be in favor of those who were abused as children and have given judgments to cover the cost of legal fees and therapy. This movie does a superb job of bringing out the kind of abuse that takes place in a home where a parent or parents are physically and/or psychologically abusing the children. Notice how all the children end up having some problems from the abuse—broken marriages, eating problems, sexual dysfunction, sleeping disorders, physical disorders, to name a few. Also notice how the brothers work very hard to keep the family secret and avoid having to deal with their own pain. Keeping the family secret can help hide the pain, but in the long run it will always come to haunt you. So denial is another primary theme in the movie. The father, especially, refuses to see the truth about the family's dysfunction. All the children have locked it away and have also refused to see the truth. Please pay special attention to the mother. Her role in the abuse is very common and so covert that the mother is often overlooked in the abusive family. It is just as abusive to see and know the abuse is taking place and do nothing as it is to be the abuser.

Year: 1993
Length: 100 min
Rating: R
Color

Under the Influence

Healing Themes:

- Living in the chaos of an alcoholic home
- Kicking up memories of an abusive parent
- Trying to make it through your teens with an abusive home life
- Avoiding following in the footsteps of an addictive parent

Cast: Thomas Carter, Andy Griffith, Season Hubley, Paul Provenza, Keanu Reeves, William Schallert, Joyce Van Patten. Director, Thomas Carter. Writer, Joyce Rebeta-Burditt.

Synopsis: An angry man with a wife, children, and a business has a drinking problem. He is often too belligerent for his family to be around him. His drinking puts him in the hospital. It comes full circle when his son follows in his footsteps.

Comments: I think this was one of the first movies of its type to deal with the effects of an alcoholic parent on the family. The individual who wrote the script was herself a recovering alcoholic. It is very apparent that she has tremendous insight; she didn't miss a trick. Notice the erratic behavior on the part of the father. Listen to how punitive he is to his family. Watching the codependency is almost painful, especially from the mother. It is also painful to feel what the family puts up with to live with this man. Notice how the children pick up the characteristics of the father and mother. Denial weaves its way through the movie, especially when the father refuses to give up the alcohol even after ending up in the hospital. If you came from a family where substance abuse was present, *Under the Influence* is going to stir up a lot of feelings. Use the movie as a tool to get out of denial and into self-recovery. By watching the movie you will experience a kind of paradoxical healing. What I mean is by watching what is wrong you can see what not to do in your life. If you are part of a support group you may want to make viewing the movie the focus of one of your meetings. This could also be a chance to bring your family out of denial by inviting them over to watch the movie with you.

Year: 1986
Length: 100 min
Rating: Unrated
Color

Unspeakable Acts

Healing Themes:
- Confronting those who would hurt children
- Getting beyond the lies
- Making sure the children are protected from molestation
- Learning the signs of sexual abuse

Cast: Jill Clayburgh, Brad Davis, Gary Frank, Season Hubley, Valerie Landsburg, Bebe Neuwirth, Gregory Sierra, Terence Knox. Director, Linda Otto. Writers, Alan Landsburg, Hesper Anderson, and Joanne Strauss.

Synopsis: A husband and wife team, Laurie and Joe Braga, child advocates, who lobby for children's rights, are informed of a case of child abuse. The abuse is more widespread than originally reported; they interview the children and the full story comes out.

Comments: Child abuse has become of paramount concern in our country. It is difficult for most of us to imagine that anyone would take advantage of a child in any way, let alone for sexual purposes. This movie opens the door to some of the issues. What is portrayed in this movie is fairly accurate. However, therapists who do the interviewing have been criticized over the last few years with respect to leading the child into saying something that never happened. Listen to the therapists talk to the child. Do the therapists' words lead the child into believing or saying something that didn't really happen? Do the therapists put words in the child's mouth? Some years ago a case made national news involving children in Huntington Beach, California. After months in trial it turned out that the original account was false. Possibly you were abused as a child. Do you still have problems in your life today because of what took place in your childhood? When we push memories such as these deep down inside of us they will emerge in ways that will have a negative effect on our lives: obesity, alcoholism, anorexia, sexual dysfunction, etc. If you are someone who is struggling through the pain and guilt of sexual abuse there are support groups and help available. You may be the parent. You may feel rage and guilt over what happened to your child. Don't keep it inside.

Year: 1990
Length: 100 min
Rating: Unrated
Color

Victims for Victims: The Theresa Saldana Story

Healing Themes:

- When you are stalked by someone
- Dealing with feelings of helplessness
- Recovering and moving on
- Using your misfortune to create a positive result

Cast: Theresa Saldana, Adrian Zmed, Lelia Goldoni, Lawrence Pressman, Linda Carlson, Mariclare Costello. Director, Karen Authur. Writer, Arthur Heinemann.

Synopsis: Theresa is a young actress whose life is suddenly changed when a mentally disturbed fan attacks her. She recovers from some of her wounds, but physical and emotional scars remain. She organizes Victims for Victims to help those who have experienced acts of violence.

Comments: This is a true story. Theresa Saldana not only played the lead but she lived though the nightmare. What courage it must have taken to re-enact her own attack. I heard her talk about the incident. She spoke of the healing she experienced as she went through the pain of working on the project. Theresa almost died from the injuries inflicted upon her by this obsessed fan. Others have died in similar cases. Don't let the fact that this story involves an actress get in the way of understanding that the story is also about stalking. Each year men and women are stalked by people who are emotionally ill, obsessed with another human being or object they feel they have the right to have. (Note: more women are stalked than men.) Some are murdered because the other person will not submit themselves to the stalker's obsessions. *Fatal Attraction* and *Play Misty for Me* will give you some more insight about the stalker. This story also deals with victim's rights. You can almost feel Theresa's frustration as she begins to understand that she remains a victim of the system, the same system she thought would protect her. She experiences rage as she tries to handle her own protection because the system is not doing what she thought it would. Give this movie a try. If you are being stalked you may learn a trick or two about your rights and how to protect yourself. Consider giving some time to organizations such as this one. You will feel a sense of accomplishment in helping those who could use your support.

Year: 1984
Length: 100 min
Rating: Unrated
Color

Wall Street

Healing Themes:
- Getting caught up in greed
- Becoming a work-aholic
- Losing self-respect and/or the respect of a parent or parents
- Regaining dignity by doing the right thing
- Choosing the right role models

Cast: Michael Douglas, Charlie Sheen, Martin Sheen, Darryl Hannah, Sean Young, James Spader, Hal Holbrook, Terence Stamp, Richard Dysart, John C. McGinley. Director, Oliver Stone. Writers, Stanley Wiser and Oliver Stone.

Synopsis: A stockbroker, Bud Fox, makes a big score when he gets the account of high roller, Gordon Gekko. The account comes with some hooks, breaking up the airline where Bud's dad works. Bud stops the takeover but is arrested for illegal trading. Bud regains his dignity by doing the right thing.

Comments: Call it what you will, this is a movie about morality and obsession. I have known people who were willing to do anything to get to the top. Like *The Closer*, they lose sight of what life is all about. Notice how Bud compromises himself little by little, refusing to listen to his father, and loses the morals and ethics that he gained as a child. I can recall being at war with myself on more than one occasion with this dilemma. "Why tell them they gave me too much of a refund on that shirt? They can afford it." "So, they forgot to charge me for the extra work. Well, they wouldn't be honest with me." Sound familiar? Well, hear the big message: I'm honest first for me and second for them. That's when I know I'm being straight with myself; that's what lets me sleep at night. When we sell our souls, we corrupt ourselves and those around us. Notice the young artist. She sends a message about the role of women in business that's quite disconcerting: Ladies, if you want to make it to the top you've got to prostitute yourself. That's a myth. Nothing is worth losing your dignity for. You have to wake up with yourself in the morning. Don't give yourself any reasons to regret the day. Just play it straight and enjoy all that life has to offer.

Year: 1987
Length: 126 min
Rating: R
Color

The War of the Roses

Healing Themes:

- Living in a love-hate relationship
- Taking things too far
- Saying things you'll regret later
- Realizing you can't take it with you
- Ignoring good advice
- Going too far just to win
- Letting greed get the best of you

Cast: Michael Douglas, Kathleen Turner, Danny DeVito, Marianne Sagebrecht. Director, Danny DeVito. Writer, Michael Leeson.

Synopsis: Barbara and Oliver are divorcing but cannot come to agreement about their assets, which include each other. Along the way the children, their businesses, and the relationships with their friends are profoundly affected. Things go too far. Barbara and Oliver become casualties of their own war.

Comments: I think this one should be mandatory viewing for all couples-to-be. I can't begin to tell you how many people have come to see me who could have been the inspiration for this movie. We see what can happen when communication is lost and obsession takes over. Oftentimes relationships like the one in *The War of the Roses* turn violent. One of the important things to see is how the relationship deteriorates over time. It is difficult for people to see how their love was lost to fighting and arguing. Another important point is how these two characters place so much importance on their possessions. That's how they've come to define themselves, by their possessions. This couple used their possessions as a way of avoiding their real feelings. They lost sight of what they were doing, which eventually cost them their lives. We have many cases on record where individuals in a relationship commit murder out of total frustration; they can't live with each other and they can't live without each other. What's a person to do? Learn to let go. Relationships don't fall apart overnight. They won't heal overnight, either. They take a lifetime of work. Use this movie as a model of what not to do in your life. What a great gift to give yourself.

Year: 1989
Length: 116 min
Rating: R
Color

The Way We Were

Healing Themes:

- Bringing back loving memories
- Falling in love with the person of your dreams
- Respecting each other's beliefs
- Going your separate ways

Cast: Barbra Streisand, Robert Redford, Bradford Dillman, Viveka Lindfors, Herb Edelman, Murray Hamilton, Patrick O'Neal, James Woods, Sally Kirkland. Director, Sydney Pollack. Writer, Arthur Laurents.

Synopsis: A man and woman who knew each other in college meet again some years later, fall in love, and marry. They are in love, yet have strong philosophical differences. Their individual beliefs cause them to divorce, though they are still very much in love with each other.

Comments: I've included this movie to help you get in touch with the past and the healing that comes with moving on after losing someone you love. You may be in a very loving relationship today, but that doesn't mean you can't feel the feelings that come with the memories of a lost love. It's okay to experience those feelings with a mate. If you are truly in love, if you are open and supportive, sharing feelings can only bring you closer. Did you get in touch with any emotions over the way she was treated in school? How many of you can acknowledge how different you were then versus now? I remember how I felt being on the outside of the in-group. Today my life is very different. I know I belong and I can choose to be a part of any group that I want to be in. There is also the issue of their difference in the philosophy of life. Can you see what a constant barrier this is for them? This is an area that I find most couples have a very difficult time with. It's important to accept the other person's beliefs. But it's also paramount that you maintain your integrity and not give up your beliefs just to be with the other person. Healthy, nurturing relationships are grounded in mutual respect for each other's philosophies. And as in this case, maintaining your beliefs can come at a very high price.

Year: 1973
Length: 118 min
Rating: PG
Color

What About Bob?

Healing Themes:

- Setting limits
- Living with a neurotic
- Realizing your therapist is human
- Being pushed to the limit

Cast: Richard Dreyfuss, Bill Murray, Julie Hagerty, Charlie Korsmo, Tom Aldredge, Roger Bowen, Fran Brill. Director, Frank Oz. Writer, Tom Schulman.

Synopsis: A newly published, narcissistic psychiatrist has a full psychiatric practice. Bob is a neurotic, so consumed with what he believes to be the doctor's power to cure him that he follows the doctor and his family on their vacation. Bob slowly drives the doctor to seek psychiatric care.

Comments: Well, I think you all deserve a break—everyone, including therapists, counselors, etc. This one's a chance to have a little fun and do some work at the same time. You won't know what hit you. While the movie is an exaggeration of the client/patient/therapist relationship, it does offer us some interesting insights. One of them is the concept of transference and countertransference: The patient puts his or her issues onto the therapist or vice versa. When the issues of the neurotic patient come to the surface, the therapist is forced to look at his own stuff. The better Bob gets, the sicker the therapist becomes. We can also see, in truth, that therapists have their own issues to deal with. These issues often make their way to the surface in therapy. If the therapist is not careful, they will stand in the way of the treatment process. I believe a good therapist is always working on growing as a person. Without personal growth the therapist will eventually stagnate, be unable to reach out to his or her clients. Also note how the family feels about him. They live with this neurotic psychiatrist. They know the truth. The neurotic patient is classic when he shows us problems related to obsessions and compulsions and all the fears and rituals that go with them. There is something to be gained from this humorous perspective of relationships in therapy. We can all use a little humbling. Have fun with this one.

Year: 1991
Length: 99 min
Rating: PG
Color

What's Eating Gilbert Grape

Healing Themes:

- Having to be an adult before your time
- Opening up to a healthy relationship in spite of family obstacles
- Finding that special someone
- If there is nothing to live for but food
- Seeing the prejudice against those with a weight problem

Cast: Juliette Lewis, Johnny Depp, Mary Steenburgen, Leonardo Dicaprio, John C. Reilly. Director, Lasse Hallstrom. Writer, Peter Hedges.

Synopsis: Gilbert Grape, the eldest child, has taken over the responsibility of the family, including a mother who is too obese to leave the house and a retarded brother. He meets a young girl. After some difficulties, they realize they are destined to be with each other.

Comments: This is a movie with a lot of wonderful, healing messages. Notice how Gilbert has become the parent, especially to his brother. Children should not be responsible for taking care of the family. The sexual relationship Gilbert is having with a married woman is not acceptable behavior and, in some ways, he is being molested. There are a number of mixed feelings that will arise relating to the mother. We can all relate to her depression, although it is difficult to forgive her for putting the entire burden of the family onto the children. When the father committed suicide, they were also abandoned by their mother. We get a bird's-eye perspective of how mean people can be to those who suffer from obesity. Watch how the children literally feed her disease the same way people enable an alcoholic. Next, notice how time-consuming it is to take care of someone who is mentally challenged. Feel the frustration and guilt that Gilbert goes through over hitting his retarded brother. Have you ever been behind someone in a wheelchair and been angry at them for being in your way, while feeling guilty at the same time? Finally, do Gilbert's sisters seem lost to you? I'll bet you barely remember them. We heal when we get in touch with feelings that we don't want to deal with. Take a look at what's happening to Gilbert Grape and take a look at yourself at the same time.

Year: 1994
Length: 120 min
Rating: PG
Color

When a Man Loves a Woman

Healing Themes:

- Seeing that an alcoholic has a profound effect on the family
- Sticking with a commitment
- If you grew up in a home where drinking took place
- Working together to solve a problem

Cast: Meg Ryan, Andy Garcia, Laurne Tom, Philip Seymour Hoffman, Tina Mayorino, Mae Whitman, Ellen Burstyn. Director, Rob Reiner. Writer, Nora Ephron.

Synopsis: Alice drinks most of the time and she has forgotten what life is like without alcohol. When her husband confronts her, Alice agrees to go into a treatment center but fights her recovery. Eventually she has to see who she is and what she has done to her family.

Comments: This movie may be the best entry to date to deal with the real issues and emotions that go along with being an alcoholic and their families. No matter who you are or what your issue, you can't help but hear the message: Alcohol and alcoholics have a profound effect on the family. If you grew up in an alcoholic family you will be deeply affected by this movie. Watch Alice's behavior. Does it look at all familiar? Do you see either of your parents in her? How about Michael's codependent behavior? Does that remind you of anyone in your family? If you are recovering from an addiction, you will see the denial in yourself as she looks the other way when it comes to dealing with her own problems. Notice how she hides her alcohol, has to have a drink after work, and can't have a good time unless she drinks. Now that's denial! What I found heart-rending is the process she goes through in her recovery. It's terribly painful to heal the wounds caused by the drinking. And we do not want to overlook the healing that her husband and children have to go through. This movie will spur you forward on your own recovery, whether you have been sober one day or ten years. Maybe it will be your first step towards putting down that drink and calling Alcoholics Anonymous. This movie is a must. Try showing this movie to someone who you think needs to get the message. It can't hurt, that's for sure.

Year: 1994
Length: 126 min
Rating: R
Color

When Harry Met Sally

Healing Themes:

- Learning how to be friends with the opposite sex
- Helping your friends through relationship break-ups
- Finding that love was right under your nose
- Recognizing that life and love have their ups and downs

Cast: Billy Crystal, Meg Ryan, Carrie Fisher, Bruno Kirby, Steven Ford, Lisa Jane Persky, Michelle Nicastro, Harley Kozak. Director, Rob Reiner. Writer, Nora Ephron.

Synopsis: Harry and Sally share a ride from college. He suggests that men and women can't be just friends. She disagrees. Years later they meet and try to become "just friends." The friendship turns into a romance but the relationship becomes strained. On New Year's Eve, they find each other and love prevails.

Comments: Because the movie spans time, it allows you to experience your own memories about lovers and friends through Harry and Sally. One classic moment comes when they deal with the idea that men and women can never be just friends. Have you lost a friendship after you became intimate with her or him? What did you learn from that experience? I think it's important to keep friends and lovers separate. But when the time comes to make a commitment, it is important to be each other's best friend and lover. Is your lover also your best friend? Was there a time when that was the case but somehow the love and friendship slipped away? What are you doing to get that back? Also notice the behavior of their friends. Can you relate to the bonding that takes place between the men and the women? This is a great movie to watch alone or in a group. If you watch it in a group discuss openly your feelings on topics such as male and female friendships and losing old lovers and friends. Maybe this is a chance for you and your significant other to bring back some of the times that brought the two of you together. You will be surprised at the positive influence this movie can have on your relationship. By the way, the idea for meeting at the Empire State Building came from *An Affair to Remember*. You may want to give that one a try along with *Sleepless in Seattle*.

Year: 1989
Length: 95 min
Rating: R
Color

When You Remember Me

Healing Themes:

- Standing up for your rights
- Refusing to accept abuse from a caregiver
- Accepting that your child may need more care than you can give
- Living with your limitations, but doing all that you can do

Cast: Fred Savage, Ellen Burstyn, Kevin Spacey, Richard Jenkins, Dwier Brown, Lee Garlington. Director, Harry Winer. Writers, Jerry McNeely and Cynthia Whitcomb.

Synopsis: After trying to take care of her son at home, a mother makes the decision to place him in a nursing home. He has muscular dystrophy but his mind works just fine. In the nursing home he experiences injustice and degradation. He rallies for patient rights and common decency.

Comments: For those of you who saw *One Flew Over the Cuckoo's Nest*, you will appreciate this movie even more. This is the real thing. I've been in places such as the one depicted in this movie. We have worked hard for patient rights, especially in settings where patients are easily victimized by their caregivers. There are some problems that are important to deal with in this movie that are not so obvious. First, could you give your child up to an institution? I can assure you this decision would not come without a great deal of pain. As parents struggle to deal with a physically or mentally challenged child, they are pushed to the limit. It's a twenty-four-hour-a-day job with no holidays and no relief. The stress is enormous. What about the caregivers? It is hard to imagine they could be abusive to those who cannot defend or take care of themselves. Yet, this is a real problem. (It's also a problem for the elderly who live in convalescent hospitals.) I often wonder about the character of such an individual. Were they abusive and not caring before they got the job or did they become that way because of the type of work they do? Give this movie a try. I believe you will be more compassionate towards those who must live in these environments and towards the parents who have no other choice but to place their children in places such as this one. You may want to watch *Lorenzo's Oil* for a slightly different perspective.

Year: 1990
Length: 100 min
Rating: Unrated
Color

Whore

Healing Themes:

- Selling yourself for sex
- Trying to make it on the streets
- Running away from an abusive home
- Being mistreated by those who say they love you

Cast: Theresa Russell, Benjamin Mouton, Antonio Fargas, Sanjay, Elizabeth Morehead, Michael Crabtree, John Diehl, Jack Nance, Tom Villard, Ginger Lynn Allen. Director, Ken Russell. Writers, Ken Russell and Deborah Dalton.

Synopsis: Liz is a whore who walks the streets at night making her living by selling herself to anyone who can pay her price. She goes from one bad experience to the next. In spite of all her chaotic encounters, Liz continues with the only life she has ever known.

Comments: First, I want to warn you about this movie. There may be some of you who are offended by its contents. Both the language and the sex scenes are quite explicit. In fact, there are several versions of this movie. It was censured for viewing in the United States. The European version is uncut and far more explicit. So...viewer beware. The reason I put this movie in the book is because of the harsh and accurate portrayal of life on the streets. Hundreds of teenagers run away each year hoping to find a happier, more caring existence than the one they have at home. Some are simply looking for excitement. Others are running away from abuse, neglect, or both. This movie gives us, especially women, a look at what street life is really all about. While this movie is explicit and graphic, part of me wishes it would be mandatory viewing for all high school students. I am not going to point out a particular scene that might offer some special message. The whole movie is the message: Stay off the streets and stay in school. If there are family problems, seek counseling before your children run away. If you or your children can't come to terms, seek support from local halfway houses or government regulated foster care programs. The streets should never be a life choice.

Year: 1991
Length: 85 min
Rating: R
Color

The Wild Child

Healing Themes:

- Growing up on your own
- Feeling as if you don't belong
- Being treated like a freak
- Trying to survive in society

Cast: Francois Truffaut, Jean-Pierre Cargol, Jean Daste, Paul Ville. Director, Francois Truffaut.

Synopsis: A French doctor hears of a boy who raised himself in the forest without any human contact. The boy tries to learn from the doctor but is unable to grasp the idea of a civilized world. He is eventually placed in a home where he is destined to live a frustrated and unfulfilling life.

Comments: This is an extraordinary film that shows us the reality of what happens to those who are isolated at birth from other humans. This movie is a true and well-documented story. Unlike the story of Tarzan—who is a myth—this boy displays the results of societal deprivation. Oddly enough, the year this movie was released, a girl (I believe her name is Jeanie) was discovered after being kept locked in a room for ten years. She had no people contact except when she was fed. The repercussions on her development were disastrous. Her life is documented in a film under the same name as this one, *Wild Child*. This movie offers a wonderful opportunity for the therapist to get a close look at this problem. You will be able to observe the behavior of the child and what the researchers went through to understand and communicate with him. In the case of Jeanie, the researchers experienced great difficulties in trying to gain the necessary grant support to work with her. Some of the researchers were chastised for turning Jeanie into a laboratory study instead of treating her like a human being. However, no matter what your background, you will be fascinated with both the film and the documentary. Your heart will go out to both of these most unfortunate human beings. The movie *Nell* deals with the same problems. I would suggest that you add it to your movie list.

Year: 1969 (French)
Length: 85 min
Rating: PG
Color

Wildflower

Healing Themes:

- Reaching out to someone who needs your help
- Growing up in an abusive home
- Finally getting a chance at life
- Breaking the bonds of illiteracy

Cast: Beau Bridges, Susan Blakely, William McNamara, Patricia Arquette, Reese Whitherspoon, Collin Wilcox Paxton. Director, Diane Keaton. Writer, Sara Flanigan.

Synopsis: It's the mid-1930s. Two children sneak onto a property and discover a girl kept in a cage. She is illiterate and suffering from epilepsy. Little by little they begin to educate her behind the backs of her abusive stepfather and submissive mother. The children work to free her from her oppressive stepfather.

Comments: I was very personally touched by this movie. It brought out memories and emotions in me that I had no idea existed. I realized immediately that I had to include this one in my book. There are several issues presented in this movie. Notice the way you feel when you watch the abusive stepfather with his wife and stepdaughter. Maybe you grew up in a home where one of your parents submitted to the whims and demands of the other parent. Did you find yourself getting caught up in the abuse? Now compare the two families: the family of the adolescents who are trying to help versus the abusive family. As you were growing up did you find you became confused about other families and the way they operated when you compared them to your own family? Finally, and this is a difficult feeling to get in touch with, what of the girl being locked up? What about her illiteracy? Possibly you were left behind in school. Maybe you had a learning problem that always made you feel stupid. Or maybe you couldn't keep up with the other kids and you were rejected by them because you didn't get the help and support you needed. When you are done watching the movie, be with your feelings for a while. Don't try to run away from them. Get in touch with your courage and use this child as an inspiration to get beyond the abuse to a healthier place in your life.

Year: 1991
Length: 100 min
Rating: Unrated
Color

The Wizard of Oz

Healing Themes:

- Recognizing you have the ability within you to get what you want
- Listening to your inner self
- Good winning over evil
- Realizing that there is no place like home

Cast: Judy Garland, Margaret Hamilton, Ray Bolger, Jack Haley, Bert Lahr, Frank Morgan, Charley Grapewin, Clara Blandick, Mitchell Lewis, Billie Burke. Director, Victor Fleming. Writers, Edgar Allan Woolf, Noel Langley, and Florence Ryerson.

Synopsis: Dorothy and her dog Toto are carried by tornado to the land of Oz. She journeys to see the Wizard, meeting three unusual characters along the way. When they find out the Wizard is no wizard at all, they all learn the answer to one of life's big questions.

Comments: Frank Baum wrote about a girl who goes on a journey of self-discovery. She is trying to heal herself and fill in the missing piece(s) in her life. I began writing this book with *The Wizard of Oz*. I wrote forty pages. Needless to say there was no way I was going to fit many movies in the book at that rate. So here are a few things to look for, but by all means don't stop looking for more meanings in this movie. Dorothy escaped to a fantasy world to deal with her problems. She is confronted by good and bad witches who are really both sides of her. The good side wants her to find her way through her problems, the bad wants her to fail and not make it down life's "yellow brick road." The dark forest and the poppy fields are her roadblocks. Along the journey she confronts her fears: "Lions and tigers and bears, oh my." Others who go with her to see the Wizard are really parts of Dorothy that she's struggling with in her inner self: her heart, her brain, her courage. The Wizard is just another mortal like a therapist, or minister, or teacher, all of whom are on their own journey in life. She comes to see the way home—the way to healing—was with her all the time. The symbolism in this move is extraordinary. When you watch from that perspective you will appreciate what Baum was trying to convey to us. We are all our own wizards, and Oz is where we are at the moment.

Year: 1939
Length: 93 min
Rating: Unrated
Color/B&W

Woman Under the Influence

Healing Themes:

- If you feel as if you can't take it anymore
- When you can't get the support you need from your spouse
- Searching for the answers to life's questions
- Looking for ways to help your spouse
- Realizing that you're not alone in life

Cast: Peter Falk, Gena Rowlands, Katherine Cassavetes, Lady Rowlands, Fred Draper. Director, John Cassavetes. Writer, John Cassavetes.

Synopsis: A woman feels like the earth is dropping out from under her feet. She doesn't know where to turn. She seeks her husband's support, but he can't seem to be there for her. When all else fails she turns to herself for the answers and resolves her own issues.

Comments: This movie is for everyone, but it is especially for couples, married or otherwise. I don't care who you are or how stable you think you are, at some time in each of our lives we experience some down times or depression, moments when we feel as if we can't or don't want to go on. There is no way of truly predicting those moments. The problem is how do we prepare ourselves for those times? How does the partner of a person going through a depression prepare for the experience? *Woman Under the Influence* can open the door to understanding this kind of relationship dilemma. As you can see, her husband has no idea what it is like to reach out to his wife to give her the support she so desperately needs. Listen to him try to push her into coming around and being the woman that he wants her to be. You will also gain some insight by looking at some of his body and facial expressions. This is what I call "body oozing." When messages like those are sent they create a lot of confusion and have nothing to do with a caring, healthy relationship. If you are having trouble coping with a life experience that your mate is going through, watch this movie. Learn to be loving, compassionate, and patient, not condemning and judgmental. There will come a time when you will need the same compassion and understanding. Sit down as a couple and give this movie a chance to teach you a few things. You will grow in the process.

Year: 1974
Length: 155 min
Rating: R
Color

A Woman's Tale

Healing Themes:
- Getting control over your life
- Never giving up your dignity
- Confronting your fears of dying
- Standing up tall
- Growing old gracefully

Cast: Sheila Florance, Gosia Dobrowolska, Norman Kaye, Chris Haywood, Ernest Gray, Myrtle Woods, Bruce Myles, Alex Menglet. Director, Paul Cox. Writer, Paul Cox.

Synopsis: Martha, a seventy-eight-year-old woman, is suffering from cancer. Wishing to leaving this earth with dignity and pride she struggles with the process of dying and how her life will end. With great effort Martha maintains her dignity in spite of the efforts of her son to put her in a nursing home.

Comments: *A Woman's Tale* is one of just a few I was able to find that deals with issues relating to the elderly. *The Trip to Bountiful* is another movie with a similar theme. Here we see a woman's struggle to maintain her dignity in her old age. You can see Martha's emotional turmoil and pain as she knows she doesn't have much time left. She deals with the harsh realities that come with cancer and at the same time the feelings that arise from knowing she doesn't have the control over her life she once thought she had. Listen to the way people deal with her now that they know she is dying. They seem to dance around Martha and her illness in an attempt to deal with their own awkwardness. How does it make you feel when you listen to them talk to her? What did you learn from watching their behavior? And what of the reality behind death and dying? There is an emotionally healthy way to die and a painful, unhealthy way to die. If we accept that we all must die, we can learn to be emotionally prepared for the process when it happens. After watching this film I think you will be a better person for taking the time to deal with this most difficult issue. You may find that along the way you gain some compassion and respect for the elderly and all that they must feel and endure.

Year: 1991
Length: 93 min
Rating: PG-13
Color

The Women of Brewster Place

Healing Themes:

- Breaking through barriers in your life
- When your children turn their backs on you
- Coping with people who can't accept your sexual orientation
- If you have lost a child
- Fighting your way back from depression
- Picking yourself up and starting all over again

Cast: Oprah Winfrey, Mary Alice, Olivia Cole, Robin Givens, Moses Gunn, Jackée, Paula Kelly, Lonette McKee, Barbara Montgomery, Phyllis Yvonne Stickney, Paul Winfield, William Allen Young, Cicely Tyson. Director, Donna Deitch. Writer, Karen Hall.

Synopsis: In a low rent district outside of New York, Matty raises her illegitimate child who ends up abandoning her. Matty gains strength by helping her neighbors, then decides she will fight against the walls that have held her back, breaking them down forever.

Comments: Looking back at my own life, I'm amazed at what I've done and what I've been through. I have run into some of the same walls as Matty, but somehow I dug deep inside and captured the courage to get the job done. And isn't that what Matty teaches us? She reminds us that we have to use our courage to keep going no matter what happens. What walls stand between you and your dreams? Maybe your wall is fear or guilt or regret. Work towards destroying those walls and moving forward with your life. There are many healing stories in this movie. You can learn that there is life after losing a child. Maybe you have felt betrayed or abandoned by your own children. Possibly you're in a relationship where your partner is here today and gone tomorrow. Matty reminds all of us to keep going. Like *The Joy Luck Club, Eating,* and *Chantilly Lace, The Women of Brewster Place* reminds us that when women come together they can gain a special bond that gives them courage. Make this a movie for the whole family. Afterwards begin the process of taking down the walls in your life, one brick at a time.

Year: 1989
Length: 180 min
Rating: R
Color

Women on the Verge of a Nervous Breakdown

Healing Themes:

- Understanding how you got to where you are in life
- Trying to hang on to your sanity
- Learning to cope with life's pressures
- Living in a non-supportive relationship

Cast: Carmen Marua, Antonio Banderas, Julieta Serrano, Maria Barranco, Rossy De Palma. Director, Pedro Almodovar. Writer, Pedro Almodovar.

Synopsis: Marua, an actress, learns that her lover of many years has abandoned her. She feels as if she is going crazy. She looks to her friends for support. Marua begins to realize that her friends are no more stable than she and becomes more frustrated than ever.

Comments: This movie has a lot to offer women, especially those who are dealing with a crisis. When crisis and chaos hit in Marua's life, she goes on a journey of self-discovery and healing. One of my favorite concepts in this movie is that those around us aren't as together as we may think they are. Everyone's got problems at different times in their lives. In addition, those who we thought were not together suddenly look pretty stable. In either case it can take a crisis to gain that understanding. In times of crisis, don't go to your family and friends for advice; go to them for emotional support. Look for people who will sit and listen, will let you bend their ear, and will offer you a hug. Think about it. If they're not stable, how can they help you? Even worse, if they offer you advice and you take it, who will be responsible when the advice does not work out? In the movie, notice how this once beloved boyfriend falls from grace. How could he be so good one moment and such a jerk the next? Life consists of transitions and growth, and part of the process is accepting other people's life choices. Beating people up, verbally or physically, because you cannot accept their life choice has no value. It's important to let them be free to make their own choices. This is a great movie to watch with a group of your friends and some popcorn. Healing happens when we get honest with ourselves and with those around us.

Year: 1988 (Spanish)
Length: 88 min
Rating: R
Color

Working Girl

Healing Themes:

- Going for the brass ring
- Becoming everything you can be
- When you feel as though you are being treated like an object
- Hanging in there when someone tries to steal your fire
- Meeting someone who respects you for who you are

Cast: Melanie Griffith, Harrison Ford, Sigourney Weaver, Joan Cusack, Alec Baldwin, Philip Bosco, Ricki Lake, Nora Dunn, Olympia Dukakis, Oliver Platt. Director, Mike Nichols. Writer, Kenin Wade.

Synopsis: Tess McGill, is bright, but because she is a secretary she is overlooked. Her boss, Katharine, has an accident. Tess puts together a deal with Jack, only to have it backfire when her boss returns. Tess maneuvers around her boss's lies and makes it to her dream.

Comments: We have several good messages in this movie that are worth looking at by both men and women. We have created a few stereotypes about women that are simply not true. Blonds are just as smart as everyone else and men and women are equally as intelligent and capable. Now let's look at the idea of hanging in there. That message is very strong in this movie. We have an opportunity to learn that when someone says "no," what that really means is "no" from that person's point of view. You must learn to hear the messages for what they are or life will be a quick series of shutdowns before you ever get started. Listen to the lies that take place. Some people live by those lies. When someone lies, they're giving you a message, telling you not to trust them. There's no need to learn that lesson more than once. What about the affair Tess catches her boyfriend in? An affair is never acceptable and there's no excuse for having one. If you're unhappy with your relationship, having an affair is not the answer. Honesty and communication will solve the problem. Our working girl handles the problem correctly. She boots him out of her life. Notice the way that affair creates space for her to let someone who is healthy and supportive into her life. Growth comes when you let life's messages in, learn to listen to your intuition, and trust in yourself. That's healing.

Year: 1988
Length: 115 min
Rating: R
Color

PART TWO

Using Movies In Therapy

USING MOVIES IN THERAPY

Watching movies with consciousness can reveal our underlying pain to help us heal and find our joy and wholeness.

—Wayne Kritsberg

If you are a therapist, counselor, educator, or minister, you can use *The Motion Picture Prescription* to help those with whom you are working on their healing journey. For the first time you have at your fingertips a comprehensive list of movies to help your patients and clients. Each movie brings to the surface one or more issues to help you with your clients' recovery.

When I started writing this book some years ago I had the idea of including the diagnostic presentation portrayed through the characterizations made by the actors. For instance, when I wrote about *Sybil* and *The Three Faces of Eve*, I placed my original therapeutic focus on presentation of multiple personality disorder. In the case of *Mr. Jones* and *Sophie's Choice*, I directed my analysis towards manic depression, substance abuse, and the potential for general medical conditions. The overall tone of these movies excluded the lay person; they leaned away from the wonderful healing messages the movies had to offer.

The Benefits of Movie Therapy

Today the focus of my work affords the general public and the therapeutic community at large an opportunity to utilize all the movies as healing tools. But while the book is written for the general population, as treatment facilitators you now have an additional therapeutic device to use as a springboard for treating your patients and clients. Additionally, all the movies can act as an excellent teaching tool for

223

students and therapists to identify a wide range of diagnostic problems. With some two hundred movies at your disposal and more on the way, you will find diagnostic conditions ranging from substance abuse, depression, and character disorders, to autism and schizophrenia. I have also included movies dealing with problems relating to AIDS, adoption, abortion, death and dying, and much, much more.

I have no doubt that most of you use movies in your practice. I know I have experienced a tremendous amount of success in treating clients and patients using the movies you will find in my book. Of the therapists I have worked with and others whom I have talked to about my book, all of them agreed that having a comprehensive list of movies dealing with therapeutic problems is a positive addition to the body of work in the area of client treatment. In speaking with therapists about their use of movies as a form of therapeutic intervention I found that all of them had their favorite movies to help them deal with various patient/client problems. For the most part, however, their list of movies was not documented. Whenever they believed a movie would be helpful in treating their clients they simply pulled the movies off the top of their head. Well, here's a tool for all of us to use with our clients.

If you are in private practice you can use *The Motion Picture Prescription* as a handy and easy-to-use reference tool to quickly identify those problems you're treating in your clients. If you oversee support groups and therapy-based treatment groups, I would suggest you use the movies as a vehicle to open up the group to dialogue about anything from relationships and family issues to abortion, adoption, and homosexuality. This is also true for hospitals, treatment centers, and halfway houses. The movies make an excellent entree into issues of addiction, sexual abuse, and abandonment. For those of you who are specializing in jail and prison treatment, there are numerous movies appropriate for your setting. If you are an educator I would strongly suggest using movies to reach those children, adolescents, and young adults who you find have difficulty opening up. Movies such as *Sid and Nancy, Drugstore Cowboy, Less Than Zero, Benny and Joon,* and *St. Elmo's Fire,* to name but a few, can pry open the doors to issues that young people have trouble communicating about and otherwise turn their backs on.

You can effectively use movies for individuals, couples, families, and group work. Movies such as *The Wizard of Oz* and *Field of Dreams* can reach those who are feeling stuck and can't seem to move on with their life. *Ultimate Betrayal, Men Don't Tell,* and *Prince of Tides* address issues of rape and abuse while *Sarah T: Portrait of a Teenage Alcoholic, The Boost,* and *Bright Lights, Big City* can bring your clients out of their denial over drugs and alcohol.

I have worked to create a list of movies that includes all the issues we might uncover while working with our clients. *The Big Chill, Over Forty,* and *Same Time Next Year* are all great for growth and maturity issues in individuals, couples, and groups, while *Beaches, The Trip to Bountiful,* and *Terms of Endearment* lead our clients through life's transitions all the way to death and dying. And *Ordinary People* and *Parenthood* help deal with family treatment issues. All of the movies I have embraced look at the issues from both the male and female perspectives.

Tips for Therapists for Using Movies with Your Clients

• If you are just getting started with a client, wait a few sessions before introducing movies as a form of therapeutic intervention. Your clients need to feel comfortable and confident in you before they can let you in. You don't want to miss any of their reactions to the movies because you have moved too quickly. They may feel like they're just not ready to let you into the part of their life that the movies may bring to the surface.

• Try not to recommend too many movies at one time. If you're seeing a client once per week, I would recommend that you prescribe one or two, but certainly no more then three at a time. If you over-prescribe the number of movies for them to watch, they may become overwhelmed with the assignment, which could be a set-up for failure.

• Be sure the movie(s) you prescribe is appropriate for the client. If you are not familiar with a particular movie you're prescribing, read the movie synopsis and comments sections first. If you send them down a false path they may feel as if you're not really in touch with their issues. Be careful not to prescribe a movie if a client is not ready to deal with the issue. Movies such as *Closet Land* and *Fatal Attraction* may cause them to have a reaction they're not prepared to handle.

• Be patient if they don't or can't follow through with watching the movie. There can be some fear tied to seeing the movies because of the subject matter and because of the feelings the movie might bring to the surface. It may take prescribing a movie two or three times before they're ready to give it a try.

• Be sure to follow up with some questions about the movies during the next few sessions. If you don't mention anything they may feel as if you don't really care or that prescribing the movie had no value.

• Ask them to keep a journal of their thoughts and feelings about the movie. You will find that their responses to the movies will open up the doors to some client communications you may never have thought possible.

• In some cases, recommend that they see the movie with a spouse, friend, family member, or a group. Ask them to give you some feedback about their feelings and the feelings of the people with whom they saw the movie.

• The most important thing of all is that you enjoy the healing process along with your client. Have fun with the movies and take the journey with your clients. If your clients feel as if you're involved, you can experience some dynamic progress.

• One final note, to assist in prescribing the movies I have included two easy-to-use prescription forms: a motion picture prescription pad and a motion picture prescription list. Both of these tools will make prescribing movies a professional way to treat your clients.

MOTION PICTURE PRESCRIPTION LIST

Therapist: _____ **Date:** _____

Client(s):_____

I would like you to watch the follow movie(s) by _____

About Last Night _____
Accidental Tourist _____
Accused _____
Adam _____
Alice in Wonderland _____
Alien _____
All That Jazz _____
An Affair to Remember _____
Baby Boom _____
Baby M _____
Barfly _____
Beaches _____
Benny and Joon _____
Big _____
Big Chill _____
Boost _____
Boy With Green Hair _____
Boys in the Band _____
Breakfast Club _____
Bright Lights, Big City _____
Broadcast News _____
Burning Bed _____
Call Me Anna _____
Carnal Knowledge _____
Chantilly Lace _____
Child's Cry for Help _____
Christmas Carol _____
Clean and Sober _____
Closer _____
Closet Land _____
Color Purple _____

Come Fill the Cup _____
Cries From the Heart _____
Crimes of the Heart _____
Cry for Help: The Tracey
　　Thurman Story _____
Dad _____
Damage _____
Dante's Inferno _____
Darkness Before Dawn _____
David's Mother _____
Days of Wine and Roses _____
Dead Poets Society _____
Defending Your Life _____
Dialogues With Madwomen _____
Do You Know the Muffin
　　Man? _____
Doctor _____
Dollmaker _____
Dr. Jekyll and Mr. Hyde _____
Drop Dead Fred _____
Drugstore Cowboy _____
Duet for One _____
Dying Young _____
Eating _____
Enchantment _____
Extremities _____
Face to Face _____
Falling Down _____
Family of Strangers _____
Fatal Attraction _____
Father of the Bride _____

Fear Inside ____
Ferris Bueller's Day Off ____
Field of Dreams ____
Fisher King ____
Flat Liners ____
For the Love of Nancy ____
Forrest Gump ____
Four Seasons ____
Frances ____
Gambler ____
Gathering ____
Ghost ____
Good Mother ____
Grand Canyon ____
Great Santin ____
Great Sinner ____
Guess Who's Coming to
    Dinner ____
Harvey ____
He Said, She Said ____
Hellraiser ____
Hot Spell ____
I Know My First Name
    Is Steven ____
I Never Sang for My
    Father ____
I'm Dancing as Fast as I Can ____
Immediate Family ____
In the Best Interest of the
    Child ____
Ironweed ____
It's a Wonderful Life ____
Jason's Lyric ____
Jo Jo Dancer, Your Life Is
    Calling ____
Joy Luck Club ____
Jungle Fever ____
Karen Carpenter Story ____
Kate's Secret ____
Kramer vs. Kramer ____

Lady Sings the Blues ____
Less Than Zero ____
Life of the Party:
    The Story of Beatrice ____
Long Way Home ____
Longest Runner ____
Looking for Mister Goodbar ____
Lost Weekend ____
M.A.D.D.: Mothers Against
    Drunk Driving ____
Made in Heaven ____
Man with the Golden Arm ____
Man Without a Face ____
Memories of Me ____
Memory of Us ____
Men Don't Tell ____
Men's Club ____
Miracle Worker ____
Mission ____
Mommie Dearest ____
Morning After ____
Mr. Destiny ____
Mr. Jones ____
My Breast ____
My Name Is Bill W ____
Naked Lunch ____
'Night, Mother ____
9 1/2 Weeks ____
Not My Kid ____
Nuts ____
Nutty Professor ____
On Golden Pond ____
One Flew Over the Cuckoo's
    Nest ____
Ordinary People ____
Our Very Own ____
Over Forty ____
Parenthood ____
Paris Is Burning ____
Philadelphia ____

Picture of Dorian Gray ____
Play Misty for Me ____
Postcards From the Edge ____
Pretty in Pink ____
Pretty Woman ____
Prince of Tides ____
Radio Flyer ____
Rain Man ____
Rape and Marriage: The Rideout
    Case ____
Rape of Richard Beck ____
Rapture ____
Regarding Henry ____
Rocket Gibraltar ____
Rocky ____
Roe vs. Wade ____
Ryan White Story ____
Same Time Next Year ____
Sarah T: Portrait of a Teenage
    Alcoholic ____
Secret Life of Walter Mitty ____
She Said No ____
Shirley Valentine ____
Sid and Nancy ____
Silence of the Lambs ____
Six Weeks ____
Sleeping with the Enemy ____
Sleepless in Seatle ____
Something About Amelia ____
Sophie's Choice ____
St. Elmo's Fire ____
Stanley and Iris ____
Star Wars ____
Steel Magnolias ____
Stella ____
Stranger in the Family ____
Summer of '42 ____
Sybil ____

Taking Back My Life:
    The Nancy Ziegenmeyer
    Story ____
Tales of Manhattan ____
Terms of Endearment ____
That's Life ____
Thelma and Louise ____
This Boy's Life ____
Three Faces of Eve ____
To Kill a Mockingbird ____
Torch Song Trilogy ____
Toughlove ____
Trip to Bountiful ____
Ultimate Betrayal ____
Under the Influence ____
Unspeakable Acts ____
Victims for Victims:
    Theresa Saldana Story ____
Wall Street ____
War of the Roses ____
Way We Were ____
What About Bob? ____
What's Eating Gilbert Grape ___
When a Man Loves a Woman ___
When Harry Met Sally ____
When You Remember Me ____
Whore ____
Wild Child ____
Wildflower ____
Wizard of Oz ____
Woman Under the Influence ____
Woman's Tale ____
Women of Brewster Place ____
Women on the Verge of a
    Nervous Breakdown ____
Working Girl ____

MOTION PICTURE PRESCRIPTION PADS

Here are two motion picture prescription pads. I would suggest you use them as follows: Make copies and create a pad of blank prescriptions. Next, fill out the prescription pads for your clients, giving them the name of the movie you want them to watch or attaching the master movie prescription list. Finally, give the prescription to your clients as an assignment in their treatment. I'm sure you will find this approach to be an effective way to help them on their healing journey.

Motion Picture Prescription

Date _____

Name _____

Watch the movies listed below
by your next appointment: _____

1. _____

2. _____

3. _____

Prescribed by _____

Motion Picture Prescription

Date _____

Name _____

Watch the movies listed below
by your next appointment: _____

1. _____

2. _____

3. _____

Prescribed by _____

Note: Author authorizes duplication of this page of *The Motion Picture Prescription* book.

GLOSSARY

Abandonment. Issues relating to the desertion of an individual, couple, or family, in either the emotional or physical sense.

Abuse. Physical, verbal, emotional, or psychological mistreatment to others or to the self, including the use of drugs, alcohol, food, smoking, gambling, etc.

Adoption. Taking responsibility for raising a child or young person as one's own.

Alcohol. A chemical compound that, when ingested, causes the brain to respond to its intoxicating effects, making it a mind-altering drug. Misusing alcohol may lead to one being an alcoholic who suffers from alcoholism. [Also see Drugs.]

Boundary(ies). A limit or line where one limit or boundary ends and another begins, as in space and interactions between people.

Codependency. The dysfunctional or malfunctional relationship that individuals may have with others; how they feel or act in the world as a function of how someone else feels or acts to the point of being unhealthy.

Death/Dying. The end of life as we know it, including the emotional issues associated with death: grief, loss, fear, abandonment, and life after death.

Denial. Choosing not to see or feel an experience; the conscious and\or unconscious act of avoiding truth or reality.

Drugs. Substances such as cocaine, heroin, marijuana, speed, crank, crack, uppers, downers, etc., which may be of legal or illegal nature and are used to alter the state of one's consciousness. [Also see Alcohol.]

Dysfunction/Malfunction. Abnormal or impaired behavior; behavior that is socially unacceptable or outside social norms.

Enable. To give power or authority; to empower. Paradoxically, keeping someone from being accountable for their actions.

Family. Anyone related to someone else through marriage, birth, or friendship, as in "A family of man," or, "She's lived with us for years. She's like family."

Gambling. The act of placing a wager or bet in anticipation of gaining a return greater than the original wager.

Healing. To make sound, well, or healthy again; to cure or get rid of a disease. Becoming emotionally self-aware on the road to recovery.

Inspiration. Something that motivates one to move in one direction or another.

Mental/Emotional Illness. As used in this book, major or minor psychological or emotional disorders, personality disorders, character disorders, etc.

Recovery. The return to consciousness; the regaining of balance, control, and composure. The ultimate goal in the process of self-healing.

Relationships. A sense of connection with one or more people either as friends, family, or intimate partner.

Sex/Sexuality. One's gender, male or female, or an act of sex such as intercourse, oral sex, etc. Sexuality is the interest in or concern with sex; sexual drive or activity.

Therapists. A large group of people who practice the discipline of administering therapy; psychiatrists, psychoanalysts, psychotherapists, or counselors.

Index

Abandonment: Accused; An Affair to Remember; Baby Boom; Beaches; Big; Boy With Green Hair; Rape of Richard Beck; Call Me Anna; Closer; Color Purple; Cries From the Heart; Darkness Before Dawn; David's Mother; Dead Poets Society; Doctor; Drop Dead Fred; Drugstore Cowboy; Eating; Falling Down; Family of Strangers; Field of Dreams; Fisher King; Flat Liners; Forrest Gump; Four Seasons; Gathering; Grand Canyon; Hot Spell; I Know My First Name Is Steven; I Never Sang for My Father; In the Best Interest of the Child; It's a Wonderful Life; Jason's Lyric; Jungle Fever; Karen Carpenter Story; Kramer v. Kramer; Life of the Party: The Story of Beatrice; Long Way Home; Looking for Mister Goodbar; Memories of Me; Mommie Dearest; Mr. Jones; My Breast; Nuts; Ordinary People; Our Very Own; Philadelphia; Postcards From the Edge; Pretty in Pink; Prince of Tides; Radio Flyer; Rain Man; Regarding Henry; Ryan White Story; She Said No; Shirley Valentine; Six Weeks; Sophie's Choice; Stanley and Iris; Stella; Sybil; Tales of Manhattan; This Boy's Life; To Kill a Mockingbird; Under the Influence; War of the Roses; Whore; Wildflower; Wizard of Oz; Women of Brewster Place; Women on the Verge of a Nervous Breakdown; Working Girl

Abuse: Accused; All That Jazz; Boost; Burning Bed; Call Me Anna; Christmas Carol; Closet Land; Color Purple; Cry for Help: The Tracey Thurman Story; Damage; Days of Wine and Roses; Do you Know the Muffin Man?; Dr. Jekyll and Mr. Hyde; Enchantment; Extremities; Falling Down; Family of Strangers; Fear Inside; Frances; Great Santini; Hellraiser; Hot Spell; I Know My First Name Is Steven; Jason's Lyric; Jo Jo Dancer, Your Life Is Calling; Jungle Fever; Karen Carpenter Story; Lady Sings the Blues; Less Than Zero; Longest Runner; Looking for Mister Goodbar; Men Don't Tell; Mission; Mommie Dearest; Morning After; Mr. Jones; Naked Lunch; 9 1/2 Weeks; Not My Kid; Nuts; On Golden Pond; One Flew Over the Cuckoo's Nest; Ordinary People; Play Misty for Me; Prince of Tides; Radio Flyer; Rape and Marriage: The Rideout Case; Rape of Richard Beck; Ryan White Story; She Said No; Sid and Nancy; Silence of the Lambs; Sleeping With the Enemy; Something About Amelia; Sophie's Choice; Summer of '42; Sybil; Taking Back My Life: The Nancy Ziegenmeyer Story; Tales of Manhattan; Thelma and Louise; This Boy's Life; Ultimate Betrayal; Under the Influence; Unspeakable Acts; Victims for Victims: The

Theresa Saldana Story; Wall Street; War of the Roses; What's Eating Gilbert Grape; Whore; Wildflower

Adoption: Baby Boom; Baby M; Color Purple; Family of Strangers; Immediate Family; In the Best Interest of the Child; Kramer vs. Kramer; Long Way Home; Our Very Own; Radio Flyer

Alcohol: Accused; All That Jazz; Barfly; Boost; Bright Lights, Big City; Call Me Anna; Carnal Knowledge; Clean and Sober; Color Purple; Come Fill the Cup; Darkness Before Dawn; Days of Wine and Roses; Drugstore Cowboy; Family of Strangers; Fisher King; Frances; Harvey; Hot Spell; In the Best Interest of the Child; Ironweed; Jason's Lyric; Jo Jo Dancer, Your Life Is Calling; Jungle Fever; Lady Sings the Blues; Less Than Zero; Life of the Party: The Story of Beatrice; Looking for Mister Goodbar; Lost Weekend; M.A.D.D.: Mothers Against Drunk Driving; Man With the Golden Arm; Men Don't Tell; Morning After; My Name Is Bill W.; Naked Lunch; Not My Kid; Postcards From the Edge; Prince of Tides; Rapture; Sarah T: Portrait of a Teenage Alcoholic; Sid and Nancy; Sophie's Choice; St. Elmo's Fire; Stella; Sybil; Tales of Manhattan; Terms of Endearment; Thelma and Louise; This Boy's Life; Toughlove; Ultimate Betrayal; Under the Influence; When a Man Loves a Woman; Whore

Codependency: Accidental Tourist; All That Jazz; Barfly; Benny and Joon; Boost; Bright Lights, Big City; Burning Bed; Call Me Anna; Carnal Knowledge; Clean and Sober; Closer; Cry for Help: The Tracey Thurman Story; Damage; Darkness Before Dawn; Days of Wine and Roses; Drop Dead Fred; Drugstore Cowboy; Eating; Family of Strangers; Fatal Attraction; Fisher King; For the Love of Nancy; Four Seasons; Frances; Gambler; Gathering; Great Santini; Great Sinner; Harvey; Hellraiser; Hot Spell; Jason's Lyric; Jo Jo Dancer, Your Life Is Calling; Jungle Fever; Kate's Story; Lady Sings the Blues; Less Than Zero; Lost Weekend; Made in Heaven; Man With the Golden Arm; Men Don't Tell; Men's Club; Miracle Worker; Naked Lunch; 'Night, Mother; 9 1/2 Weeks; Not My Kid; Nuts; On Golden Pond; Ordinary People; Our Very Own; Parenthood; Play Misty for Me; Pretty in Pink; Prince of Tides; Radio Flyer; Rapture; Sarah T: Portrait of a Teenage Alcoholic; Sid and Nancy; Something About Amelia; Sophie's Choice; St. Elmo's Fire; Stanley and Iris; Stella; That's Life; Three Faces of Eve; Toughlove; Ultimate Betrayal; Under the Influence; War of the Roses; What About Bob?; What's Eating Gilbert Grape; When a Man

Loves a Woman; Wildflower; Wizard of Oz; Women of Brewster Place; Working Girl

Death/Dying: Accidental Tourist; Adam; Alien; All That Jazz; Beaches; Big Chill; Chantilly Lace; Closer; Color Purple; Crimes of the Heart; Dad; Damage; Dante's Inferno; Dead Poets Society; Defending Your Life; Doctor; Dollmaker; Duet for One; Drugstore Cowboy; Dying Young; Family of Strangers; Field of Dreams; Flat Liners; Ghost; Forrest Gump; Hot Spell; I Never Sang for My Father; It's a Wonderful Life; Jason's Lyric; Joy Luck Club; Jungle Fever; Karen Carpenter Story; Lady Sings the Blues; Long Way Home; M.A.D.D.: Mothers Against Drunk Driving; Made in Heaven; Mission; 'Night, Mother; Ordinary People; Philadelphia; Rain Man; Rocket Gibraltar; Ryan White Story; Sid and Nancy; Six Weeks; Sleepless in Seattle; Sophie's Choice; Steel Magnolias; Summer of '42; Tales of Manhattan; Terms of Endearment; That's Life; Three Faces of Eve; Torch Song Trilogy; Trip to Bountiful; War of the Roses; Woman's Tale; Women of Brewster Place

Denial: About Last Night; Accidental Tourist; Alien; All That Jazz; Bright Lights, Big City; Broadcast News; Call Me Anna; Carnal Knowledge; Clean and Sober; Closet Land; Color Purple; Come Fill the Cup; Cries From the Heart; Cry for Help: The Tracey Thurman Story; Damage; Darkness Before Dawn; Days of Wine and Roses; Defending Your Life; Do You Know the Muffin Man?; Dr. Jekyll and Mr. Hyde; Drop Dead Fred; Drugstore Cowboy; Dying Young; Eating; Face to Face; Falling Down; Fatal Attraction; Fisher King; Flat Liners; For the Love of Nancy; Four Seasons; Frances; Gambler; Gathering; Grand Canyon; Great Santini; Great Sinner; Guess Who's Coming to Dinner; Harvey; Hellraiser; Hot Spell; I Know My First Name Is Steven; I Never Sang for My Father; Immediate Family; Jason's Lyric; Jo Jo Dancer, Your Life Is Calling; Jungle Fever; Karen Carpenter Story; Kate's Secret; Lady Sings the Blues; Less Than Zero; Lost Weekend; M.A.D.D.: Mothers Against Drunk Driving; Made in Heaven; Man With the Golden Arm; Memories of Me; Men Don't Tell; Men's Club; Mission; Mommie Dearest; Mr. Jones; My Breast; My Name Is Bill W.; Naked Lunch; 'Night, Mother; 9 1/2 Weeks; Not My Kid; Nuts; On Golden Pond; One Flew Over the Cuckoo's Nest; Ordinary People; Parenthood; Picture of Dorian Gray; Play Misty for Me; Postcards From the Edge; Pretty in Pink; Prince of Tides; Rain Man; Rape and Marriage: The Rideout Case; Rapture; Sarah T: Portrait of a Teenage Alcoholic;

Shirley Valentine; Something About Amelia; Sophie's Choice; St. Elmo's Fire; Steel Magnolias; Stella; Stranger in the Family; Tales of Manhattan; Terms of Endearment; That's Life; This Boy's Life; To Kill a Mockingbird; Toughlove; Ultimate Betrayal; Under the Influence; Wall Street; War of the Roses; What About Bob?; What's Eating Gilbert Grape; When a Man Loves a Woman; Whore; Wildflower; Wizard of Oz; Woman Under the Influence; Women of Brewster Place

Divorce: Accidental Tourist; An Affair to Remember; Call Me Anna; Carnal Knowledge; Damage; David's Mother; Falling Down; Good Mother; Kramer vs. Kramer; Prince of Tides; Shirley Valentine; Tales of Manhattan; War of the Roses; Way We Were

Drugs: All that Jazz; Boost; Breakfast Club; Bright Lights, Big City; Call Me Anna; Clean and Sober; Closer; Color Purple; Darkness Before Dawn; Dr. Jekyll and Mr. Hyde; Drugstore Cowboy; Fisher King; Frances; I'm Dancing as Fast as I Can; In the Best Interest of the Child; Jason's Lyric; Jo Jo Dancer, Your Life Is Calling; Jungle Fever; Lady Sings the Blues; Less Than Zero; Life of the Party: The Story of Beatrice; Looking for Mr. Goodbar; Naked Lunch; Not My Kid; Nutty Professor; Postcards from the Edge; Sid and Nancy; Toughlove; Whore; Wizard of Oz

Family: Accidental Tourist; Adam; All That Jazz; Baby Boom; Baby M; Beaches; Benny and Joon; Big; Boost; Boy With Green Hair; Broadcast News; Burning Bed; Call Me Anna; Christmas Carol; Clean and Sober; Closer; Color Purple; Cries From the Heart; Crimes of the Heart; Dad; Damage; Darkness Before Dawn; David's Mother; Days of Wine and Roses; Dead Poets Society; Do you Know the Muffin Man?; Doctor; Dollmaker; Drop Dead Fred; Eating; Enchantment; Falling Down; Family of Strangers; Fatal Attraction; Father of the Bride; For the Love of Nancy; Forrest Gump; Frances; Gathering; Grand Canyon; Great Santini; Guess Who's Coming to Dinner; Harvey; Hot Spell; I Know My First Name Is Steven; I Never Sang for My Father; I'm Dancing as Fast as I Can; Immediate Family; In the Best Interest of the Child; It's a Wonderful Life; Jason's Lyric; Joy Luck Club; Jungle Fever; Karen Carpenter Story; Kate's Story; Kramer vs. Kramer; Long Way Home; Longest Runner; Lost Weekend; M.A.D.D.: Mothers Against Drunk Driving; Made in Heaven; Memories of Me; Memory of Us; Men Don't Tell; Men's Club; Miracle Worker; Mission; Mommie Dearest; Mr. Destiny; My Name Is Bill W.; 'Night, Mother; Not My

Kid; Nuts; On Golden Pond; Our Very Own; Parenthood; Postcards From the Edge; Pretty in Pink; Prince of Tides; Radio Flyer; Rain Man; Rape and Marriage: The Rideout Case; Regarding Henry; Rocket Gibraltar; Ryan White Story; Sarah T: Portrait of a Teenage Alcoholic; Sid and Nancy; Six Weeks; Sleepless in Seattle; Something About Amelia; Sophie's Choice; St. Elmo's Fire; Stanley and Iris; Steel Magnolias; Stella; Stranger in the Family; Sybil; Taking Back My Life: The Nancy Ziegenmeyer Story; Tales of Manhattan; Terms of Endearment; That's Life; This Boy's Life; Three Faces of Eve; To Kill a Mockingbird; Toughlove; Trip to Bountiful; Unspeakable Acts; Ultimate Betrayal; Under the Influence; War of the Roses; What About Bob?; What's Eating Gilbert Grape; When a Man Loves a Woman; When Harry Met Sally; When You Remember Me; Wildflower; Wizard of Oz; Woman Under the Influence; Woman's Tale; Women of Brewster Place; Women on the Verge of a Nervous Breakdown

Food: Eating; For the Love of Nancy; Hot Spell; Karen Carpenter Story; Kate's Secret; Ultimate Betrayal; What's Eating Gilbert Grape

Friends: About Last Night; Barfly; Beaches; Big; Big Chill; Boy With Green Hair; Boys in the Band; Breakfast Club; Bright Lights, Big City; Chantilly Lace; Christmas Carol; Clean and Sober; Color Purple; Dead Poets Society; Doctor; Drop Dead Fred; Duet for One; Drugstore Cowboy; Eating; Face to Face; Family of Strangers; Ferris Bueller's Day Off; Field of Dreams; Fisher King; Forrest Gump; Four Seasons; Good Mother; Grand Canyon; Great Sinner; He Said, She Said; It's a Wonderful Life; Jo Jo Dancer, Your Life Is Calling; Less Than Zero; Life of the Party: The Story of Beatrice; Longest Runner; Mr. Destiny; My Name Is Bill W.; One Flew Over the Cuckoo's Nest; Our Very Own; Over Forty; Paris Is Burning; Philadelphia; Pretty in Pink; Prince of Tides; Regarding Henry; Ryan White Story; She Said No; Sleepless in Seattle; Sophie's Choice; St. Elmo's Fire; Steel Magnolias; Stella; Summer of '42; Tales of Manhattan; Thelma and Louise; Three Faces of Eve; Torch Song Trilogy; Way We Were; Wildflower; Wizard of Oz; Woman's Tale; Women of Brewster Place; Women on the Verge of a Nervous Breakdown; Working Girl

Gambling: Gambler; Great Sinner

Mental/Emotional Illness: Boost; Burning Bed; Call Me Anna; Closet Land; Cries From the Heart; Cry for Help: The Tracey Thurman

Story; Damage; David's Mother; Dialogues with Madwomen; Dr. Jekyll and Mr. Hyde; Extremities; Face to Face; Falling Down; Family of Strangers; Fatal Attraction; Fear Inside; Field of Dreams; Fisher King; For the Love of Nancy; Frances; Gambler; Harvey; I Know My First Name Is Steven; In the Best Interest of the Child; Jungle Fever; Karen Carpenter Story; Mommie Dearest; Mr. Jones; 'Night, Mother; Nuts; On Golden Pond; One Flew Over the Cuckoo's Nest; Ordinary People; Picture of Dorian Gray; Play Misty for Me; Prince of Tides; Rain Man; Sid and Nancy; Silence of the Lambs; Sleeping With the Enemy; Sophie's Choice; Sybil; Three Faces of Eve; Victims for Victims: The Theresa Saldana Story; War of the Roses; Wizard of Oz; Woman Under the Influence

Physical Illness: All That Jazz; Beaches; Boy With Green Hair; Dad; David's Mother; Doctor; Duet for One; Dying Young; Family of Strangers; For the Love of Nancy; Ironweed; Jo Jo Dancer, Your Life Is Calling; Longest Runner; Miracle Worker; My Breast; My Name Is Bill W.; On Golden Pond; Rapture; Regarding Henry; Ryan White Story; Six Weeks; Steel Magnolias; Stranger in the Family; Terms of Endearment; That's Life; What's Eating Gilbert Grape; When You Remember Me; Wildflower; Woman's Tale

Relationships: About Last Night; Accidental Tourist; Accused; Alien; All That Jazz; An Affair to Remember; Baby Boom; Baby M; Beaches; Benny and Joon; Big; Big Chill; Boost; Boy With Green Hair; Boys in the Band; Breakfast Club; Bright Lights, Big City; Broadcast News; Burning Bed; Call Me Anna; Carnal Knowledge; Chantilly Lace; Clean and Sober; Closer; Color Purple; Come Fill the Cup; Cry for Help: The Tracey Thurman Story; Dad; Damage; Darkness Before Dawn; David's Mother; Days of Wine and Roses; Dead Poets Society; Defending Your Life; Doctor; Dollmaker; Drop Dead Fred; Duet for One; Drugstore Cowboy; Dying Young; Eating; Enchantment; Extremities; Falling Down; Family of Strangers; Fatal Attraction; Father of the Bride; Fisher King; Forrest Gump; Four Seasons; Gathering; Ghost; Good Mother; Grand Canyon; Great Santini; Guess Who's Coming to Dinner; He Said, She Said; Hellraiser; Hot Spell; I Know My First Name Is Steven; I Never Sang for My Father; I'm Dancing as Fast as I Can; Immediate Family; Ironweed; It's a Wonderful Life; Jo Jo Dancer, Your Life Is Calling; Jason's Lyric; Joy Luck Club; Jungle Fever; Kate's Secret; Kramer vs. Kramer; Lady Sings the Blues; Less Than Zero; Longest Runner; Looking for Mister Goodbar; Lost Weekend; Made in Heav-

SUGGESTION BOX

Please fill out the form below and mail it to:

THE MOVIE DOCTOR
OREGON PSYCHOTHERAPY CONSORTIUM
12311 NE GLISAN
SUITE 165
PORTLAND, OR 97230
(503) 255-4990

Date:_____

Name:_____(Optional)

In what part of the country do you live? _____

How old are you?_____

Are you a practicing therapist? Yes _____ No _____

Did you find this type of therapy to be helpful? Yes _____ No _____

What is your opinion of the book? _____

Here are some of the movies I would like to see you include in the next edition of your book:
1. _____
2. _____
3. _____
4. _____

I WOULD LIKE A MOVIE DISTRIBUTOR LIST. I HAVE ENCLOSED A CHECK/MONEY ORDER FOR $2.50.

MY NAME AND ADDRESS ARE

_____
(Name)

_____
(Mailing Address)

_____
(City, State, Zip+4)

TO CONTACT THE MOVIE DOCTOR™

Dr. Gary Solomon is available for speaking engagements, conferences, and lectures throughout the country. His presentations are both enlightening and entertaining. He brings his audiences to a new level of self-awareness and takes them on a wonderful journey with his healing stories.

To contact Dr. Gary Solomon
please write:

THE MOVIE DOCTOR
OREGON PSYCHOTHERAPY CONSORTIUM
12311 NE GLISAN
SUITE 165
PORTLAND, OR 97230

Or call
1-503-255-4990

Support, Recovery, and Out-Reach Organizations

In *The Motion Picture Prescription* I recommended you make contact and become involved with support, recovery, and out-reach organizations to help you, your family, and friends in the healing process. Below is a partial list of some of those organizations. Most organizations offer their support at no charge. Please keep in mind that the names of the organizations will vary from city to city, throughout the world. Check with your local directory service for the proper listings and phone numbers. Don't hesitate to call directory assistance and tell them what you are looking for. Most city phone services have a master list to refer to in dealing with these sensitive, personal issues.

Anonymous Groups

Alcoholics Anonymous (AA)
Alateen Anonymous
Overeaters Anonymous (OA)
Narcotics Anonymous (NA)
Smokers Anonymous (SA)
Cocaine Anonymous (CA)
Pills Anonymous (PA)
Artists Anonymous
Gamblers Anonymous (GA)
Sex Anonymous (SA)
Families Anonymous (FA)
Hookers Anonymous (HA)
Debtors Anonymous

Support Groups

Alanon
Adult Children of Alcoholics
Anger Management
Incests Survivors
MADD: Mothers Against Drunk Drivers
Victims for Victims
Toughlove
Parents with autistic children
Gays/Lesbians

Hotlines and Treatment Centers

Crisis Hotline—local & 800#
Rape Hotline—local & 800#
Teen Crisis Hotline—local & 800#
Pregnancy Hotline—local & 800#
Runaway Hotline—800#
Local hospitals
Addiction & trauma treatment centers
Police support lines
Homeless shelters
Battered women's shelters
Schools and Colleges
Therapists/Psychotherapists/ Counselors
Religious and spiritually based organizations
AIDS Hotline—local & 800#
Suicide Hotline—local & 800#